Is Gay Good?

Is Gay Good?

Ethics, Theology, and Homosexuality

Edited by
W. DWIGHT OBERHOLTZER

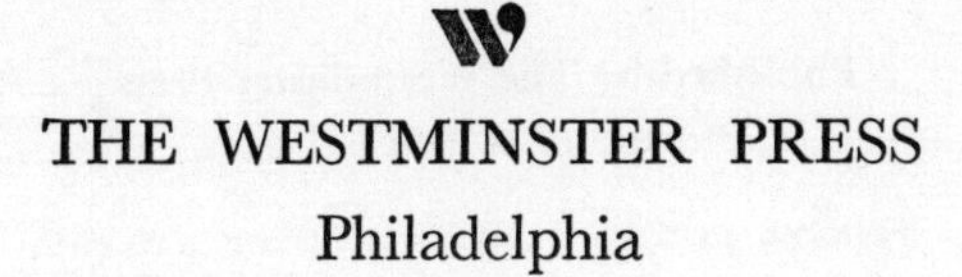

ISBN 0-664-24912-4

LIBRARY OF CONGRESS CATALOG CARD NO. 75-141202

BOOK DESIGN BY
DOROTHY ALDEN SMITH

Published by The Westminster Press®
Philadelphia, Pennsylvania

PRINTED IN THE UNITED STATES OF AMERICA

Contents

Preface

The problems we sweep under the rug or push back out of sight always cost us more headaches, because we sidestepped them. Reading through the contributions to this book, as a nonparticipating or balcony observer, I am struck afresh by the foolishness of our moral and cultural evasions and rigidities. For the question at stake here is among the most acutely human ones, and the ability to look at it with person-centered concern instead of moralism and legalism is what will spell our failure or our success.

It is possible, I grant, that a "theology of homosexuality" is needed, but why construct separate theologies, so that a theology of heterosexuality and a theology of autosexuality and a theology of nonsexuality would be needed to complete the series? It may be that we are not so much lacking in good theologizing about homosexuality but are suffering the obfuscations of a traditionally weak and twisted theology of sexuality as such. New and constructive theological reflection on sex and on the richer, deeper phenomenon of sexuality will, I believe, put the homosexual into a realistic and humane perspective which conventional church talk and thought is unable to achieve.

The "revelation" and the "tradition" have alike been antihomosexual all along. To escape this ancient and malicious mind-set will mean that we have to drop the almost obsessive-compulsive addiction of typical theologizers to the Bible in Protestant circles and to tradition in Catholic circles. Both bibliolatry and orthodoxy have failed to help us in searching for a relevant, humane, and person-oriented ethics. (Thomas Maurer goes straight to the heart of the matter.)

A thoughtful reading of von Rohr's and Harvey's chapters will illustrate the logical difficulties and inherited baggage of conventional theologizers. Both papers are carefully worked out: Harvey's tidier, orthodox, and more articulated; von Rohr's reaching for depth and exposing an almost painful conflictedness. Von Rohr's position paper went through a lot of unnecessary thrashing around with the archaic notion of "naturalness" before he could conclude that "there is really no *peccatum contra naturam*" in homosexual and, presumably, other acts of a noncoital kind. The Archbishop's statement quoted by Coleman ("Homosexual acts are always wrong") is a sample of ethical legalism, but at least his actual language avoided the natural-law quagmire.

The reader will find several different viewpoints and styles in this book, from the conventional but very genuine piety of Henry to the "way out" opinion of Lyon and Martin. It is plain that von Rohr has succeeded in his task of provoking responses. Professor Oberholtzer is on the right track in getting such knowledgeable people to delve into the theological and moral issues at stake. I am impressed by the almost utter absence of scientific agreement about homosexuality's cause and incidence, and inclined to be doubtful about the assumptions and the costs of studies such as the new one which the National Institute of Mental Health is funding for a Kinsey research with five thousand homosexuals in the San Francisco Bay Area.

Suppose, for example, we find that the cause of sexual orientations is chromosomal, or psychogenic, or something else; what difference would it make morally? More inquiries along this book's line are needed to find the right questions to ask and then to get some sensible answers. I could illustrate what I mean by just one minor but ethically freighted question: Has a girl lost her virginity with her first sexual act (other than masturbation) if it was with another girl? What is virginity? Would different answers be proposed by homosexuals and heterosexuals?

We don't have forever to work it out. Homophile groups are now launched overtly into political action. It was more than ten years ago that a model code of the American Law Institute proposed legalization of homosexual acts between consenting adults. Why are the United States and the Soviet Union so much more repressive on this score than most of the world? Draft boards may inquire into a draftee's sexual life, and make records available to prospective employers. Homosexuals are ineligible for government jobs, and, in some states, for schoolteaching; private employers discriminate. In some states they are compelled to register as psychopaths, losing their civil rights and forced to undergo medical treatment. These things remind us of the interdependence of law and ethics, and show how real and pressing the whole question is for millions of human beings.

Church groups as separated in doctrine as the American Lutherans and the Unitarian Universalists have lately faced the issue. The Lutherans declare that homosexuals are no more (and no less) "sinners" than other people. And the Unitarian Universalists have approved laws allowing homosexual relations between consenting adults. Meanwhile, on the East Coast a computer-dating service for homosexuals is in full operation.

It would be legitimate, I believe, to end this welcome to a new book with a candid confession of my own present judgment on the issue (without the reasoning). It seems to me that there is no ethical objection to homosexuality as such, even though some of us have aesthetic objections of a personal order. There is, I would hold, nothing intrinsically good or evil per se in any sexual act. Whether it is right or wrong depends on its situation, and what is sometimes right is other times wrong. Homosexual acts can be morally objectionable in some situations, in exactly the same way that heterosexual acts can be.

Love validates sex. Sex is not self-validating or inherently right and good—not in any of its variant forms. A truly loving homosexual relationship is morally justifiable as an unloving heterosexual relationship is not—not even when licensed by marriage. Indeed, marriage as well as sexual acts is validated by authentic loving concern, not by either moral or civil laws. As I see it, this applies to all sexual activity—auto, hetero, or homo—in any truly Christian ethics. Pittenger puts it succinctly when he says that what he calls sin is both "a refusal to love" and "a violation of love." But the discussion needs to continue before any judgment can offer firm ground, pro or con.

JOSEPH FLETCHER

Introduction

Subduing the Cyclops—A Giant Step Toward Ethics

W. Dwight Oberholtzer

The lights are coming up on a concealed world. Once-shadowed, diligently hidden cities are appearing in the glare of invading, unrelenting searchlights. Uncovered by novelists, journalists, scientists, and criminologists, publicized on the covers of *Time* magazine and the *Berkeley Tribe,* the secret world of the homosexual is interviewed, interpreted, and, finally, labeled. Americans may gawk with voyeuristic pleasure or blush with embarrassed chagrin. But "the gay world" has been found.[1]

Found but not understood. Each single spot, each interpretation, lights up a different, even novel gay world. According to *Life,* for instance, the movie industry produced or released over a dozen films in 1968, all claiming to nudge back the shadows from homosexual experience.[2] Each, however, created its own gay world. And scientific reports, viewed collectively, heighten this disturbing divergence. Is it the gay world of Bergler or Schofield, Cleckley or Hoffman, that is the illusion? Each light on the subject stands as a one-eyed Cyclops. Left uncoordinated, the concealed world of the homosexual remains hidden behind these various separate efforts that have been made to illumine it.

A concealed gay world exists, however, only for naïve or befuddled outsiders. Insiders—and they number in the millions—readily recognize its side streets and street corners. Some are seasonal residents. Ten percent of the white male population is "more or less exclusively homosexual for at least three years, between the age of 16 and 65." [3] For these men and for their female counterparts, gay life is anything but concealed. Others hold full citizenship. One to 3 percent of the single female population and 4 percent of the white male population are exclusively gay for most of their lives.[4] They have searched the streets of the *City of Night,* felt the intimacy of *Giovanni's Room,* and crossed the borders of *Another Country.*[5] Still others spend only weekends, drifting sporadically in and out of the gay world.[6] But who could count the added millions who reluctantly enter because a son, father, daughter, mother, wife, husband, fiancée, or friend is gay? When hesitant visitors and resolute residents are totaled, the secret world of the homosexual is not so secret after all. A large minority tune in.

But, yet, what a silent minority it is. And for good reason: 63 percent of the country, reports a Harris Poll, believe homosexuality is "harmful to American life." [7] The prevalence of this opinion supports the blackmail, dishonorable discharge, and job insecurity that many homosexuals face.[8] Many, although not all, Americans detest homosexuality and homosexuals. This is enough to explain initially the silence of the minority; it goes a long way toward explaining much behavior in the gay world, too. Parents, consequently, do not publicize their son's marriage—to another man. Few parents confide to neighbors why their eligible daughter remains single.

Even fewer men with security clearances recount their weekend gaiety for superiors. In this society, gay is bad—assumed so, thought so, and taught so. Current social taboos have inhibited discussion. The result is often an agony of silence for millions who writhe between what Baldwin calls their "troubling sex" and public opinion.[9] Thus, Martin Hoffman can rightly term homosexuality "perhaps *the most serious undiscussed problem* in the United States today."[10] The "unrecognized minority" has been without spokesmen, either good reformers or good spies.[11]

Since Hoffman wrote in 1968, the silence has steadily lifted. As reflected in this volume's bibliography, scientific winds have shifted and blown away some benign neglect. Box-office attendance at least indicates some chatter in the popular gallery. But in spite of this more vigorous, even serious discussion, all is quiet on the ethical front. An occasional church convention rustles a newspaper's fourth section with its earthshaking statement on sex and the family. It takes seconds, however, to list the authors of book-length ethical analyses of homosexuality, the titles of edited collections, and the authors who obliquely confront the gay world at the ethical level. Single-sentence slogans are more likely to capture public attention. The Gay Liberation Front in Berkeley shocks the most equalitarian with "Gay is Good," while the *Berkeley Tribe* titillates the newsstand audience with its front-page come-on "Gay is Bad." Simplistic moral slogans raise eyebrows, sell papers, or bring catharsis to those who shout them. But in their presence "the most serious undiscussed problem in the United States today" remains, ethically, just that.

So much for setting the general scene. Ethics, the hero

of this volume, enters. To be sure, he may become, depending upon the perspective, the scoundrel, the buffoon, the heroine, or another less expected character. But he does, wearing the costume each essayist provides, answer the question that scientific description and explanation must necessarily beg: Is gay good? Hopefully, the collection will begin to fill the current vacuum and move toward what must be eventually an interdisciplinary discussion.

Christian ethics draws from a wide range of resources. The Bible, church tradition, contemporary experience, a definition of the "natural" and the "valued"—all these and other elements are potential resources for the ethicist. Some of the contributors to this volume reject one or most of them. Traditional Christian ethics, however, claims that personal, existential, or, to use H. Richard Niebuhr's term, "inner" experience makes sense around the life and meaning of Jesus, the Christ.[12] Ethicists administer other resources in varying dosages, but the meaning of Christ—as varied as this may be from author to author—is central to the evaluation of human action. This introduction argues for another resource: social science. It does not defend a particular ethic, although it does imply that any ethic will self-destruct without scientific information. The completed essay provides: (1) prolegomena for any ethic of the gay world but also (2) an introduction to the other essays in this volume, (3) an introduction to the gay world, and (4) an introduction to the scientific literature.

A Commitment to Understanding

Ethical evaluation of homosexuality, regardless of the other tools it employs, demands commitment to the homosexual world. Left to its own devices, of course, this brief statement of the essay's thesis will confuse any careful reader. Is it necessary to be homosexual in order to do Christian ethics properly? Is the commitment to homosexuality? For some in the gay community, that would be a happy solution. But that is exactly the kind of commitment that is neither meant nor needed. The commitment is just as assuredly not to heterosexuality. Careful ethicists are committed or pledged, as they begin their work, to understanding the gay world. Ethicists enter the homosexual world with open ears and minds, not with painted signs or reformers' slogans. And they do this both for the sake of becoming informed and for the sake of their subsequent ethic.

An ethic that doesn't understand the gay world totters on rotten timbers. First, this uninformed ethic often suggests that the homosexual deny his own integrity, his own sense of what is reasonable and responsible. Because it is not designed either for the dilemmas or for the delights that he confronts daily, such an ethic sounds written in a foreign tongue. Just as African women could make no sense of the blouses and the bras that American missionaries scolded them to wear, homosexuals are puzzled, some are maddened, at the ethical costumes they are compelled to prefer. An insensitive ethic makes unintelligible and inappropriate demands. It seems impossible that a homosexual could be held ethically responsible for doing what he considers unreasonable. Exchanging personal decision for another's demand seems, in fact, the height of irresponsibility. This does not imply that an ethic for the homosexual—indeed, for any person—should feel warm and cozy; certainly, what homosexuals ought to do may be quite uncomfortable. But the ethic must be appropriate to decisions made in the gay world.

Second, an uninformed ethic puts prognosis before diagnosis. It is not simply a matter, then, of what this kind of ethic forces the homosexual to do. The ethic itself suffers from a procedural fault. In this case the M.D. —Doctor of Morality—prescribes medicine without knowing the patient. This revokes licenses in other professions, but, strangely enough, ethicists feel immune.

Third, without diagnosis of the gay world's actual dangers, the prescribed cure may be an overdose, killing the patient. For instance, a lesbian woman with, surprisingly, latent heterosexual tendencies may be directed in therapy toward full heterosexual adjustment. In the gradual process, however, she may become so dependent upon her therapist that, in effect, she has exchanged, possibly at her ethicist's suggestion, relative self-determination in the gay world for psychological serfdom in the straight. The cure, quite conceivably proposed on the uninformed assumption that the gay world is homogeneous—homogeneously sick, at that—has, at a most significant level for ethical accountability, killed the patient.[13]

Fourth, an ethic unchastened by conversation with homosexual persons has not even the slightest guarantee that it will be anything more than the uncritical perpetuation of cultural prejudices.

Fifth, even worse, an uninformed ethic spawns what Herbert Blumer calls in a different context, "the worst kind of subjectivism." [14] Cultural prejudices at least have latitude. They are shared with others and rooted in common, although partial, experience. An ethicist who knows little of the gay world, however, fills in the gaps of the cultural distortion with his own personal tastes, with his own eccentric surmises. And this subjectivism begets a serendipitous arrogance. The uninformed ethicist practices theology, the so-called queen of the sciences, in a closet. He makes the insidious claim from his darkroom—the fact that he is straight or gay himself makes no difference—that he knows more about gay life than anyone else. He then advises others, using this ignorance. Such "closet queens" have their own problems.

Good reasons exist, then, for asserting that an uninformed ethic is highly dangerous. But simply to counterclaim that an ethicist should be informed leaves important unanswered questions. What kind of understanding is he after? The understanding of the social reformer, of the man on the street, of the policeman? In all these cases the answer is an emphatic "No!" The ethical task, in its initial stages, calls for the work of a good spy.

The successful spy reports. He doesn't moralize, simplify, or condemn, leaving that to appropriate reformers, laymen, and policemen. He neutralizes his personal biases in an effort to both accurately and comprehensively unmask the gay world.[15] What would happen if spies wrote intelligence reports about Communist China to coddle the prejudices of superiors or to proof-text their own personal beliefs? The result would support personal ambition or personal ideology, but it would not faithfully portray China's insides—a distortion that could have disastrous effect upon subsequent military or political policy. The truly professional spy reveals how "tenable," to reapply David Matza's word, or workable, or, indeed, beautiful the gay world is *for those who prefer to live there.*[16] He also brings back information concerning the "ungay" or unhappy or ugly aspects of homosexual life, again, for those who experience them. In other words, he sensitizes himself to gay life in all its dialects, in all its meeting places, in all its joys, and in all its frustrations.[17] Good public policy or good ethical analysis stems from the unbiased, exhaustive, many-eyed investigation of the careful spy.

Bad espionage, on the other hand, is the work of a one-eyed Cyclops. Like the Homeric giants who were fabled to inhabit Sicily, poor intelligence squints through a single eye, unaware of depth and breadth. The reports of one-eyed agents, furthermore, have telltale traits. They are simplistic, fictitious, static, and ideological.

To be more specific, Cyclopean analysis traffics in unsophisticated stereotypes. The simpleminded spy reports from the gay world, for instance, that all male homosexuals are effeminate, immediately recognizable as they mince down the street, swishing, limp-wristing, and—certainly—lisping. Shockingly, 29 percent of the population consider this kind of information accurate.[18] But, as a sweeping generalization, it is as artless as its counterpart regarding "butch" or masculine women and lesbianism. Wardell Pomeroy, for twenty years a much better investigator on the staff of the Institute for Sex Research at Indiana University, corrects this myopia when he writes, "About 15 percent of the males and 5 percent of the females with extensive homosexual histories are identifiable." [19] To employ the popular fable, then, in buttressing an ethical argument is clearly ludicrous. The Cyclops tempts us to do just that. To distort in the other direction—to claim that all male homosexuals have no problem with femininity—however, is equally the result of crude intelligence. As John Gagnon and William Simon reveal, some homosexual men struggle through a "crisis of femininity," dragging out female attire and affecting female behavior.[20] Balanced, faithful espionage includes both or many sides. It evades the simple, popular caricature and thus provides a more sure foundation for ethics. Simplification betrays bad research.

Faulty espionage also jams people into categories that don't fit. It overlooks the ripping seams. To illustrate, many people believe that homosexuals live an unconscious parody of the state of heterosexuality from which they have fallen. The uninformed informer pampers this prejudice by reporting that all gay couples combine "active" (masculine) and "passive" (feminine) roles. One plays the husband, the other the wife, both in bed and out. Thank goodness for better spies with fewer fictions. After investigating thirty male homosexuals for eight years, Evelyn Hooker, of UCLA, reported: no correspondence exists for the majority between their sense of masculinity or femininity and their particular sexual patterns.[21] Commonsense categories used in the heterosexual world, therefore, are not necessarily helpful in comprehending the gay world. Fictitious transfer betrays faulty research.

In fact, unqualified use of any category distorts. Wide-angle vision, not tunnel vision, is the remedy. But, sadly, accounts often arrive from the gay world in neat, categorical, and static packages without benefit of spectrum. In the study both of social deviation in general and of sexual deviation in particular, ticky-tack box reports are suspect.[22] As Kinsey's research demonstrated incontestably, many men and women are neither exclusively heterosexual nor exclusively homosexual. Only 61 to 72 percent of the unmarried female population are exclusively straight; only 1 to 3 percent of the single female population are exclusively gay. Among white males, 53 to 78 percent are totally straight; 4 percent are exclusively gay.[23] Many Americans fervently believe that only two possibilities exist: straight or gay. Not so. Over their lifetimes millions swing in between. If these two static categories can misrepresent, concealing middle terms, what about the assumed stone wall between the gay world and the straight world? What about the highly respected but small-angle distinctions between male and female,[24] sick and well, natural and unnatural, normal and abnormal,[25] criminal and noncriminal,[26] and even good spies and bad spies? To see overlap is to see life. Static categories constrict.

Primitive analysis is the result of unchastened ideology.[27] Personal beliefs cloud over the gay world's variety. For the heterosexual, the imposition of straight terms, values, and attitudes upon the gay world is the clue to this. Although this has ethical implications by itself,[28] it also results in misunderstanding and a distorted ethic. But personal, uncriticized dogma may also infest an ethic constructed by a homosexual. Many gay men and women, pointing to the concentration of homosexuals in the arts, ardently believe that gay persons are constitutionally less aggressive, more sensitive or (in a good sense) softer than the average heterosexual—a laudable reason, so the ideology implies, for applauding homosexuality in general. The fact that Indian fighters and cowboys in the nineteenth century—a group not notorious for its tenderness—were some of the most overtly homosexual men in America does not dent the ideological armor. Secondly, some in the gay community conclude publicly or privately that homosexual couples have the only real love. Theirs is the only true, uncoerced affection because heterosexual marriage is propped up by external supports such as convention and legality. The divorce rate supposedly alchemizes this assumption into fact. But ideology of this kind simply compares the best of one with the worst of another, ignorant of or unwilling to see either the spontaneous love in some straight marriages or the compulsive love in some gay marriages. Distortions lurk in the gay world, too.[29] Finally, homosexuals attending symposia on the gay life-style often express the opinion that fascination with sex in the gay world is simply a heterosexual assumption. Again, as Hoffman's study at least of the male homosexual indicates, this ideology misses the diversity of behavior—some highly sex-oriented—in the homosexual subculture. It is necessary to neutralize biases on all sides. Ideology perverts.

Yet, the neutral spy is also a human spy. And the knowledge he gains is always, to use Michael Polanyi's phrase, "personal knowledge." [30] Complete neutrality is, to the dismay of many, humanly impossible. The personal selection of a world to investigate, the personal interpretation of what is seen and heard there, even the theories selected for testing and confidence in the worth of scientific inquiry—all these factors betray individual assumptions and preferences that are extrascientific. Assumptions play no less a part in constructing an ethic after the spy work is completed or in writing this essay. The crucial question is: Are personal biases acknowledged and checked? Are they used to probe the gay world better or to distort it? [31] Perhaps the best insurance against a contorting ideology is, in Howard Becker's words, "close contact with the people we study," [32] a cross fire of research and opinion, and sensitivity to the work of the Cyclops: unchecked bias, simplification, fictitious transfer, and hardened categories. To subdue the Cyclops is to take a giant step toward good ethics.

Process in the Gay World

What commitment to understanding implies should now be clear. This second section of the essay begins to answer the question, What does homosexual experience include? The focus, it must be emphasized, is uncompromisingly upon *homosexual* experience. Not heterosexual experience. Not what straights think homosexual experience is or should be, but gay experience from the inside. What does becoming and being homosexual mean for the gay person? [33]

Viewed from behind the homosexual's eyes, becoming gay is a gradual, explorative, natural, interpersonal, and human process. Each word is significant. But no word is an ethical judgment, either of the process or of the product. An illustration is appropriate. Jack is a stable, twenty-four-year-old husband with two children. He loves his family, enjoys sex with his wife, and counts on continuing both. His sex life is conventional and fulfilling, although he and his wife find oral intercourse distasteful. He has, since college days, hated "queers" and "fags," although he has never known a homosexual personally. His only homosexual experience, which he now tosses off as an adolescent phase and prefers to forget, took place during his teen-age years with a very close school friend. If anyone were to ask him how he currently defines himself sexually—which, certainly, because of his two children no one does—he would confidently and quickly respond: "Are you kidding? I'm straight!"

What would happen if Jack were to become exclusively gay? Contrary to what might be thought, this is not an idle question, although it does suggest an extreme case. Changes of this kind do take place, although Kinsey's studies suggest that the chance for this is greater among married males than among married females. The most general, and maybe to some the most obvious, answer to this question is: a radical shift must occur in the meaning that Jack's wife, family, friends, sexual behavior, and self-definition presently have. That sums up the end result. It intimates correctly that meaning is the crucial factor. But it does not make the process toward homosexuality more transparent. That task is next.

Becoming gay is as slow a process as getting to know one's wife—indeed, as becoming straight. Dissimilarities between the two processes abound, certainly. But for Jack the move from straight father to gay lover, the process between his before and after, is as gradual. Granted, he is not the average homosexual. And, as an adult, he is aware of his development in a way that the emerging adolescent homosexual is not. But, at the same time, both are conscious and for both the process progresses inch by inch. To become homosexual is not to be turned on as a light bulb—push button, light's on. The human drugstore has no instant gay.[34]

Jack's shift, *if*—and this is a crucial word—it takes place, processes through at least three stages: (1) being open, (2) being able, and (3) being committed. In the first stage Jack's heterosexual world is no longer taken for granted but becomes problematic; [35] he becomes psychologically open to the possibility of gay encounter. In the second stage he moves from thinking to doing, a movement that demands opportunity and the cooperation of others.[36] In the third stage Jack defines homosexual activity as worthwhile; he identifies himself as gay and now takes for granted the appropriateness of his new sexual role. No stage is airtight or takes place overnight. Each shades into the next. And each includes a complex, sequential combination of personal experience with others, interpretation, subsequent personal experience with others, reinterpretation, and on into the infinite detail of human life. It is only afterward, when ice tongs hold the completed process between before and after, that the radical shift in meaning can be seen. How might this radical reinterpretation take place?

Generally speaking, through a shift in Jack's social encounters—his experience with its initial and subsequent interpretation.[37] Concretely speaking, he may slowly build a Platonic—in the popular sense of that word—relationship with Paul, a colleague at work. He may develop, in other words, affection for another man—simply affection, not sex. He may—and this need not be in relationship to Paul or, indeed, may be without Paul's friendship—discover, as one in every two men do, that he is occasionally erotically attracted to other men.[38] He may find, through reading or conversation, that 37 percent of the male population have "at least some overt homosexual experience to the point of orgasm between adolescence and old age."[39] This puts his embarrassing adolescent behavior and his present sexual feelings in a new context. A new interpretation may spring out. He may be away from his wife with a group of men for a long period. He may gradually change his opinion, through lunch-hour conversations with straight colleagues, about oral-genital sexuality. He may become open to such contact with his wife. He may come to know a homosexual male who batters his previous stereotype. He may have thought flashes like these: "He has strange lips; I wonder what kissing him would be like? He certainly is well built; I wonder what touching him would be like? I wonder what he looks like in the shower?" He may in innumerable ways edge toward being open. He may, but he *need not,* have all or some or other experiences; the experiences may build and cluster in his mind or remain isolated and forgotten. Indeed, the experienced speed of the progression may vary. Although the whole process is gradual, Jack's participation in a particular sequence of events may move him more rapidly toward homosexual identity, slow him down, stop him, or redirect him. These experiences only illustrate. They are not mandatory, sequential, or inclusive.[40] The conclusion at this point is twofold: (1) homosexuality develops gradually [41] in relationship to other persons and changing personal views; [42] (2) becoming gay happens neither despite one nor without others—responsibility is two-shouldered. But it should be added: at this juncture discussion focuses simply upon the subtle approach toward the first stage or, in Baldwin's more elegant words, toward the tug of "insistent possibilities." Innumerable opportunities for experience and interpretation exist at each stage. At each gradual, potential step justifying reasons, moral views, and religious beliefs change.[43] And at each step Jack may be turned on, off, or out.

In other words, the process is one of exploration, not preordination. Even after Jack becomes open, he may not become able. He may not know the right people, interpret his sexual experiences homosexually, have enough courage, or he may lack something else. At each progressive point, especially in the overt movement toward being gay (being able and being committed), the process of testing, evaluating, and retesting his highly intricate. Jack may probe with subtle questions about sex in general, hoping to hear about homosexuality in particular. He may be rejected in his physical advances, never to try again. He may be rejected, never to stop trying. David's first homosexual experience with Joey in *Giovanni's Room,* taking seven pages to describe, hints at the provisional, experimental, even accidental development of gay experience.[44] Without hearing and seeing the conversations unfold, without viewing the shifts in social setting, and without listening to Jack as he mulls his new experiences over in his mind, it is impossible to portray adequately the uncountable range of possibilities. Certainly, the short span of this essay prohibits detailed discussion of each equally complex stage. It is enough to say that homosexuality is tentatively constructed. The process is dependent upon the facilitation or lack of it that others offer and upon personal responses to opportunities.

Because of the gentle, shaded, and personal character of the transition, it is often called "natural" by those who have gone through it.[45] Jack, going through the process as an adult—although in relation to his youthful past—would interpret it differently from the way an eighteen-year-old would as he "comes out." But, for both of them, there has been no artificial, external interruption. No one has given them either gay shots or antigay shots. Personal rebuffs, even violent ones perhaps, to their homosexual exploration have occurred. Agonizing decisions accompany their insistent feelings. But they are unaware of what is facilitating their attractions, and these feelings seem to have naturally bubbled up from inside as from a hidden, natural spring. The reason for this has two parts: (1) the process is gradual, and, because of this, their *experienced* part and the part of others in the natural emergence is slight; (2) the process is to a large degree *unplanned;* no one, heterosexual or homosexual or bisexual, sits down on a specific day with pencil and pad to scheme, move by move, the capture of his sexuality. Social science, being true to its method, may attempt to understand rationally how people become gay, but the homosexual process is neither totally cognitive nor totally noncognitive. This implies something for those concerned with the relation of sexuality, be it hetero or homo really, and responsibility. To pursue this is important.

Many gay persons think their gayness is caused. No single person forces them to become homosexual, of course. "Insistent possibilities" are simply felt to surge uncontrollably upward. Evelyn Hooker, in her research with male homosexuals, reported that "the majority believe either that they were born as homosexuals or that familial factors operating very early in their lives determined the outcome."[46] D. W. Cory concurs from his subjective standpoint when he writes:

> No teacher but life itself could have convinced me that homosexual passions do not come and go at will, but cling relentlessly to the last breath of life. When I awaken today and feel devoid of the drive that has dominated my personality, I smile and merely await its inevitable return.[47]

The basic question, however, is, To what degree is this true from other perspectives?

From Sartre's standpoint and on the basis of the foregoing description of becoming gay, belief in the necessity of one's homosexuality is both "bad faith" and good faith.[48] It is bad faith to pretend that homosexuality is necessary when it is in fact partly conscious and voluntary. Gay attractions are not sneakily created while Jack is out of the room. He becomes gay with his consent, although not without the consent of others. Jack's contributions and the contributions of others are recognized only when the gradual process of becoming gay is stretched out again and examined as it took place originally. Gay persons remember only what happened. They forget what *might have happened.* Thus, instead of remembering the choice among possibilities that was actually experienced in the past, they fasten upon the single action chosen and baptize it as inevitable—an exercise in bad faith.[49] How differently they view the present, which is simply the past of tomorrow, with its relatively open possibilities.

It is good faith to claim, on the other hand, that present reconstruction and redirection of this sexual development is very difficult if not impossible, especially for the exclusive homosexual. What was relative freedom may now be forever lost. Pomeroy, in support of this view, writes, "There is only a small likelihood that persons who have been in the 5 or 6 category [predominantly homosexual, only incidently heterosexual; exclusively homosexual] on the rating scale for any appreciable period of time—five to ten years—will ever work down the scale, although homosexuals who are highly motivated to change may be able to do so." [50] Responsibility makes sense only in relation to perceived possibility. And the agonizing, personal question remains: Do I perceive as impossible what is, for me, really a painful possibility? This raises the ethical question; it does not solve it.

To return to the major theme of this section, the process of becoming and being gay is an interpersonal and human process. That means it is a meaningful process undertaken in relation to others. At the most general level, human beings, in some contrast to other mammals, manufacture complex symbols; with language they interpret and respond to their environment in ways that billiard balls never do. The shift from heterosexual to homosexual meaning is traceable in four analytically distinct areas: (1) the interpretation of one's identity, (2) the interpretation of one's values and interests, (3) the interpretation of one's intended and completed action, and (4) the interpretation of one's situation in relation to others.

But to speak in these terms does not capture the human turmoil that a change of this magnitude in our society may bring. The emotional implications are monumental. Only a reader who can spiral his way down through the *o*'s and *a*'s on the printed page toward empathy with the homosexual will begin to fathom the turbulent human feelings. In *Giovanni's Room,* when David and Giovanni make love for the first time, Baldwin closes the scene with these poignant words:

> He [Giovanni] pulled me against him, putting himself into my arms as though he were giving me himself to carry, and slowly pulled me down with him to that bed. With everything in me screaming *No!* yet the sum of me sighed *Yes.*[51]

The difference between parts and whole—so little, yet, for the homosexual, so agonizingly and so beautifully much. Regardless of the ethical verdict, it should never be forgotten that good spies find human beings in the gay world, not "perverts" or "queers." [52]

The focus has been upon the gay person. Admittedly, becoming gay and being gay are interpersonal processes. That has been said also. But an account at the face-to-face level is still fragmentary. The homosexual is part of American society. The door to this wider dimension is opened by D. W. Cory when he declares:

> The dominant factor in my life, towering in importance above all others, is a consciousness that I am different. In one all-important respect, I am unlike the great mass of people always around me, and the knowledge of this fact is with me at all times, influencing profoundly my every thought, each minute activity, and all my aspirations. It is inescapable, not only this being different, but more than that, this constant awareness of a dissimilarity.[53]

Most homosexuals would agree with this statement. But why the constant awareness of difference? Why is the sexuality of the gay person not simply different, as an apple from an orange, but highly problematic?

The best answer is: Society has so ruled. The dominant norms of American society scream, "Thou shalt not be homosexual." The legal norms intone, "Thou shalt not commit homosexual acts." Heterosexuals are rule-bound too, certainly. Relatively precise public admonitions dictate the when, where, and with whom of their sexual expression. These public regulations are presently battered by private morality. But, regardless of this ambiguity, no one questions the basic rightness of straight sexuality itself. No one gets anxious over latent heterosexuality. Gay persons live in different glass houses. Society—and this always means people—directly and indirectly throws boulders. Sixty-three percent think "Gay is Bad."

For this reason, the homosexual fights through a crisis of self-acceptance [54] undreamed of by straights.[55] The central issue in that struggle is that many homosexuals have learned their moral ABC's quite well. They often agree that they are bad. As crucial as human sexuality is and as important to self-acceptance, this wracking conflict between social no's and personal yes's devastates. At the same time, the crisis of self-acceptance is, for the individual homosexual, one of the most far-reaching he must face. Schofield's study of some three hundred persons—homosexual and nonhomosexual, in prison and out, under psychiatric care and not—concludes that "the ability to come to terms with the situation" reduces the need for psychiatric help, participation in public homosexual acts, and involvement in sex crimes.[56] Hoffman suggests that the high rate of promiscuity in the male gay world is the product, at least in large part, of self-hatred.[57] This self-hatred is the refracted result of society's rejection.

Yet social censorship comes in many shades. The rejection surfaces publicly in state laws and local law enforcement; [58] the activity of prosecutors, judges, and juries; federal employment practices; [59] the induction and discharge procedures of the Armed Forces; the mandatory registration of homosexuals; [60] and the official position of church organizations. It is less audibly expressed in whispered conversations about "one of them," jokes and cartoons about "queers" and "fairies," the reluctant contact with or the express avoidance of a gay man or woman, the number of jobs lost or parties unattended because "you just don't seem to fit here," the cold shoulder at church gatherings, the tenacity of the distorting stereotype, the possibility for and the actual incidence of blackmail, and the generally unreported vicious beatings of alleged homosexuals by self-appointed judges.

But the ambiguity in the social rejection is also striking. Thirty-seven percent of the country believe homosexuality is less than harmful to American life. Contrary to some gay ideology, the public reaction is not unanimous. This ambivalence emerges in state laws and their application. Viewed nationally, no agreement exists over the severity of a first offense; penalties range from one year to one life.[61] No consensus is possible over the definition of the homosexual act; it ranges from "any lascivious act" to "anal intercourse." [62] No consistency exists in the application of the laws by policemen. And, to cap the process off, almost no one goes to jail when the ambiguous laws are applied.[63] This having been said, however, it should be added that the relation between lawbooks and current opinion is nebulous. Current arrest records and actual convictions are better indicators of present opinion.

Contemporary reactions are also mirrored in prevailing stereotypes. Sociologist J. L. Simmons questioned 134 adults who reflected America's citizens. He asked them to select traits which they thought most homosexuals possessed. Seventy-two percent thought gay persons "sexually abnormal." Fifty-two percent thought them "perverted." Forty percent thought them both "mentally ill" and "maladjusted." Twenty-nine percent thought them "effeminate." [64] This negative image may be inaccurate, but it informs a label that refuses to meet homosexuals as persons.[65] Simmons found, in a separate project, that people also felt more socially removed from lesbians and male homosexuals than from any of the other groups listed.[66]

At the same time, striking changes in public opinion are also evident. Explanations are not yet conclusive. But the organization and militancy both of homosexual and homophile groups [67] and of those sympathetic to the gay cause are contributing factors. Shifts in cultural values, sexual mores, male-female roles, and family structure are also significant.[68] Several scattered events indicate the change in attitude toward the homosexual. Since the beginning of 1967, applicants for jobs in New York City government need not confess their homosexuality. Increasing numbers of clergymen, lawyers, and other professional persons are willing to champion reform publicly. The New York State Liquor Authority has ruled that bars are no longer prohibited from serving homosexuals. The San Francisco Tavern Guild has achieved similar gains in California. Current movies, plays, and novels developing homosexual themes parallel the shift in public perspective. Several Protestant denominations are in the process of rewriting old statements on homosexuality; the July, 1970, resolution by the Unitarian Universalists' meeting in Seattle is one of the most recent liberalizations. Finally, the Harris Poll meters are jiggling slightly. In 1965, 70 percent of the population thought homosexuality was harmful to American life; that percentage is now 63. Different winds are blowing.

It is dangerous to speak of a social reaction anyway. Both rejection and acceptance—with whatever middle terms—are pocketed. No unanimous response exists. John Kitsuse's study of undergraduates uncovered relatively "mild reactions" to homosexuals." [69] As sociologists have known for years, a person's place in society and the persons with whom he associates influence his response. Kinsey said, for instance, that women with gay histories were more willing to accept other gay men and women than were straight women.[70] In conclusion, however, social rejection, regardless of its ambiguity and regardless of the ameliorating influences, inhibits the homosexual's self-acceptance at every turn.

To summarize this section, becoming and being gay is a highly intricate process. It is not static or simple but dynamic and complex. Personal interpretations and commitments slowly emerge. Associations and their meaning gradually change. Social reactions of various kinds play an important role at every stage. Being turned on or being turned off is the result of tentative exploration. In short, homosexual life is a fluid, many-faceted process. To understand this is to defeat all simplification.

Variety in the Gay World

To return to the essay's major theme, ethical evaluation of homosexuality demands commitment to the homosexual world. This means to the whole world, not to a part of it. The simplifier, in contrast, believes a drum is an orchestra. When spying in the gay world, he finds hairdressers and calls them "the gay community." The truth is he has not seen the world at all. Variety is the hallmark of real gay life. The "Final Report of the Task Force on Homosexuality" commissioned by the National Institute of Mental Health describes this actual heterogeneity: "Homosexual individuals can be found in all walks of life, at all socioeconomic levels, among all cultural groups within American society, and in rural as well as urban areas." Others concur with this rudimentary fact.

More subtle confusions of part with whole creep in. Bad spies shove all the gay world's residents either onto a barstool or into a steam room. This falsification leaves the impression that the notorius public places are the only places. Certainly, to deny their part would be distortive. Bars, streets, parks, public toilets, all-night restaurants, bus stations, steam rooms, movie houses, after-hours clubs, hotels, and many other settings help to make up the homosexual world. Each has its own clientele, atmosphere, dangers, and rewards. Each offers an entrance into the gay world. And for researchers who have other private doors slammed, the public sector of the gay world is relatively easy to enter. Furthermore, each is a legitimate arena for investigation and description.[71] Much has been learned, especially about the male homosexual, through the study of this sexual marketplace. Extrasexual dimensions to this public scene also have been uncovered. Evelyn Hooker, for instance, suggests that the gay bar is a "communication center" for current gay gossip as well as an "induction center" for the novice.[72] In addition, the public scene exposes the dangers of police entrapment, the male fascination with sexuality, the need for anonymity, the quest for the perfect lover, the high regard for youthfulness and attractiveness, subcultural norms for behavior, and other elements that are an important part of the gay world.

The public scene, nonetheless, is not the whole scene. It may have great impact on the male life-style, but only a minority frequent this sector at any one time. A quick comparison of gay bar attendance on a given night with Kinsey's estimation of the total gay population in an area makes the point. Hoffman speculates—and speculation is the only possible course—that 6,000 male homosexuals frequent the 40 gay bars in San Francisco at the midnight to 1 A.M. peak. Between 50,000 and 100,000 gay men live in the Bay Area.[73] The number not in bars —given popular notions about gay life-styles—is astounding. Furthermore, focus upon the public sector brackets out other crucial portions of the total gay environment. The female homosexual for whom barhopping is rare, the majority of young men and women under twenty-one,[74] the nonbar married homosexuals, and, in general, the private sphere—none of these significant groups is touched. Research on sex in public toilets is certainly possible,[75] but, given the distorting tendency to see the whole gay world through a "glory hole" or from a barstool, it is laudable only if it puts itself in context. How does the public toilet fit into the whole gay world? No one answers that question.

In fact, no one knows much about the nonpublic gay world. Yet, gay people have careers. They have straight friends. They have mothers and fathers. They have sons and daughters. They celebrate Thanksgiving and Christmas. They eat out and laugh and cry and argue. They have indigestion and unmown yards. They are affronted and befriended. They pay taxes, go to school, attend church, and have birthdays. In short, they have an everyday[76] just as straights do. This day doesn't last from 8 P.M. until 1 A.M. when the bars are full. Their lives aren't all spent in bed, in tears, in therapy, in prison, or in ecstasy. But what is known about this? Little or nothing.

Storytellers, nonetheless, continue to pass on one-sided tales. Some suggest that the gay world is populated only with psychotics—latent if not overt. Edmund Bergler (*Homosexuality: Disease or Way of Life?*) gives this impression. So do Hervey Cleckley (*Caricature of Love*), Irving Bieber (*Homosexuality: A Psychoanalytical Study*), and other psychiatrists. And the impression holds—for some homosexuals. Some need and desire psychiatric help. The Bergler-Bieber cases document this. No contest. But the whole world doesn't recline on a couch.[77] Evelyn Hooker began demonstrating this in 1957. Using attitude scales, projective techniques, and life histories, she matched the records of thirty homosexuals with thirty heterosexuals, both groups being drawn from the general, not the couch, population. Two experts read and compared the records of the matched pairs. Their task was to distinguish straight from gay. Neither judge was able to do more than guess. Hooker concluded that "some homosexuals may be very ordinary individuals, indistinguishable, except in sexual pattern, from ordinary individuals who are heterosexual" and that homosexuality, hence, "may be a deviation in sexual pattern which is within the normal range, psychologically." [78] After interviewing 157 male homosexuals, Martin Hoffman asked, Are there a substantial number who cannot be considered mentally ill, using reasonable clinical standards? He writes: "The answer which I have found to this question is unequivocally in the affirmative. I have interviewed numerous men (and in many cases have extensive corroborating data from their friends and associates) who simply cannot be diagnosed mentally ill on the basis of any clinical psychiatric criteria known to me." [79] Again, this does not deny that neurotic homosexuals exist or that social pressure may create great opportunity for neurosis. But investigation of the whole gay world should no more judge it on the basis of psychiatric records alone than sociologists should judge the American family solely on the basis of divorce court proceedings.

It also is a mistake to assume that the gay world in America is the only gay world or that current attitudes toward homosexuality are the only possible ones. Comprehensive exploration means opening doors to the past and to other societies. As D. J. West concludes, gay life is as "old as history," emerging in Greece, in Rome, in China, and in most other areas of the world.[80] A wide range of societies tolerates homosexuality in some form. Ford and Beach in their *Patterns of Sexual Behavior,* which draws upon the Human Relations Area Files at Yale, reveal that in "49 (64%) of the 76 societies other than our own from which information is available, homosexual activities of one sort or another are considered normal and socially acceptable for certain members of the community." [81] Only 28 of the 76 societies indicate the absence, rarity, or secrecy of adult homosexual practices.[82] This comparative evidence proves that the American reaction to homosexuality is not the only one, that it is a rather severe one, and that a surprising number of other societies allow for homosexual expression in some form or another. The specific form varies. Generally, female homosexuality is permitted more than male homosexuality.[83] Such cross-cultural data place the world of the American homosexual in a more comprehensive context.

Finally, in opening up the variety in the gay world, homosexual life is not simply sexual activity. The labels or stereotypes that the general public applies to the gay person entrenches the impression that he is simply a "sex pervert." The homosexual's everyday is consequently deformed. Those everyday aspects, those activities which overlap with the rest of the population's, are forgotten. Whatever he says professionally, accomplishes in the community, or hopes for in the future are all squeezed through his sexuality. Straight laymen do this repeatedly. But so does scientific research taking the public-toilet approach. The obsessive concern for the cause of homosexuality and the fascination with the notorious places betrays this myopia and will continue to subvert attempts to know the whole, everyday gay world.

After voicing these cautions, however, we can raise a legitimate question: How important to the homosexual everyday *is* sex? The gay world as a whole gives no unanimous reply. Variety halts generalization. But the research of Kinsey, Hoffman, Gagnon, and Simon suggests that, at least for a significant *segment* of the male gay world, sex itself is highly important. This is *not* to say that sex is the only concern or that every gay male regardless of age and other influences is always sex-happy. That unidimensional view is incorrect. But, for a large number of males at certain points in their biographies, the one-night stand or, better, a series of one-night stands with casual acquaintances is important. Kinsey's first report began to document this dimension of the homosexual world when it concluded, "The homosexual male is more often concerned with finding a succession of partners, no one of whom will provide more than a few contacts, or perhaps not more than a single contact."[84] Only 51 percent of the males whom Kinsey studied had had sexual contact with only one or two partners. Twenty-two percent had had sex with over ten partners. And, if the sexual prowess of the gay male—judged in quantitative terms—is in doubt, some men have had more than two hundred contacts.[85] The most adventurous heterosexual would have difficulty keeping pace. This does not say that all male homosexuals are running with over two hundred men. It is not saying that the 51 percent should be overlooked. But it is suggesting that for apparently half the male gay population a lot of partner-changing is going on or has gone on. This reflects part of gay experience, but an influential part. Hoffman's study of 157 "reasonably conventional" gay men in San Francisco brought him to the conclusion which Kinsey had reached twenty years earlier: "The *most serious problem* for those who live in the gay world is the great difficulty they have in establishing stable paired relationships with each other.[86] This opinion is further buttressed by Gagnon-Simon's investigation of 550 homosexual males. They found, first of all, that between 43 to 51 percent had had 60 percent or more of their sexual relationships with partners they contacted only once. Secondly, between 7 to 19 percent of this group had picked up their sexual partners at public terminals; a larger percentage told of similar contacts in other semipublic or public settings.[87] Sex is thus separated from other personal commitments and had with a wide range of casually chosen cohorts. The prevalence of this activity is reflected in the high rate of venereal disease among male homosexuals.[88] In other words, in trying to answer the original question provisionally, sex itself is an important enough experience to make emotional attachments or other nonsexual considerations—at least for the period of the one-night stand—unimportant.

It is false to imply, however, that heterosexual males would not like to do the same thing with females or that, without more evidence, gay males are more interested in sex than straight males. It seems correct to conclude that homosexual men have more opportunity for casual sex and take advantage of it. The difference between what the female in our society allows sexually and what the male allows is the pivotal factor. Nonetheless, "straight" sex is a noticeable part of the male gay scene.

Members of the gay community—especially those interested in public relations—heatedly debate the Hoffmans and the Kinseys over how big this part is. Many claim that homosexual men have fewer orgasms in their lifetimes than heterosexual men—something Kinsey documented in 1948 [89]—and are, thus, demonstratively less concerned with sex than straight men. Others deny that so-called promiscuity is actually an important issue; what society does to the homosexual is the real problem. Still others assert that only a minority engage in promiscuous behavior. And these objections have some weight. Since the total gay world is not known, it is impossible to determine accurately the exact percentage of promiscuous men. Also, current research has not comprehensively tapped the world of the gay marriage, nor has it determined whether the male homosexual goes through stages, e.g., promiscuous while young but nonpromiscuous when older or when married. Finally, no one has compared the so-called gay overconcern for sex with the concern of the straight male. It may well be that straight males talk about sex as much and would like to have it as often but are simply prohibited by the female and by social custom. However, it seems, with protests from some, that until additional research is available—quite possibly the work done in San Francisco in 1960–1970 by the Institute for Sex Research [90]—the present findings are the more accurate.

Other available information suggests a striking and

provocative counterpoint. In contrast to what is known about the male homosexual, the female gay woman is surprisingly nonpromiscuous. With no legal sanction for her relationship and with much less than overwhelming support, 71 percent of the females whom Kinsey questioned had had sexual relations with only one or two partners. In contrast to 22 percent for the men, only 4 percent of the women had had sexual contact with over ten partners.[91] This is a notable comparison which defeats all effort to melt the gay world into a single ingot. The nonpromiscuous character of female relationships is highly significant for the ethicist who wishes to assess the part that homosexuality plays in behavior. The female's stability means that homosexuality and promiscuity are not necessarily bed partners. Why the difference between male and female? In pressing toward an initial answer, we will further document the variety and complexity of the gay world.

Promiscuity in the male emerges in relation to three interconnected factors: (1) the psychophysical, (2) the personal, and (3) the social.[92] At the first level, the male, in contrast to the female, quickly responds sexually to physical stimuli. Here homosexuality has nothing to do with it. For the *male,* visual contact, for instance, is enough to start fires burning. Sexual arousal may easily precede any physical contact or it may come with very little physical contact. Male sex needs little context. Females, on the other hand, tend to be aroused after relatively extended contact with the potential partner. Pornography, for this reason, is produced only for men. Well, almost. Be it in movie, literary, or photographic form, men are almost the exclusive buyers—even of lesbian books. Furthermore, men are more exclusively interested in and more exclusively stimulated by the sight of genitalia.[93] The sex organs can become for the male an end in themselves. Men are also more often content with ejaculation for its own sake and can reach orgasm both easily and quickly. They can separate the sex act from contact with the rest of the body or from emotional attachment. Fellatio through "glory holes" in public toilets epitomizes these capacities. Women, in comparison, find visual stimuli by themselves relatively uninteresting, integrate genital contact with bodily contact, and, most significantly, put their sexual activity within an emotional framework. Lester Kirkendall in his study of premarital intercourse found that at every level of liaison, from the casual pickup to the formal engagement, women tend to see the sexual encounter in terms of a permanent relationship and eventual marriage.[94] The Vedder-King study of lesbianism in the female prison also uncovered this nonpromiscuous tendency.[95] The low rate of partner exchange documents this in the wider lesbianism community. Evidence suggests, finally, that cross-culturally men combine their sexual propensities with interest in a variety of sexual partners; women do not.[96] This is to say simply that transcultural responses with psychophysical foundations lead men toward easy promiscuity. Without the female counterweight, therefore, in the male gay marriage or in the bar subculture the male tendency is doubled. Instability is understandable.

But male sexuality is not simply the product of relatively involuntary reactions. The gay man interprets his sexual feelings. He relates them to his understanding of his sexuality, of himself, and of his situation. These interpretations may check or allow promiscuity. Male sexuality, to consider the second major factor, is personally managed. The gay man may think himself a product of uncontrollable, amoral sexual drives which must be gratified for their own sake. He may define his situation as one in which immediate gratification is easy. The lengths to which he goes reflect how important sexual contact is for his self-definition, for who he thinks himself to be. It appears, then, that rapid bed-hopping is done by men whose sexuality is, and is expressed as being, crucial to their self-image. It seems that the male gay world allows and perpetuates the validity of this self-definition more than the female-influenced heterosexual world.

The conflict for the gay male who defines himself primarily in sexual terms is great. Selfhood is continually, irrevocably wasting away just by living, just by aging. John Rechy captures the existential trauma:

> The end of youth is a kind of death. You die slowly by the process of gnawing discovery. You die, too, in the gigantic awareness that the miraculous passport given to the young can be ripped away sadly by the enemy Time. . . . Youth is a struggle against—and, paradoxically, therefore a struggle *toward* death: a suicide of the soul.[97]

Yet, "suicide" is not the right word; suicide implies a willful act of death over which the individual has some control. In this relationship among the self, sexuality, loss of youth, and death, the sexual self has no control. The self is uncontrollably dying just by living; life in a real sense is death, and time is its second. This provides the clue to what is called "the crisis of aging" in the gay world. If sexual vigor were not as important to homosexual males, then the crisis of growing old would not be as central to their world.

At the same time, this is somewhat simplistic. Every gay man does not believe himself to be a penis. For others, even a large number, this is close to the truth. Hoffman calls this "sex fetishism." But, concurrently, many males are in search of the Perfect Lover, the ultimate and faithful companion.[98] For many the "constant searching for a vague ideal, just around the corner but never quite in sight," is a countering reality.[99] The self-definition "I am alone" wars silently with the self-definition "I am sexual." Rechy says it graphically:

> Now, beyond the spilled sperm—if nothing more than sex is possible—are we like enemies in that spent battle field of fugitive sex—in which there is every intimacy and no intimacy at all?[100]

Every physical intimacy, yes. Every intimacy, no. The intimacy of the lasting relationship is lacking.

Indeed, intimacy itself is not crucial here. Duration is. Further, it is incorrect to assume that all cruising homosexuals know only sexual intimacy. Intense affairs develop, if only over a weekend or two, in which much more is shared than raw sex. Heterosexuals have similar, brief encounters in which each partner opens himself up personally to the other. Circumstances in the gay world or the social rejection of the gay world often preclude this for the male homosexual. But it does happen. Therefore it is not emotional intimacy that is missing. What is lacking is duration, a lasting intimacy—the extended time to know someone extensively.

Factors at the psychophysical and personal levels inhibit this kind of intimacy. The male tendency toward promiscuity—fed by quick arousal and an interest in variety—and a sexual self-definition fight the lasting relationship. A war rages between "the frantic needs of Inside—Now!!" and "wanting to feel wanted."[101]

The gay male is not an isolate, however. The personally experienced conflict between promiscuity and fidelity is also perpetuated and created by the society in which he lives. The social dimension to the problem has two sectors. The first is the male gay world itself. Here quite a few homosexuals may celebrate their marriage in the privacy of their homes and patios. Gay men may ardently wish for and passionately talk about marriage in gay bars and baths. But this world of steam rooms and barstools does little to support it actively. The value system and the normative structure, in fact, push in opposite directions. The priority given youth, physical attractiveness, sexuality, "basket size," and sexual endurance mixed with a normative structure condoning one-night stands, allowing a rapid turnover of clientele and expecting frequent divorces, creates a social structure in which extended intimacy is greatly inhibited. At this level the female world stands out again in some contrast. The floor plan of the lesbian subculture has little space for public terminals, bars, steam rooms, street-corner prostitution and other male trappings. Consistent with female sexuality, the world of the lesbian does not promote casual physical encounters. Some instability exists in female relationships,[102] a great deal of emotional investment is sometimes made in short-term friendship, but this is not heightened, as it is in the male world, by dominant subcultural norms and values.

The rejection by the larger society, nonetheless, is the most important single factor in understanding the gay man's dilemma. Hoffman correctly views the centrality of this second part of the social dimension. He writes, "To put the matter in its *most* simple terms the reason that males who are homosexually inclined cannot form stable relationships with each other is that society does not want them to."[103] The fear of being found out and the consequent need for anonymity is the product, in large measure, of social condemnation. Sex in darkened parks is the quick and logical antidote that social rejection prescribes. It's fast; it's easy; it's safe; and, maybe most importantly, it's rapidly forgotten. No constant reminder of personal tendencies or incriminating evidence for others to see survives. Briefly, society condemns the promiscuity its prohibitions create. This does not render an ethical verdict. It simply reports accurately the mutually dependent relationship between behavior in the gay world and social control. The major implication is that any comprehensive ethic of the gay world must be at the same time an ethic of the straight world. In other words, the "black problem" is at the most significant level the "white problem." Commitment to the homosexual world demands putting it in its social context. It means seeing the effects of unrelieved, condemnatory labeling.

This labeling threatens extended intimacy at most turns. Male gay marriage is not the least affected. American attitudes render any closeness between males suspect. When two men live together for any period of time, hold hands in public, dance together, kiss, embrace, or even spend a great deal of time together, public conscience immediately accuses. How different it is for the female. If two men do marry, the relationship is not supported legally, religiously, or socially. Their relationship has no tax breaks, and public celebration of the marriage is not permitted—two supports for straight marriage. On the contrary, married men often must fear for their jobs, reputations, parents' love, and friends' respect. The bar subculture does not build their relationship up, and they have neither children nor public opinion to keep them together. In fact, most public values and norms encourage the destruction of their marriage. Is it any wonder that many gay men claim that all they really have and need is love, even if this does fudge somewhat? [104]

The lesbians' problems are certainly different. The female tendency to mix affection with sexual expression is not the only factor in reducing instability. Lesbians don't offend the public conscience as much. Who interrogates two women holding hands, kissing, or living together? Of course, these activities don't infallibly betray homosexual relationships. But the fact is: no one considers them queer. This less violent reaction to lesbianism in our society jibes with cross-cultural information. Julia Brown reveals that only 33 percent of the societies she measured punish female homosexuality. Strikingly, 68 percent of those societies punish the male.[105] The implication is not that the lesbian has an easy time in our society. This is decidedly not the case. The lesbian does encounter, however, less severe condemnation than the male does. The lighter stigma may account for the relatively high degree of self-acceptance among lesbians.[106]

In summary, a great variety exists in the gay world. Diversity prevails in occupation, cultural background, economic level, religion, and psychological adjustment. Female and male life-styles, subculture, and social acceptance also differ. But, at the same time, patterns emerge, especially in relation to lesbian and male marriages. Factors at the psychophysical, personal, and social levels help to account for the relative instability in male relationships. But variety is always around the corner.

Additional information may uncover more stability in the male gay world and less stability in the female. Yet the contrast between them will remain significant. Certainly, further understanding will call for commitment both to the intricate processes and to the striking variety in homosexual experience.

Implications for an Ethic of the Gay World

When attempting to analyze microscopically the process of becoming and being gay, when trying to understand the lesbian's world or the world of the male gay marriage or, indeed, the wide range of experiences in the homosexual everyday, we find that complete information is sorely lacking. The temptation is to abdicate from ethical decision. Three members of the Hooker Task Force for the National Institute of Mental Health succumbed, refusing to make policy suggestions. Others do also. Although information about the gay world is provisional—as repeatedly said in this essay—the decision not to decide has serious flaws. First, all the information will never be in; if complete reports are demanded, no decision will ever be made. Second, fascination with how little is known may become novocaine for the mind; the immensity of the task immobilizes further study. Third, the refusal to make informed decisions allows the uninformed, and usually eager moralist to leap easily into the vacuum; tentative but informed decisions give way to absolute and uninformed decisions. Fourth, enough information is available to provide, when correlated, some helpful guidelines for action; the cross-cultural incidence and the treatment of homosexuality offer some direction, for instance. Finally, and this is the most important, decisions are being made, have to be made in the midst of the present ambiguity. Teen-agers struggling with their sexual feelings, families finding out about their homosexual daughter, adults living with threatened careers, legislators voting on law reform, psychiatrists and ministers counseling homosexuals—all these persons can't, won't, and don't wait until all the information is in. The informed citizen can only chasten his tentative opinions with great concern for the homosexual, great concern for American society, and a healthy awareness of his own relative perspective.

Several implications for ethical decision stand out:

1. Sound ethics clamps down hard on bias. Because feelings run high in this area, scientific information, which eventually strains out blatant subjectivity, is most useful. Thoughtful sifting of many opinions, both scientific and nonscientific, is purifying. Contact with representative homosexuals is mandatory. If the ethicist shows little acquaintance with scientific reports, other person's opinions, and actual homosexuals, he is probably manufacturing his own fantasy.
2. The ethicist can no longer overlook the insistent problems of the 7 to 15 million homosexuals and their countless friends.
3. Homosexuals as a group are no more moral or immoral, religious or nonreligious, selfish or unselfish, sensitive or insensitive, sexy or unsexy, loving or unloving, than heterosexuals as a group. No ethic should claim that they are.
4. In fact, homosexuals are more like heterosexuals than not. Contrary to some, they are human beings. They become gay through an interpersonal process which differs only in content from the process of

becoming straight. Much more uncertainty exists for the gay person as he explores his sexuality, but his basic humanity transcends his particular sexual preference. Only surrealistic architecture builds cities on one brick. Certainly an ethic must have a wider foundation than sexual preference.

5. No sound ethic can condemn homosexuality for its unreal fruits. Homosexuality—in contrast to the rejection of it—does not by itself cause mental illness or criminal careers.
6. An ethic of the homosexual world must take seriously male sexuality and the bar-world subculture, both of which allow for and even perpetuate sex fetishism and barnyard morality.
7. An ethic must be sophisticated enough to deal with and speak persuasively to the actual conflicts in the gay world. Many homosexuals see no way out of the battle between their sexuality and their conscience. Many find it tortuous to face what their private life includes and what their public life excludes—both, they feel, of necessity. Many men especially see no door out of the struggle between their present sexual needs and their long-term need for love.
8. Serious consideration must be given to the near impossibility for an exclusive homosexual to change. An ethic must weigh heavily the demand that possible change makes upon economic resources, time, desire, and energies.
9. An ethic that cannot appreciate the joy, the beauty, and the variety in the gay world is sadly uninformed. It takes little effort or understanding to emphasize the real and imagined ugliness.

10. Any suggested treatment of the homosexual should be chastened by the wisdom of other societies.
11. The prevalence of homosexuality as a natural (existent) phenomenon does not make it good. Cancer exists, too; so do bombs for death and balms for life. The choice between explosives and medicine is not based upon their existence but upon what is valued.[107]
12. An ethic of the gay world must also be an ethic of the straight. Heterosexual parents helped create their homosexual sons. The severity of social rejection drives males especially to impersonal, anonymous sex and away from extended intimacy.
13. Ethical evaluation, regardless of its brand, cannot be uniform. The gay world is too heterogeneous. The ambivalent teen-ager is not the seasoned adult. The male homosexual is not the female. The bed hopper is not the faithful lover. The adjusted homosexual is not the unstable homosexual. The weekender with a home and family is not the exclusive gay person. The honest one-night stand is not the dishonest gay marriage. The one-timer at a convention is not the gay hustler. The homosexual Boy Scout leader is not the gay lawyer. Activity in a public toilet is not gay activity in a private home. Behavior is heterogeneous; ethics must speak to the variety.
14. A Christian ethic should be concerned both with God's will and with how this God appears to the homosexual who must live with his imperatives.
15. Is homosexuality itself the most crucial ethical issue? What of sexuality? Indeed, living with *plurality* in an emerging world society may be the larger

> problem. Variety exists. That's certain. Is it valuable? That's uncertain. The implication for ethics and theology are uncountable.

The rest of the book is now ahead. What's in store? First, in answering that question, distorting labels must be avoided. For this reason, it is enough to say, secondly, that the collection is and was designed to be highly diverse. In answering the moral question, "Is gay good?" the spectrum stretches from celibacy to celebration, from use of the Bible to distrust of it, from finding homosexuality natural to finding it unnatural. As indicated in the biographical sketches, the professional background of the authors is highly varied. This accounts for the variety of opinion.

John von Rohr, of the Pacific School of Religion and the Graduate Theological Union, Berkeley, begins the discussion. Since the symposium is dialogical, the other authors then respond to von Rohr's presentation. An author's entrance is determined by his contrast with the previous essayist. Von Rohr closes the volume with his second thoughts. His lead essay was originally written in 1965 for the Pacific Coast Theological Group. The present edition is a revised, shortened version but continues to speak to the salient theological and ethical issues. The other authors suggest how well.

The collection is now yours. It's diverse. It's open-ended. It's provocative. It's unsettling. In being a cross fire of opinion, a plurality of ideas and frames of reference, it goes a long way, at the ethical level, toward subduing the single answer.

Notes

1. "The Homosexual: Newly Visible, Newly Understood," *Time,* 94:56–67 (Oct. 31, 1969); *Berkeley Tribe,* II, June 19–26, 1970; Martin Hoffman, *The Gay World* (Bantam Books, Inc., 1968). The term "gay" is as old as sixteenth-century France. It means "homosexual," although it did not originally carry with it an echo of the effeminate stereotype. "Straight" means "heterosexual." For other slang terminology, see Gordon Westwood, *A Minority* (London: Longmans, Green & Co., Ltd., 1960), Appendix C.

2. See Richard Schickel, "Shock of Seeing a Hidden World," *Life,* 65:34–38 (Nov. 1, 1968). Schickel's review explicitly mentions *The Fox, The Legend of Lylah Clare, Therese and Isabelle, Les Biches* ["The Does"], and *The Killing of Sister George.* For an indication of film treatment previous to 1968, see *Social Action,* 34:45 (Dec., 1967). More recent cinematic portrayals by Richard Burton and Rex Harrison in *Staircase,* Elizabeth Taylor in *Secret Ceremony,* and Rod Steiger in *The Sergeant* combine with *The Boys in the Band, Midnight Cowboy,* and *Satyricon* to fashion a current, colorful, but confusing light show.

3. Alfred C. Kinsey *et al., Sexual Behavior in the Human Male* (W. B. Saunders Company, 1948), p. 651. The Kinsey reports are weak at several notorious points. Nonetheless, they remain the only works of their kind. Until something better is printed, they must suffice as a starting point.

4. Alfred C. Kinsey *et al., Sexual Behavior in the Human Female* (W. B. Saunders Company, 1953), p. 474. Kinsey, *Male,* p. 651.

5. John Rechy, *City of Night* (Grove Press, Inc., 1963);

James Baldwin, *Giovanni's Room* (Dell Publishing Co., Inc., 1956); James Baldwin, *Another Country* (Dell Publishing Co., Inc., 1962).

6. Thirty-seven percent of the white male population and 19 percent of the female population have had "at least some overt homosexual experience to the point of orgasm between adolescence and old age." See Kinsey, *Male,* p. 650, and Kinsey, *Female,* pp. 453–454.

7. This conclusion reached in October, 1969, is reported in *Time,* 94:61 (Oct. 31, 1969).

8. See Edwin Michael Schur, *Crimes Without Victims* (Prentice-Hall, Inc., 1965), pp. 82–85.

9. Baldwin, *Giovanni's Room,* p. 223.

10. Hoffman, *The Gay World,* p. 1. (Emphasis in the original.)

11. See Donald Webster Cory, "The Unrecognized Minority," in Charles H. McCaghy, *et al.* (eds.), *In Their Own Behalf: Voices from the Margin* (Appleton-Century-Crofts, 1968), pp. 70–82.

12. See H. Richard Niebuhr, *The Meaning of Revelation* (The Macmillan Company, 1962), Ch. 2.

13. This raises a question for ethicists that should be continually unsettling: Are not they accountable for the cures they propose and for the effects, both in the lives of individual persons and in societies, that these cures produce?

14. See Herbert Blumer, "Society as Symbolic Interaction," in Arnold Rose (ed.), *Human Behavior and Social Processes: An Interactionist Approach* (Houghton Mifflin Company, 1962), p. 188.

15. Neutralization of strong prejudice may take overcompensation, as in the case of Howard Becker's "unconventional sentimentality," designed to combat an overly romantic or conventionally sentimental view of the deviant. See Howard S. Becker (ed.), *The Other Side* (The Free Press of Glencoe, Inc., 1964), p. 4. Furthermore,

neutralization is not emasculation; the spy retains his moral values but employs them after he is back with accurate information.

16. David Matza, *Becoming Deviant* (Prentice-Hall, Inc., 1969), p. 43.

17. The homosexual's circumstances are crucial. But this is not a commercial for situation ethics or for any other ethic. The source for ethical norms, found either in or outside the life situation, remains for others to debate.

18. See Jerry Laird Simmons, *Deviants* (The Glendessary Press, 1969), p. 29.

19. Wardell B. Pomeroy, "Homosexuality," in Ralph W. Weltge (ed.), *The Same Sex: An Appraisal of Homosexuality* (The Pilgrim Press, 1969), p. 11. Less systematic evidence from journalists even betrays surprise at finding so few "queens" in gay bars, indeed at finding so many masculine-looking male homosexuals. See William J. Helmer, "New York's 'Middle-Class' Homosexuals," in *Harper's,* 226:85–92 (March, 1963).

20. John H. Gagnon and William Simon, "Homosexuality: The Formulation of a Sociological Perspective," in Mark Lefton, *et al.* (eds.), *Approaches to Deviance: Theories, Concepts, and Research Findings* (Appleton-Century-Crofts, Inc., 1968), p. 356.

21. See Evelyn Hooker, "An Empirical Study of Some Relations Between Sexual Patterns and Gender Identity in Male Homosexuals," in John Money (ed.), *Sex Research: New Developments* (Holt, Rinehart and Winston, Inc., 1965).

22. See Matza, *Becoming Deviant,* esp. Ch. 3, "Pathology and Diversity."

23. Kinsey, *Female,* pp. 474, 485; Kinsey, *Male,* p. 651.

24. For a discussion of the current breakdown in the exclusive male and female role, see Charles E. Winick, *The New People: Desexualization in American Life* (Pegasus, 1970).

25. For authorities who question the traditional duality between mental illness and mental health, especially in relation to schizophrenia, see Norman O. Brown, *Love's Body* (Vintage Books, 1966) ; R. D. Laing, *The Politics of Experience* (Ballantine Books, 1967) ; and Thomas S. Szasz, "The Myth of Mental Illness," in Lefton (ed.) , *Approaches,* pp. 79–89.

26. See Austin T. Turk, "Prospects for Theories of Criminal Behavior," in Lefton (ed) , *Approaches,* pp. 362–374.

27. Here "ideology" means "knowing corrupted by wanting or believing." See Gwynn Nettler, *Explanations* (McGraw-Hill Book Company, Inc., 1970) , Ch. 6.

28. It means the falsification, even the denial or destruction of another's life experience.

29. This does not deny the normative support that straight marriage has nor overlook the part that its lack plays in breaking up gay marriages. Gay relationships are kept together, however, by more than pure affection. See note 104.

30. Michael Polanyi, *Personal Knowledge: Toward a Post-Critical Philosophy* (Harper Torchbooks, 1964) .

31. It would be helpful for spys, for ethicists, and for their readers to spell out assumptions along with conclusions. How many ethicists do that? This essay presupposes the following: (1) People put in separate categories often have more in common than not. (2) A man's values, self-image, and behavior are shaped by his position in society. (3) The gay world is highly heterogeneous. (4) Legislation against homosexual activity represents an inordinate overkill and has denied basic civil liberties to consenting adults. (5) Meaning, meaning shifts, and decision are at the core of human existence. (6) God is best conceptualized in relation to the future, meaning construction, and value judgment. (7) Absolute differences are the result of conflict among relative interpretations. (8) Re-

pressive life within a pluralistic world is the major current dilemma threatening man's existence.

32. Howard Saul Becker, *Outsiders: Studies in the Sociology of Deviance* (The Free Press of Glencoe, Inc., 1963), p. 176.

33. What follows is admittedly impressionistic. No one has reported these processes specifically, systematically, or conclusively. Gagnon and Simon, "Homosexuality," *loc. cit.,* are beginning to fill in the "homosexual life cycle," to trace the life of the adult homosexual through stages labeled "coming out," "the crisis of femininity," "the crisis of aging," and so forth. But the present analysis probes to a more microscopic level. Older sociological formulations (e.g., Max Weber's conception of *verstehen* and George H. Mead's conception of time) and current developments in the sociology of deviance inform what follows. In general, see John Lofland, *Deviance and Identity* (Prentice-Hall, Inc., 1969), and Matza, *Becoming Deviant.* For background insights into adult change, see the chapter "Becoming a Marihuana User," in Becker, *Outsiders,* pp. 41–58, and "Personal Change in Adult Life," in Warren G. Bennis, *et al.* (eds.), *The Planning of Change* (Holt, Rinehart and Winston, Inc., 1969), pp. 255–267.

34. The simple decision to wear something to a party offers a cameo of process analysis. Early in the afternoon the potential partygoer puts on a pair of pants and a shirt, thinking: "It's important that I dress up tonight in order to impress Jane, but I'll change later. These clothes are more comfortable anyway for now." The afternoon may move in an unplanned direction; friends come over and stay to talk; the car takes longer to clean than expected, supper takes longer to prepare than usual. In short, life flows ahead. But the hour gets surprisingly late. At the moment to decide, these thoughts emerge: "I sure don't want to be late. I haven't time to iron my shirt. Maybe Jane won't be there anyway. Who will notice what I wear?

It'll be dark, and I'll leave early. Forget it." The meaning of the clothes change shifted in relation to shifting events. That's the clue, although sexual change isn't like putting on a clean shirt.

35. This word and others in the present section hide a complex theoretical background developed lucidly by Alfred Schutz, "Choosing Among Projects of Action" and "Phenomenology and the Social Sciences," in *Collected Papers,* Vol. I, *The Problem of Social Reality,* ed. by Maurice Natanson (The Hague: Martinus Nijhoff, 1962), pp. 67–96, 118–139.

36. Sociologists call this the passage through "opportunity structures." See Richard A. Cloward and Lloyd E. Ohlin, *Delinquency and Opportunity* (The Free Press of Glencoe, Inc., 1960).

37. The validity of this situational approach to adult sexual change—in contrast to but not in contradiction of interpretations emphasizing early childhood—is strengthened by studies of prison behavior. Under such dramatically changed social conditions widespread homosexuality emerges in both male and female institutions. See especially David A. Ward and Gene G. Kassebaum, *Women's Prison: Sex and Social Structure* (Aldine Publishing Company, 1965). Jack's situation is quite different and prison gay life is not representative of the gay world. But prison homosexuality documents the impact of situational factors.

38. Kinsey, *Male,* p. 650.

39. *Ibid.*

40. Certainly, they are not presented to frighten anyone. Developing a friendship with another man does not *necessarily* lead a husband, son, or friend to homosexuality. Neither do all of these illustrative experiences together. It is unfortunate that so many people share with Peter and Barbara Wyden, authors of *Growing Up Straight: What Every Thoughtful Parent Should Know*

About Homosexuality (Stein & Day, Publishers, 1968), an inordinate fear of homosexuality. Also, contrary to what the Wydens claim, homosexuality in both male and female appears to have numerous, even contradictory, causes. Given the present state of social scientific knowledge, no accurate method for predicting the emergence of homosexuality exists. To pretend differently is to raise both false fears and false hopes.

41. Baldwin captures the subtle slowness of this process—as seen from the gay person's perspective—when he portrays David's flight from his homosexuality, a process that, in its speed, is similar to becoming gay. David says: "And yet—when one begins to search for the crucial, the definitive moment, the moment which changed all others, one finds oneself pressing, in great pain, through a maze of false signals and abruptly locking doors. My flight may, indeed, have begun that summer—which does not tell me where to find the germ of the dilemma which resolved itself, that summer, into flight. Of course, it is somewhere before me, locked in that reflection I am watching in the window as the night comes down outside. It is trapped in the room with me, always has been, and always will be, and it is yet more foreign to me than those foreign hills outside." (Baldwin, *Giovanni's Room,* pp. 16–17.) Only completion of the process and a selective interpretation of the past provides the clue to those crucial moments. How often past conversions are reinterpreted indicates the nonfinal character of so-called final decisions.

42. Choice of sex object is *learned.* According to the latest scientific information, it is neither biologically preordained nor hormonally induced. See N. Parker, "Homosexuality in Twins: A Report on Three Discordant Pairs," in *British Journal of Psychiatry,* 40:489–495 (1964), and J. D. Rainer, *et al.,* "Homosexuality and Heterosexuality in Identical Twins," in *Psycho-somatic Medicine,* 21:251–258 (1960). For a discussion of origins, see Hoffman, *The*

Gay World, Chs. 7 and 8, and Donald James West, *Homosexuality* (Aldine Publishing Co., 1968), Chs. 7, 8, and 9. Physiological factors, speaking broadly, influence sexual *performance* (the workability of the sex organs and their capacity for activity) and sexual *desire* (whether one feels well or up to it), but they do not determine sexual *preference*—the choice of male or female. Physiology, thus, does not determine object choice, but this preference is not developed independent of physiological factors. The child has at birth, in Hoffman's terms, an "undifferentiated sexual potential," a free-floating, unattached sexuality (Hoffman, *The Gay World,* p. 121).

43. For an excellent illustration of the kind of subtle shift in morality that takes place but in a different area, see Donald R. Cressey, *Other People's Money: A Study in the Social Psychology of Embezzlement* (The Free Press, 1953), Ch. 5. See also Jack D. Douglas, "Deviance and Respectability: The Social Construction of Moral Meanings," in Jack D. Douglas (ed.), *Deviance and Respectability* (Basic Books, Inc., 1970), pp. 3–30, and Lofland, *Deviance and Identity,* pp. 84–93.

44. See Baldwin, *Giovanni's Room,* pp. 10–16. How similar this sounds—except for the choice of sexual partner—to the first sexual experience had by adolescent heterosexuals.

45. The traditional natural law ethicist speaks from a different dictionary, a dictionary not as closely tied in this case to what is experienced as to what ought to be lived.

46. Evelyn Hooker, "Male Homosexuals and Their 'Worlds,' " in Judd Marmor (ed.), *Sexual Inversion: The Multiple Roots of Homosexuality* (Basic Books, Inc., 1965), p. 102.

47. Cory, "The Unrecognized Minority," in McCaghy (ed.), *In Their Own Behalf,* p. 77.

48. The verbatim of a gay man reported by J. R. Parker, "How They Began," in Aron M. Krich (ed.),

The Homosexuals: As Seen by Themselves and Thirty Authorities (Citadel Press, 1954), p. 74, captures the stance between complete determinism and complete voluntarism expressed here: "As soon as I went to school, *I developed* deep affection for those of my school fellows who were well-built, and handsome; and spent much time in devising means of meeting them. With one boy in particular I was very friendly, having for him a strong sexual passion, which I did not understand, nor did he, though we used to creep into one or the other's bed every night. I suffered from erections at the thought of handsome boys since the age of eight, though I did not understand anything about sexual matters till I was fifteen." (Emphasis added.) Not understanding "sexual matters" and the facilitation of a friend does not deny the part of "*I* developed."

49. In Alfred Schutz's terms this confuses the subjective, "in-order-to" motive in present experience with the objective, "because" motive applicable to past experience. See Alfred Schutz, "Choosing Among Projects of Action," in Natanson (ed.), *Collected Papers,* Vol. I, pp. 69–72.

50. Pomeroy, "Homosexuality," in Weltge (ed.), *The Same Sex,* p. 7. He continues: "The important part to remember is that no matter where they stand on the scale, they cannot become more heterosexual by attempting to renounce or give up their homosexuality." The transfer must be made—the crucial word again—gradually. The most optimistic report on treatment—more frequently quite low success is reported—comes from Irving Bieber and his colleagues. See Irving Bieber, *et al., Homosexuality: A Psychoanalytic Study of Male Homosexuals* (Basic Books, Inc., 1962). If the conditions are favorable, i.e., the patient is young, bisexual, willing, wealthy, and persistent, up to 27 percent of the patients may become exclusively heterosexual, according to Bieber. For a summary discussion of treatment effectiveness, see Michael

George Schofield, *Sociological Aspects of Homosexuality* (Little, Brown & Company, 1965), pp. 162–172. In the Bieber study it was noted that the best results come after 350 hours of psychiatric counseling. More than *ethical* issues are involved; this help costs about $10,000.

51. Baldwin, *Giovanni's Room,* pp. 86–87.

52. Homosexual behavior is outlandish or repugnant or mystifying mainly—to give one reason—because the straight person compares at the wrong point or from the wrong point. The comparison with heterosexual behavior is made at the end of the process, not at the beginning or along the way. How sexually similar are all human beings at birth. How human is the process of change just sketched. Gay people are monsters for many because they do not see similarities and because they have not experienced the gradual change from the inside. This does not deny or make light of the majority's negative reaction. It is real and, given their perspective, understandable; it certainly has effects in the homosexual's life. But it does not represent the only reality, the only interpretation. And the good spy is committed to exposing "multiple realities" both in their construction and in their survival. He is also aware that rejection of the homosexual is sometimes projection, a rejection of feared homosexuality in oneself. For a brilliant treatment of the problem of multiple interpretations, see Alfred Schutz, "Multiple Realities," in Natanson (ed.), *Collected Papers,* Vol. I, pp. 207–259.

53. Donald Webster Cory, *The Homosexual in America: A Subjective Approach* (Castle Books, 1960), p. 6.

54. There are other crises created for and by the homosexual in our society. In addition to the list which Gagnon and Simon are developing they are: (1) the crisis of awareness (related to self-acceptance), (2) the crisis of publication (telling the secret), (3) the crisis of "straight" sex (Hoffman calls this "sex fetishism"),

(4) the crisis of lost familial love, (5) the crisis of life goals, (6) the crisis of duration (related to what Hoffman calls "intimacy") and (7) the crisis of isolation (having only gay friends).

55. A gay lawyer once suggested that I imagine myself in a homosexual society. I did. The identity crises—even in fantasy—were enough to change my personal appreciation of the gay dilemma radically. In this case the spy dropped his guard of neutrality and was floored.

56. Schofield, *Sociological Aspects,* pp. 174, 210. For a critique of Schofield's research plan, see Martin Hoffman, Review of Schofield, *Issues in Criminology,* II, Fall, 1966, 313–316.

57. Hoffman, *The Gay World,* Ch. 10.

58. For a brief, comprehensive treatment of the legal dimension at the world level, see West, *Homosexuality,* pp. 72–84; for a chart summary of present state laws and for an excellent statement on behalf of homosexual law reform, see Gilbert M. Cantor, "The Need for Homosexual Law Reform," in Weltge (ed.), *The Same Sex,* pp. 83–94; for a detailed analysis of present legal codes, see Hoffman, *The Gay World,* pp. 77–97.

59. The treatment given Walter Jenkins, a member of President Johnson's former staff, represents the manner in which homosexuals are barred from federal employment. See Lewis I. Maddocks, "The Law and The Church vs. the Homosexual," in Weltge (ed.), *The Same Sex,* pp. 101–104.

60. See Hoffman, *The Gay World,* pp. 89–92.

61. As of 1969 the maximum penalty for the first violation of the laws proscribing sodomy in five states (California, Idaho, Missouri, Montana, and Nevada) is life imprisonment. Thirty-five states have maximum penalties of less than life but at least ten years; twelve states call for less than life but at least twenty years. Illinois (1961) is the only state in which homosexual acts between con-

senting adults in private are not punished. It is nowhere illegal, of course, to be homosexual; laws have to do with behavior. The severity reflected in these maximum penalties is matched with an equally extreme range of punishments for the initial offense. In seven states, five years is the minimum penalty; in six others (Kentucky, Louisiana, New Hampshire, South Carolina, Vermont, and Wisconsin), it is the maximum.

62. In nineteen states, the homosexual act is defined vaguely as "the crime against nature," something that must have been more obvious to the original legislators than it is today. Words and phrases such as "buggery," "any lascivious act," "unnatural copulation," and "the abominable and detestable crime against nature with mankind or beast" sprinkle the lawbooks. But the term "sodomy"—used by itself in thirteen state codes or with the phrase "crime against nature" in six others—is more regularly employed to describe the homosexual act. It isn't much more precise than its cohort "the crime against nature." The common-law or generally accepted definition of "sodomy," which is the often unexamined legacy of sixteenth-century England, renders it "anal intercourse." This definition is either inadequate or confusing for three reasons: (1) even though it is designed to distinguish and, subsequently, to extinguish homosexual activity, it can be equally applied to the heterosexual bedroom because it does not emphasize the illegality of anal intercourse with a member of the same sex; (2) it does not consider important, attenuating circumstances such as consent, adulthood, or privacy; (3) it overlooks the significant differences among anal intercourse, fellatio (oral-penile stimulation), cunnilingus (oral-vulval contact), and mutual masturbation and is, thus, insufficient. As a result of this imprecise, common-law definition, a heterosexual couple in one room is subject to arrest for sodomy, while a homosexual pair in

the next apartment performing mutual fellatio is doing nothing illegal—because the law doesn't cover it. Even if the sodomy laws were expanded—as they have been in twenty states—to include oral-genital contact, this would only mean—because the distinction is usually still not made between gay and straight activity—that half of the married heterosexual population would be up for jail terms. Kinsey indicated (*Female,* p. 399; *Male,* p. 576) that 49 percent of all married females engage in some form of oral-penile stimulation. Sixty percent of the college-educated engage in this kind of sexual activity. The theoretic although not actual result of current legislation: straight people are caught in nets laid for the gay. Furthermore, to compound and recompound the confusion, common-law definitions of sodomy—laws expressly (although improperly) designed to cope with homosexual activity—are not even used by enforcement officers. In Los Angeles County, California, for instance, 90 percent of the felony arrests were for oral, not anal, intercourse, and between 90 and 95 percent of all homosexual arrests were for misdemeanors involving "disorderly conduct," "soliciting," and "loitering." See "Project/The Consenting Adult Homosexual and the Law: An Empirical Study of Enforcement and Administration in Los Angeles County," *UCLA Law Review,* 13:643–842 (March, 1966).

63. The number of arrests fluctuates from city to city and from period to period. It is erratically determined by the pressure of local opinion, the personal inclinations of officials and policemen, and the man-power supply. In short, ambivalent laws are applied sporadically, often at the whim of personal opinion. But, yet, almost no one spends time in prison. Of the 457 felony convictions reported in the Los Angeles study, only three men were actually jailed. Whether the defendant is tried for a misdemeanor or for a felony he is usually fined, given

an immediately suspended jail sentence, and placed on probation. There are several reasons for this. Judges realize that putting a male homosexual in an all-male prison is like curing avarice by working in a bank. Judges also realize that the law is selectively applied. Since estimates indicate only twenty convictions for every six million acts, many judges feel that the person before them is the unlucky brunt of an unenforceable law.

64. Simmons, *Deviants,* p. 29. In notable contrast, heterosexual adulterers were thought "immoral" by 41 percent, "promiscuous" by 36 percent, "insecure" by 34 percent, "lonely" by 32 percent, and "sinful" by 31 percent. They were not called "mentally ill" or any other of the things homosexuals were.

65. Labels kill. They also are necessary to human life. For a study of labeling in daily life, see Norman K. Denzin, "Rules of Conduct and the Study of Deviant Behavior: Some Notes on the Social Relationship," in Douglas (ed.), *Deviance and Respectability,* pp. 120–159, and Erving Goffman, *Stigma* (Prentice-Hall, Inc., 1963).

66. *Ibid.,* pp. 31–35. This research was done in 1965 and does not necessarily reflect either the whole population at the time or current attitudes. It is suggestive, however. The other groups were: (with decreasing tolerance) intellectuals, ex-mental patients, atheists, ex-convicts, gamblers, beatniks, alcoholics, adulterers, political radicals, marijuana smokers, and prostitutes.

67. See the listing of homophile organizations in this volume.

68. This analysis emphasizes process and personal interpretation, elements close to the everyday experience of the gay person. Other treatments focus on cultural or social system factors, e.g., changing sex mores. These are important but are spatially and temporally removed from the immediate experience of the gay individual and

thus, for him, take on lesser significance.

69. John Kitsuse, "Societal Reaction to Deviant Behavior: Problems of Theory and Method," *Social Problems,* 9:247–256 (1962), esp. 256.

70. Kinsey, *Female,* pp. 479–481.

71. For further description of this public scene, see Hoffman, *The Gay World,* Ch. 3; Rechy, *City of Night;* and John Rechy, *Numbers* (Grove Press, Inc., 1967).

72. Hooker, " 'Worlds,' " in Marmor (ed.), *Sexual Inversion,* pp. 98–99.

73. Hoffman, *The Gay World,* pp. 9–10.

74. The recent reform bill before the Dutch Parliament, which advocates the legalizing of consenting homosexual relationships between those over sixteen, is sensitive to the large number of young homosexuals who, in their formative years, are outside the doors of baths and bars.

75. See Laud Humphreys, "Tearoom Trade: Impersonal Sex in Public Places," *Transaction,* VII (Jan., 1970), 11–25.

76. The word "everyday" comes from the technical term *"Lebenswelt,"* or "lived world," suggested by the philosopher Edmund Husserl and expanded by the sociologist Alfred Schutz.

77. The whole world cannot be explained by one psychiatric theory either. The Bergler-Bieber approach is under fire currently. It is vulnerable because it assumes a single cause for male homosexuality—the overprotective mother and the indifferent father. Several years ago, of course, it was the reverse—indifferent mothers and overaffectionate fathers. Drs. Kremer and Rifkin, on the basis of their in-depth study of twenty-five lesbians, found a similar reversal in the current psychiatric explanation for female homosexuality. Not affectionate fathers and puritanical mothers—the old theory—but hostile fathers and overburdened mothers have lesbian daughters.

These researchers did not, however, claim a new absolute explanation. They concluded, allowing the variety in gay experience to speak, that "homosexuality may be a final common behavioral pathway rather than a single entity with a single etiology." See Malvina W. Kremer and Alfred H. Rifkin, "The Early Development of Homosexuality: A Study of Adolescent Lesbians," *American Journal of Psychiatry,* 126:129–134, esp. 133–134 (July, 1969).

78. Evelyn Hooker, "The Adjustment of the Male Overt Homosexual," reported in Schur, *Crimes Without Victims,* p. 74.

79. Hoffman, *The Gay World,* p. 158. See also Gagnon and Simon, "Homosexuality," in Lefton (ed.), *Approaches,* p. 353.

80. See West, *Homosexuality,* pp. 21–29. For development of attitudes in the West, see Derrick Sherwin Bailey, *Homosexuality and the Western Christian Tradition* (London: Longmans, Green & Co., Ltd., 1955).

81. See C. S. Ford and F. A. Beach, *Patterns of Sexual Behavior* (Harper & Brothers, 1951), pp. 129–133, esp. pp. 130 and 129. For another infrahuman, cross-cultural perspective upon male homosexuality, see Wainwright Churchill, *Homosexual Behavior Among Males* (Hawthorne Books, Inc., 1967), pp. 60–88. Churchill supports Ford-Beach while adding (p. 72) that, in spite of the variety of social treatment of homosexuality, no society, regardless of its degree of permissiveness, has condoned exclusive homosexual practice as a permanent life-style for a large number of its adults.

82. Twsana Society, which approves female homosexuality but rejects male homosexuality, is counted in each group.

83. See Julia S. Brown, "A Comparative Study of Deviations from Sexual Mores," *American Sociological Review,* 17:135–146 (April, 1952). The Ford-Beach findings

also support the essential validity of Kinsey's heterosexual-homosexual continuum, a continuum that is also found at the level of subhuman primates and lower mammals. See Ford and Beach, *Patterns,* pp. 134–143.

84. Kinsey, *Male,* p. 632.

85. Kinsey, *Female,* p. 488. Paul Gebhard in studying a very select group of male sex offenders writes: "It was impossible to arrive at a figure for the homosexual offender vs. adults, since their promiscuity was such that they were frequently unable to give precise estimates, but we know that the median would be closer to 200 than 100 partners." See Paul H. Gebhard and others, *Sex Offenders: An Analysis of Types* (Harper & Row, Publishers, Inc., 1965), p. 637. If the median was above 100, some of these men put in remarkable performances.

86. Hoffman, *The Gay World,* pp. 7, 42, 164. (Emphasis supplied.)

87. Gagnon and Simon, "Homosexuality," in Lefton (ed.), *Approaches,* pp. 354–355. The spectrum is created by variance between groups. For example, 7 percent of the *college* educated who had *mixed* homosexual and heterosexual histories picked up tricks in public terminals; 19 percent of the *high school* educated who had *exclusively* homosexual histories did their shopping in these places.

88. Disease detectives in Massachusetts, who are some of the best organized in the nation, blame male homosexuality for 16 percent of the state's venereal disease. See *Time,* 96:36 (July 27, 1970).

89. Kinsey, *Male,* pp. 631–636.

90. The Institute for Sex Research at Indiana University, known generally as the Kinsey Institute, has recently completed an investigation of the gay community in San Francisco, funded by the National Institute of Mental Health. In-depth interviews with 1,040 homosexuals, randomly selected from some 6,000 volunteers,

were collected. The data are now being interpreted and will be published in 1971 or 1972. With publication the report will be the most thorough of its kind yet undertaken in this area.

91. Kinsey, *Female,* p. 476.

92. The following section is influenced directly by Hoffman, *The Gay World,* Chs. 10 and 11. Hoffman's work, however, only sensitizes. It lacks the systematic rigor and comprehensiveness necessary to draw certain, grounded conclusions. The present treatment is, likewise, only suggestive.

93. At the infrahuman level, males are aroused sexually when they observe other animals engaged in sexual activity. Females are not. See Kinsey, *Female,* pp. 661–662.

94. Lester Kirkendall, *Premarital Intercourse and Interpersonal Relationships* (The Julian Press, Inc., 1961), pp. 64, 88–89, 114, 119, and 137. Dr. Mary Calderone puts it succinctly: "The girl plays at sex, for which she is not ready, because fundamentally what she wants is love; and the boy plays at love, for which he is not ready, because what he wants is sex." ("How Young Men Influence the Girls Who Love Them," *Redbook,* 125:45 f. [July, 1965].

95. See Clyde B. Vedder and Patricia G. King, "Female Homosexuality in Prison," in their *Problems of Homosexuality in Corrections* (Charles C. Thomas, Publishers, 1967), pp. 27–41.

96. Kinsey, *Female,* p. 682.

97. Rechy, *City of Night,* p. 237.

98. This quest has utopian overtones. Kinsey, *Male,* pp. 632–633, documents the striking perfectionism in the male homosexual community. In the search for one-night bed partners or for the One, potential lovers may be rejected simply for the color of their hair or eyes.

99. Schofield, *Sociological Aspects,* p. 178. The very

search for stability, for the Perfect Lover, may drive males from partner to partner.

100. Rechy, *City of Night,* p. 364.

101. *Ibid.,* pp. 29, 354. In the light of this suggested conflict between promiscuity and marriage, it is significant that some married couples remain aloof from regular participation in the bar scene. It may be that they each now have a regular sexual partner and no longer need the marketplace. It also may be that the sex-oriented, single, youthful population of the gay bar is an unconscious or realized threat to their relationship.

102. Although the contrast between male and female is consistent with most current information, variety renders this no more than a significant pattern. Many gay men do not frequent the public sector and some lesbians have highly unstable relationships. For appropriate texturing in this area see John H. Gagnon and William Simon, "The Lesbian: A Preliminary Overview," in their *Sexual Deviance* (Harper and Row, Publishers, Inc., 1967), pp. 247–282, esp. 275–279. The impressionistic character of their presentation means taking the word "preliminary" in their title seriously.

103. Hoffman, *The Gay World,* p. 174. (Emphasis in the original.)

104. It is false to assume that love is the only cement —gay dogmas to the contrary. Other considerations, expressed by gay men themselves, keep the marriage together: (1) "I'm too old to start looking again"; (2) "I'm afraid to go cruising"; (3) "I don't want to hurt him by breaking us up"; (4) "At least the relationship is stable, and we're not frantically barhopping"; (5) "Two incomes are better than one"; (6) "I probably wouldn't find anyone better"; (7) "Regular sex is better than weekend sex"; (8) "I can't admit to my gay friends that we've failed"; (9) "We've got so much money tied up in our home"; (10) "I'd hate to leave all of our things

behind"; (11) "I don't want to go through the legal hassle with the deeds to the house, car and boat"; (12) "Our relationship is at least comfortable." Homosexuals who have been public defenders of the gay community and of the lasting gay marriage have additional reasons for staying married—one of the best often being, of course, that they're in love.

105. Julia S. Brown, *loc. cit.*, p. 138.

106. Kinsey found that 20 percent of the 142 exclusively homosexual women he studied regret their sexuality; 71 percent have no regret; and 6 percent have only slight regret. (Kinsey, *Female*, p. 477.)

107. The confusion of what is with what ought to be is called the "naturalistic fallacy." The discussion goes back to Hume's *Treatise* and today is spoken of linguistically as the confusion between descriptive and evaluative statements, a confusion of oranges with elephants. For debate on this point, see John R. Searle, "How to Derive 'Ought' from 'Is,' " and R. M. Hare, "The Promising Game," in Philippa Foot (ed.), *Theories of Ethics* (London: Oxford University Press, 1967), pp. 101–127. Thus, no one is justified in claiming that because homosexuality exists it is therefore good—or bad.

1

Toward a Theology of Homosexuality

John von Rohr

Throughout the centuries, Christian theology has condemned all homosexuality as sin. Concerning this type of deviation, its judgment has been quite undeviating. Corresponding social consequences have followed, ranging from ostracism within church and community to criminal legislation against all homosexual acts. Yet in recent years there have been intimations of change in these perspectives, with growing interest not only in rehabilitation of the homosexual but even more in rehabilitation of Christian thinking itself concerning homosexuality. This essay seeks simply to promote further dialogue on that important matter.

To some extent this rehabilitation involves a reappraisal of the Biblical materials presumably related to homosexuality. This is especially true of what has been looked upon traditionally as the *locus classicus* of divine wrath against homosexual behavior, the Sodom story of Gen., ch. 19. In this account the city of Sodom is reputed to have been destroyed by God for the sin of its inhabitants. And that sin has been traditionally identified as homosexual, since the narrative speaks of the men of the city clamoring for male visitors who have come into their midst in order that they might "know" them. Recent analysis,[1] however, has raised questions on two counts, wholly apart from the basic matter of the historical reliability of the narrative itself when viewed in the light of modern Biblical criticism. One notes simply that the Hebrew verb here translated "to know," judged by the preponderant manner of its usage in the Old Testament, does not necessarily imply a sexual relationship. And the other points out that the homosexual interpretation of the story actually did not develop until close to New Testament times. There are, of course, subsequent references in the Old Testament to Sodom, its sin, and its destruction, but none of these identify that sin explicitly as homosexuality. It was rather in writings around the beginning of the Christian era that this view began to emerge. The Testament of the Twelve Patriarchs spoke of Sodom as a city that "changed the course of nature." Philo saw it as a place of great lust where "men mounted males" in search of sexual gratification. And by the time of Clement of Alexandria in the second century this homosexual passion also included a "burning with insane love for boys." But all this is very late in relation to the original event and its story. A reappraisal of the Sodom narrative and its interpretation can suggest that homosexuality was an afterthought.

But though this classic Biblical case against homosexuality may be reinterpreted as an instance of at least uncertain, if not unjustified, identification, the fact still remains that where the Bible does explicitly refer to this matter it is condemnatory in its judgment. In the Old Testament the laws of Leviticus are emphatic in prohibiting male homosexual activity, even to the point of attaching the penalty of death.[2] And in the New Testament the letter to the Romans adds female homosexuality for reprimand,[3] while other passages refer to homosexuals in general as among the unrighteous who violate divine law and will be denied inheritance of the Kingdom of God.[4] Actually, the number of such Biblical references is very limited. But where homosexuality is mentioned explicitly in the Bible, the stance is one of prohibition and condemnation, a view that has then been consistently maintained in the subsequent centuries of Christian history.

Rehabilitation of Christian thinking on homosexuality, therefore, needs to recognize that new perspectives can indeed be added. The specific norms of an ancient time are subject to the modification suggested by insights and discoveries of a more modern time. It may well be that those specific norms need to be replaced by the more general Christian norm of concern for the person and the value of personal relationships. And it may well also be that contemporary psychological and sociological insights into the nature of homosexuality can assist in the development of at least some new evaluations with respect to this form of sexual life.

One contemporary consideration of undoubted importance is the now common emphasis upon the presence of a homosexual "condition" generally underlying homosexual acts. Though it is possible, of course, for homosexual behavior to be entered into by the heterosexually inclined, say for monetary reasons or for those of sheer perversion, the fact of an underlying homosexual inclination must be recognized for some persons as dominantly present. This is what the Wolfenden Report, a document prepared by an appointed commission for the

British Parliament, defined as a "sexual propensity for persons of one's own sex," [5] which then may or may not express itself in overt homosexual behavior. The existence of the "condition" was further arrestingly affirmed by this report when it stated that "solitary masturbation with homosexual fantasies" is probably the most common expression of the homosexual tendency.[6] Actually, clinical analysis indicates that homosexuality and heterosexuality are not always mutually exclusive but can be combined in a given individual. Kinsey has shown this to be true of the overt sexual behavior, distributing both male and female activity over a seven-point scale ranging from the completely heterosexual to the completely homosexual. The Wolfenden Report likewise made this point with regard to underlying impulses, saying, "All gradations can exist from apparently exclusive homosexuality without any conscious capacity for arousal by heterosexual stimuli to apparently exclusive heterosexuality." [7] But the point for the moment is to take note of the "condition" of homosexuality and the fact that it can indeed be the dominant impulse for some persons.

A further contemporary consideration makes this somewhat more specific quantitatively by noting the fairly substantial incidence of homosexual activity, as reported and surmised through clinical studies. Theological and ethical judgments, of course, cannot be based simply upon statistical data. Yet if we are to be led in time to think about the "natural" and the "unnatural" or the "normal" and the "abnormal," categories often employed in discussion of homosexuality, then perhaps the further categories of the "not too unnatural" or the "not entirely abnormal" might have some relevance. Thus the disclosures of the extent of homosexuality, as seen in contemporary studies, are not unimportant. Kinsey's figures are those most frequently utilized. His most startling statistic is to the effect that 37 percent of the total male population have at least some overt homosexual experience, to the point of orgasm, during their lifetime. This is, of course, an "accumulative incidence" figure, and thus is also deceptive since it includes individuals with only a single homosexual experience along with those for whom this is a continuous pattern. With regard to chronic homosexuality, his investigations show that 4 percent of all white males are exclusively homosexual throughout their lives after the onset of adolescence, and also that 10 percent are preponderantly homosexual for at least three years between the ages of 16 and 65. As to female homosexuality, Kinsey shows a somewhat lower "accumulative incidence" figure than for men, this being set at 28 percent. Havelock Ellis, however, has estimated that there is actually twice as much female homosexual activity as male. In any case, the figures for known overt activity are generally looked upon as representing only a small fraction of the totality of homosexual behavior. The psychiatrist, Edmund Bergler, who is convinced that Kinsey's sampling procedures were very faulty especially with regard to women and who thus sees the 28 percent figure as much too low, also makes the statement that the "ratio of visible to camouflaged Lesbians is probably one to one hundred." [8]

But this leads to one further consideration that should now be entered into the picture. Let me state it first through observations made by Evelyn Hooker, who has engaged in studies of homosexuality for the National Institute of Mental Health of the United States Public Health Service. From these studies she has published her conviction that homosexuality as known through those who come into conflict with the law or who present themselves in a disturbed state for therapy constitutes only a small portion of the totality of homosexual behavior. It is much more extensively present among persons "who live relatively discreet, stable, law-abiding (in all other respects), constructive, and socially useful lives." She writes:

> This group, whose homosexuality is well hidden and concealed from public view because of social stigma and legal penalty, constitutes the largest portion of those engaging in homosexual behavior. Criminal behavior or severe emotional maladjustment, and child molestation, are *not* more likely to be found in this group than in comparable groups of heterosexual individuals. To this group belong many of our most useful and able citizens in all walks of life.[9]

Thus we have now come to the point of observing not only that much homosexual activity is concealed and generally unknown but also that it manifests itself frequently in seemingly stable lives and further, therefore, that much of it is carried on basically in a nonpredatory, and perhaps one could say nonpromiscuous, way. The "nonpredatory" judgment would not likely be contested, for it is doubtful that any would affirm all homosexual behavior to be child molestation or some other form of aggression.

However, the judgment that this behavior is or can be nonpromiscuous, in large measure, is open to some question, especially on the part of certain psychiatrists whose clinical observation leads to contrary views, Abram Kardiner writes: "It is a noteworthy feature of homosexual unions that they are usually entered on by males who do not know one another and do not seek to continue their relationships. Most of the encounters are 'pick-ups' and 'one-night stands.'"[10] And Edmund Bergler says: "The typical homosexual is perpetually on the prowl. His 'cruising' is more extensive than that of the heterosexual neurotic."[11] But it is interesting that a different judgment arises from within the homosexual community itself. Writing in the *Mattachine Review* and discussing these allegations of promiscuity, William Raeder says, "Many homosexuals who recognize themselves as intelligent, sensitive, hard-working, serious-minded, loyal in their personal relationships and circumspect in sexual matters will wince at the charge."[12] In the same publication Luther Allen is critical of homosexual "gayety," maintaining that "this is not relatedness, but prostitution for physical release only," thus urging upon the promiscuous element within the community the more stable type of relationship that enables one "to become a different kind of homosexual."[13] And Iris Murdoch, writing in *The Ladder,* a lesbian magazine, sees no difference between homosexuals and heterosexuals in this regard: "There are plenty of neurotic and unstable homosexuals and there are plenty of promiscuous ones. But there are a great many who are none of these things and many heterosexuals who are all of them. . . . Indeed if one reflects on the extreme promiscuity of heterosexuals, both in the past and today, I doubt if any charge of exceptional promiscuity can significantly be made against homosexuals." But it is not just this matter of denial. There is also the corresponding positive affirmation: "Homosexuals in love can experience the same entire and unselfish devotion of body and soul to another which is characteristic of heterosexual love at its best." [14] So we are left with the conclusion that whereas there are types of homosexual behavior that can be designated predatory and promiscuous, there is also that which is reserved and responsible.

But now we should explore this a little more fully, for we are moving toward things more clearly relevant to Christian theology. We are dealing at this point with the realm of persons in sexual relationship, and surely Christian thought is concerned about that. Here it has become customary to employ the "I and thou" terminology in speaking about heterosexual love. Sexual relations without the personal communication and self-giving implied by such designation can turn the occasion into an exploitative "I-it" pattern and in a sense constitute rape, even though sanctioned by law. In the ideal sense there must be this depth dimension of personal communion in the sexual act. Here is the point of man's elevation above simply erotic sexuality. Sexual love will not lack its erotic element. Indeed, the *eros* of such love can be more than mere bodily pleasure, being a product also of man's spirit which finds its own measure of fulfillment in the achievements of sexual conquest, even in the marriage relationship. But spirit is likewise capable of expressing itself in self-giving, and thus man's sexuality, which conveys so many of the complexities of his existence, also becomes a vehicle of *agape*. And here then is where the "it" becomes "thou" and the communion of persons is achieved. So much of the biological and psychological literature on sex uses the term "love object" for the partner sought for the sexual relationship. Though this is not an inappropriate designation for that type of sexuality seeking simply erotic fulfillment, it can hardly be deemed adequate when carried into the language of sexual love as maintained in Christian understanding. In the most profound sense, there are subjects in such love, but not objects. And the subjects are united in body and spirit, the "one flesh" which comes to be in the marriage act. Here personhood is the key, or rather the love that truly loves and honors the person with whom love's experience is shared. And its components are at least these three: respect, self-giving, and fidelity.

So the question now becomes one of the possibility of homosexual fulfillment, or better, approximation (for fulfillment is elusive everywhere), of this kind of personal love. Miss Murdoch's earlier testimony to the contrary, there are those who question the likelihood of such realization. We recall Bergler's description of homosexuality as promiscuity on the prowl. But sheer promiscuity apart, there is the question of whether homosexual union can survive the various trials and difficulties to which it is exposed; even more, whether or not such union carries within itself a kind of necessary instability. Judge Morris Ploscowe, writing on homosexuality as executive director of the Commission on Organized Crime for the American Bar Association, feels indeed that it does. He says: "Normally there is no real permanence to homosexual relationships. The quality of emotional instability encountered in homosexuals, both male and female, makes them continually dissatisfied with their lot." [15] And Michael Buckley, though he admits the rare possibility of a permanent relationship, sees the basic picture as one of progressive disintegration, even after an "idealistic" beginning: "All too soon a pattern very familiar in homosexual circles is followed; occasional infidelities become habitual on one or both sides, and after a period of stormy recriminations and neurotic depressions they will either part company, or, as sometimes happens where there are common interests apart from sex, they may continue to share the same establishment on a 'semidetached' basis, each going his own way in his quest for an increasing variety of sexual experience." [16]

Yet there are other views to the contrary, and Miss Murdoch's claims of "entire and unselfish devotion" of "homosexuals in love" are supported from outside, as well as from within, the homosexual community. Writing in *The Encyclopedia of Mental Health,* Walter Bromberg says: "The love of a homosexual for another is as strong, as full of tenderness and passion, as that felt in heterosexual relationships. . . . One can distinguish the admiration, idealization, warmth, and companionship that exist in good marriages." [17] But all told, probably a healthy note of caution should be observed in seeking to reach some descriptive conclusion with respect to this empirical, though rather inaccessible, situation. Bromberg himself qualifies his statement about these homosexual relationships by saying, "while they last." And there is no question but that such matters as the lack of a supportive community, the absence of children, and perhaps even the criminal state of homosexuality in the eyes of the law make more difficult the permanence of such union than that of heterosexual variety—which indeed has often proved difficult enough. However, it must also be said that much as the permanence of relationship and the personal character of love are related to each other, they are not so fully to be identified that the absence of the former means the denial of the latter. Even genuine love can sometimes go wrong in this mystery and tangle of personal relationships. One should perhaps think more in terms of the reality of the present and the hope for the future in any given love experience. And here it would seem possible to say that for many a homosexual, even as for many a heterosexual, such love is personal, for embodied within it are respect, self-giving, and fidelity.

But we really have not yet come to grips with the central matter: this love of man for man and woman for woman may be personal but it is also homosexual. What of that? Tradition has certainly spoken of it as being "unnatural," and it is indeed in terms of this designation that the church has chiefly understood homosexuality to be sin. Thomas Aquinas' phrase was *peccatum contra naturam,* for *natura* was God's creation, and to act contrary to its provisions and its laws was to act in rebellion against God himself. And is not the *natura* of the thirteenth century also the *natura* of our day? Or is it? Phrased better perhaps, one can ask if the understanding of nature as held in the thirteenth century need be the understanding of nature by which we should live today. Obviously in many areas it is not. Thus what about here? Is there perhaps a modern equivalent to the myth of Aristophanes in Plato's *Symposium*? It will be remembered that there the original sexes were portrayed as three—male, female, and hermaphrodite—but that Zeus, angered by man's pride, decided to sever them all in two so that each sex was therefore left incomplete and was compelled to seek out a partner who would make it whole once more. Thus male and female homosexuality are seen to have their origin in the nature of things, as enacted by the gods, along with the seeking of man and woman for each other. Can this thought be transplanted into (or demythologized for!) the twentieth century? Can the judgments of long centuries of Christian tradition be set aside and homosexuality be deemed for those who experience it a part of the order of nature? Robert W. Wood, a clergyman concerned over these matters, has answered in the affirmative, writing, "The practicing of homosexuality by one who cannot be a heterosexual, and practicing it within the bounds of a constructive, mature life, can be a natural action of God's mortal creature." [18]

Yet there are difficulties that emerge in really reaching such a clear-cut answer when one explores more fully, and now in terms of modern insights, this relationship between the "natural" and homosexuality. Perhaps the most natural way of designating the natural is through biological and physiological reference, but here it is doubtful that homosexuality can lay claim to being a part of the natural order of creation. One does find Kinsey insisting that there is a biological variant within human life, as within some animal life, that makes for this predisposition and that some persons, therefore, are simply "born that way." But this can be subjected to serious questioning, both on the animal level, where homosexuality would actually appear to be rare and on the human level where many would find its origins in quite different factors. This physiological ground has also been more specifically set forth in theories that seek to identify precise causative factors. A chromosomal theory suggests that a male homosexual is a man with a woman's chromosomal pattern. A hormonal theory sees the presence of female hormones as providing the basis for the inverted urges of the individual who is otherwise sexually a male. But in the main such understandings of the origins of homosexuality seem not to be accepted on any large scale. Walter Bromberg writes: "Medical opinion is sharply divided although the majority of those working in this area are agreed that homosexuality does not depend on an organic component in the individual. Most psychiatrists including this writer, feel that glands or glandular products cannot direct the choice of male over female sex objects in the male, or the reverse in women. It is agreed that gland secretion can determine the degree or amount of sexual impulse. . . . However, the direction of sexual drive, whether homosexual or heterosexual, is not determined by hormones." [19] Thus it is doubtful whether homosexual tendency can be designated as a part of one's biological inheritance and therefore as physiologically "natural."

Theories at the opposite extreme speak of homosexuality as an acquired or learned habit structure. Here the emphasis is upon either early or late exposure to homosexual activitity as leading one then into this pattern of behavior. It is stressed that homosexuality is sometimes learned in schools, in camps, in the army, in prisons, wherever there is a concentration of population of a single sex, generally male. It is also pointed out that seduction can play a role here by way of introducing the individual, particularly a young person, to this type of experience. Buckley is willing to use the term "bad habit fixation" for homosexual practice, though he is similarly willing to recognize that there are also other factors which predispose the individual to such homosexuality and which diminish to some extent his degree of personal responsibility for it.[20] But for the large majority of investigators of homosexual behavior, it is these other factors, psychologically understood, which constitute the most important basis for homosexual inclination and practice.

It is interesting, however, that at this point there is no

clear and unanimous understanding as to the precise nature of the psychological developments that lead to the homosexual condition. Considerable disagreement appears among psychoanalysts as various probes are made into the homosexual's experience. Evelyn Hooker summarizes the confusion succinctly when she writes, "According to psychoanalytic theory, homosexuality . . . may be produced by (1) hostility to the mother, (2) excessive affection for the mother, (3) hostility to the father, (4) excessive affection for the father." [21] That certainly covers all the bases! Yet actually, despite the variety of theories, the main concentration of emphasis seems to be upon the role of a dominant mother in the infancy and early experience of the child. Bergler talks about the influential place of the "giantess of the nursery" in the formative experience that leads to homosexuality.[22] Kardiner notes that "one of the standard patterns to be found in male homosexuals is derived from the dominant mother who assumed the role of disciplinarian to the detriment of the paternal ideal. The father becomes feminized by comparison; the female seems inaccessible and the male becomes the sexual choice." [23] Kardiner also feels that the same dominance is responsible for female homosexuality: "The overpowering fear of the mother can compel the little girl to abandon her heterosexual objectives toward father or brother and compliantly submit to her mother. When grown up, such a female will seek orgiastic experience with another female." [24] And Bromberg writes: "Chiefly, homosexuality develops as a psychological defense against unconscious fear of women with subsequent retreat to men for sexual expression. This is the core of the psychoanalytic theory of homosexuality. . . . Early fear of women, in homosexually inclined boys, is observed by their identification with women, the 'identification with the aggressor' mechanism. Thus, men become psychologically 'safe' for them. These mechanisms are, of course, unknown to the individual." [25]

The significance of the foregoing, from the perspective of our particular analysis, is perhaps most strongly suggested by the final sentence, for, psychologically analyzed, the impulses of homosexuality are seen to develop quite unconsciously and in such manner that the homosexual "condition" emerges entirely apart from any conscious willing that it be so. This is a state of life for the presence of which the individual is not responsible, even though he may be supremely responsible for the mode of its ultimate employment. One may not be "born that way" biologically, but homosexually inclined persons would appear to be created psychologically in that manner, that is, be given the components of psychic life, at a point when maturity and responsibility begin to emerge, with this as one of the ingredients. So we are back again to our earlier question, though with some new data added: Is homosexual behavior *contra naturam,* or can the category of the "natural" be in some way applied to it?

But now let me suggest that the question is really falsely put, for in the light of the data we may not be dealing with an either/or, but with a both/and. It is difficult to see, on the one hand, how homosexuality can ultimately escape the traditional designation of "unnaturalness." God's primary order of nature would seem to lay an expectation upon men for a heterosexual life. This is the pristine order of creation, even as it is the means of that order's extension through procreation. Both the Biblical and the anatomical testify to this fundamental character of created human existence. The faith understanding of the early Hebrew community knew that in the wisdom of God the creation of Adam was quickly accompanied by the creation of Eve, that then the two became "one flesh," and that this indeed modeled God's intention for the whole of his human family. Jesus himself recalled for his day the fact that God in the beginning made them male and female and that then, as man joins wife, the two become one. In the light of this Christian understanding of the underlying intended purpose of God's creation it is indeed difficult to see how homosexual activity can fail to be designated "unnatural."

Yet, on the other hand, in the given life pattern of certain individuals this homosexual impulse and its expression are entirely "natural"—nothing could be more natural, if I read the testimonies aright. From psychological forces operative long before responsible choice is made, the molding of life has occurred in such manner that sexual propensities have been reversed, perhaps indeed in varying degrees for different individuals, but in such manner that now a homosexual "condition" truly exists and homosexual activity becomes an expression of one's "nature." It is easy to observe, of course, that such a nature is really pathological and that thus the expressions of it are entirely unnatural after all. But at that point it perhaps becomes necessary to recall the potential for abiding personal love which exists within the homosexual condition. Frankly, this I take to be a most crucial element in any attempt to reinterpret theologically for today the fact of homosexuality. Simply the presence of constitutional inclination is hardly sufficient to lead to the less judgmental perspectives proposed. Kleptomania is a compulsion, but not to be condoned. Thus the significance of the "natural" in homosexuality is that it is an avenue for the approximation of one of the intentions of God's creation, self-giving and faithful love between persons, even though the mode of expression is also "unnatural" when seen against the pristine and prevailing patterns of that creation. Yet despite all of this, there remains a question, I believe, as to the genuine capability of the categories "natural" and "unnatural" to convey with full adequacy a theological appraisal of homosexuality. Thus we might move from them to two other terms through which further observations can be made. They are "sin" and "redemption."

Homosexual practice has traditionally been designated as sin. It is *contra naturam,* and for that reason *peccatum.* But the ambivalence in the meaning of "natural" and "unnatural" suggested above may urge us also to think somewhat more broadly into this matter, raising particularly the question as to whether these categories can truly carry the weight of a thoroughgoing doctrine of man's "fall." In medieval metaphysics "nature" in man's life was conjoined with "supernature," and the fall was then viewed chiefly as the loss of the latter rather than as the vitiation of the former. So despite a doctrine of original sin, man's nature was really not sinful. Supernature was destroyed, but nature was not diseased—and thus it was possible to utilize the category of the natural in speaking of the moral, base ethics in part on a doctrine of natural law, and consequently in at least one dimension define sin (now actual, rather than original) as being that which is *contra naturam.* I think that Protestant understanding, however, has felt this to be too neat a package. Life is not quite that tidy in the midst of its untidiness, for the fall represents a more inclusive disruptiveness than this would seem to portray. The whole of man's being is affected and infected by the inturned character of his life, and there is no sanctuary of the untouched natural which can be either an epistemological or ethical haven from the ravages of sin. So the thrust of Protestant emphasis has been upon revelation and grace. And though Luther did indeed speak about natural law, it was identified by him very quickly as being the Biblical law of love. In this mode of thought then there is really no *peccatum contra naturam,* at least in the sense of the *natura* providing the decisive ground for the determination of sin. Much more significant for this understanding is the all-pervasive state of rebellion in which fallen man stands before God.

When one begins to apply this to man's sexual life, certain further consequences would seem to emerge. One has to do with the common sinfulness of all men in their sexuality, be it hetero or homo in character. There is also no refuge here free from the ravages of sin, for man's sexuality, even in marriage, gathers up within itself the complexities and paradoxes of his deepest being, the impulses of both his lust and his love. The nature of marital intercourse can be properly glorified, sanctified, and sacramentalized, as it has been in much recent writing, for this is an area of experience filled with potential for deepest personal communication and self-giving, but even here the formula, *simul justus et peccator,* applies. So this surely means that caution must be exercised in castigating homosexuality simply because one stands at the vantage point of a heterosexual haven. Paul spoke about "all" having sinned and come short of the glory of God, and this can apply to the whole of mankind in its sexual seeking and expression as well as in other aspects of its being. A disordering of loyalties is endemic to human existence in its entirety. Though the expression, *mea culpa,* is clearly not appropriate to the psychology of the marriage bed, there is no escape of even such a moment from the pervasive reality of man's sin. So there is need to be aware of common ground in sinfulness—and thus restraint in the throwing of stones.

But still more, this disengaging of the "sin of homosexuality" from a natural law rootage would seemingly make possible a clearer identification of the expression of sinfulness possible within it, namely, the violation of the personal order through aggression and exploitation. We are back once again to the issue of homosexual seduction and promiscuity (a parallel, incidentally, to heterosexual seduction and promiscuity), where clearly such impersonality of relationship is present. But also to be included are the more stable forms of homosexual behavior where domination, lust, and conquest can equally be motivating considerations, even while there can likewise be present factors of genuine personal love. So now the explicit statement can be ventured, that the sinfulness of homosexuality is not to be found in the fact that it is *homo*-sexuality, but rather in the fact that it is homo-*sexuality* in the midst of man's disordered state, where all sexuality becomes an instrument of his lust as well as of his love.

The other term is "redemption," and this can be related to homosexuality by thinking of it as referring to the provision of "new life." What is the nature of new and better life for the homosexual, particularly as envisaged from perspectives of Christian concern and faith? Three things at least seem important here. The first speaks of "cure," that is to say, the guided transition to a pattern of heterosexual impulse and behavior. Immediately the question can be raised, however, as to whether this "redemption" really fits the state of "sin" as previously described. Perhaps it does not, but it takes into account another important factor, namely, that all other things (i.e., sexual impulses) being equal, it is a lot better to live in our world as a heterosexual than as a homosexual. And there is relevance here to the subject of sin as we have been discussing it, for one can surely imagine that the strangeness and general unacceptability of homosexuality in what is largely a heterosexual society can accentuate the potentials for exploitation and promiscuity on the part of the homosexual and make much more difficult for him the realization or approximation of a lasting love relationship. The handicap in this regard of being a homosexual must be very great indeed. When one thinks of the impediments thrown up by social custom to what would otherwise be normal forms of association and expression, the furtiveness necessitated by it all, the mask of hypocrisy that must frequently be worn, and the shame so easily bestowed, one cannot help sensing the abnormal tensions, struggles, and frustrations to which the life of a homosexual is exposed. Even the changing of criminal legislation to legitimatize the private acts of consenting adults, desirable as that is, will not materially alter this societal picture. Thus there is a less tortured life in heterosexuality, and a body of evidence is developing to the effect that under psychoanalytical treatment a change in sexual direction, at least for some, can take place. Surely this should be pursued wherever, and to whatever extent, it can. But it should quickly be said that the extent is limited among other things by the degree of willingness of homosexuals to seek this form of "new life."

Some while ago an interesting exchange concerning this

took place in the *Mattachine Review*. Dr. Fink is quoted as having advocated psychotherapy for homosexuals in order that through the development of heterosexuality greater self-respect and satisfaction could be gained. Luther Allen replied: "I believe that Dr. Fink's understanding of self-respect and mine differ greatly. I cannot see any difference between psychotherapy designed to change a homosexual into a heterosexual and brain-washing. . . . But how can a brain-washed person retain his self-respect? . . . Does Dr. Fink really believe that a man can deny and crush out his deepest, strongest, and most intimate and personal and meaningful emotions and force himself to adopt the beliefs and behavior of the majority and still retain his self-respect?" [26] This is an answer, assuming that therapy itself can be successful, only for those who desire it.

So a second redemptive note must turn us fully back again to the homosexual world itself and stress that within that framework of sexual expression as within the framework of heterosexual behavior, there are the values to be sought of deep and abiding personal love. This is perhaps simply to remind us once more that the sin conveyed through man's sexuality is the sin of lust and domination and promiscuity and exploitation, the sin of disrespecting persons, and that redemption, in such degree as it is present, carries one conversely toward a love characterized by respect, self-giving, and fidelity. And thus, in this area of our concern, it involves developing the type of stable relationship which, again in Luther Allen's words, enables one to "become a different kind of homosexual." [27]

Then finally, these redemptive possibilities within homosexuality can best be actualized only as there is, among other things, a greater acceptance genuinely granted to those who walk along the homosexual way. In both church and society there is need for more wholesome restoration of the homosexual to the life of community. Just what this might mean in a variety of practical terms is not easy to envisage. Could it mean the approval and encouragement of dancing by male couples at church or community functions? Could it mean a marriage ceremony for homosexuals? Could it mean the adoption of children by married homosexual partners? The practical consequences of rehabilitated attitudes would need to be worked out with care as well as with consideration. But practical consequences manifesting acceptance there must be if acceptance itself is to be genuine and meaningful. To think here of redemption means that not only the homosexual but also the relationship of both church and society to the homosexual must be redeemed.

NOTES

1. Derrick Sherwin Bailey, *Homosexuality and the Western Christian Tradition* (London: Longmans, Green & Co., Ltd., 1955), pp. 1–28.
2. Lev. 18:22; 20:13.
3. Rom. 1:26.
4. I Cor. 6:9-10; I Tim. 1:9-10.
5. *The Wolfenden Report: Report of the Committee on Homosexual Offenses and Prostitution* (Stein and Day, Inc., 1963), par. 18.
6. *Ibid.*, par. 23.
7. *Ibid.*, par. 22.
8. Edmund Bergler, *Homosexuality: Disease or Way of Life?* (Hill and Wang, Inc., 1956), p. 261.

9. Evelyn Hooker, "Homosexuality—Summary of Studies," in E. M. Duvall and S. M. Duvall (eds.), *Sex Ways —In Fact and Faith* (Association Press, 1961), p. 172.

10. Abram Kardiner, *Sex and Morality* (The Bobbs-Merrill Co., Inc., 1954), p. 185.

11. Edmund Bergler, *op. cit.*, p. 19.

12. William Raeder, in *Mattachine Review*, Nov.–Dec., 1960, p. 17.

13. Luther Allen, in *Mattachine Review*, Oct, 1960, p. 13.

14. Iris Murdoch, in *The Ladder*, Dec., 1964, p. 22.

15. Judge Morris Ploscowe, "Homosexuality, Sodomy, and Crimes Against Nature," *Pastoral Psychology*, Nov., 1951, p. 42.

16. Michael J. Buckley, *Morality and the Homosexual: A Catholic Approach to a Moral Problem* (The Newman Press, 1959), p. 145.

17. Walter Bromberg, "Homosexuality," *The Encyclopedia of Mental Health* (New York, 1963), Vol. III, p. 757.

18. Robert Watson Wood, *Christ and the Homosexual* (Vantage Press, Inc., 1960), p. 206.

19. Bromberg, *loc. cit.*, p. 751.

20. Buckley, *op. cit.*, p. 153.

21. Hooker, *loc. cit.*, p. 170.

22. Bergler, *op. cit.*, p. 263.

23. Kardiner, *op. cit.*, p. 147.

24. *Ibid.*, p. 174.

25. Bromberg, *loc. cit.*, p. 752.

26. Allen, *loc. cit.*, pp. 13–14.

27. *Ibid.*, p. 13.

2

Toward a Theology of Homosexuality— Tried and Found Trite and Tragic

THOMAS MAURER

I welcome the desire of Dr. John von Rohr to extend the dialogue between Christian churches and the homosexual. At long last some exciting and relevant things are happening in some churches, and the interest and concern that some persons have been expressing about their traditional attitudes toward homosexuality is one example.

However, I have to say at the outset that I am disappointed in the approach that von Rohr takes to the subject of a theology of homosexuality. In fairness to von Rohr, I ought to say that it has been difficult for me to respond to any dissertation I have yet encountered on this subject. It is immediately evident that the problem is that we operate from diverse premises. The traditional premise—which seems the one from which von Rohr writes—is that to be valid a theology must be authenticated by something written somewhere in the Bible. This to me is totally untenable.

I have long since tired of theological writings that frantically seek out a morsel in the Bible that, torture and twist though they may have to, can be made to seem to validate some modern theological stance. I just don't feel the need to do that! Indeed, that to me is a woeful misuse of the Bible—or of any resource, for that matter. Even more annoying to me is his attempt to rationalize condemnatory statements made in the Bible about homosexuality. No better example exists than the statements in the twentieth chapter of Leviticus and the nineteenth chapter of Genesis and those made by Paul in his letter to the Romans. Why don't we have the courage and the candor to admit that the attitudes and opinions expressed by these ancient writers are thoroughly reprehensible and repugnant and were so even in their time, not to mention in this supposedly enlightened day? In other words, what in the world is a twentieth-century theologian doing trying to interpret the doctrine of original sin so that it can be made less damning of man in general and of the homosexual in particular? Who originated that doctrine? And what right does that primitive person, or persons, have to impose upon me these feelings of guilt? In essence perhaps what I must say is that I find it all but impossible to have dialogue with a theologian who will use as one of his premises "the pervasive reality of man's sin" as does von Rohr.

Further, what does von Rohr mean to convey by his use of the word "lust"? In fact, I would like to know what Jesus meant by his purported use of the word. If "lust" means obsession, obviously it is harmful, since to be obsessed with anything destroys one's vitality. But if "lust" connotes desire, then it is not only a necessity. It is also good. Von Rohr neither clarifies his interpretation of the word nor says whether he condemns it or approves of it. Having brought up the word, von Rohr, it seems to this writer, should have done both.

To go on: one of my theological premises is that all life and living is creative, and therefore theology ought to be creative. To me that implies that in the most meaningful sense it has to be existential, that is, to be valid, a theology has to be created out of one's own experience, out of one's own visceral being. To be sure it is only wise and prudent to avail oneself of all the resources there are back over the centuries—the Bible of course included. But to me there is no greater misuse of the Bible than to make it our taskmaster, a body of writing to which we are enslaved. I can see no validity whatsoever to the claim that something written two or three thousand years ago has any special revelance to my way of living and thinking.

I happen to buy most of what Jesus said, but not because it's in the Bible or because he said it, but rather because I find it existentially valid. And I have to be candid enough to say that there are a few things Jesus said that I can't buy.

All of this I say in order to reiterate that I don't understand why a present-day theologian would take valuable time and effort to try to explain away what is in the Bible. What if we have been misinterpreting the Sodom story? I don't care whether it condemns homosexuality or heterosexuality or sexuality or whatever. Nor do I care what Paul condemns or condones. I have no basis for presuming that these writers had any better access to God than does von Rohr. In fact, I would like to know what von Rohr thinks about homosexuality and what theology has come out of his own striving and struggling with living and what that theology has to say about homosexuality.

Then I'm afraid I have to do a bit of nit-picking with von Rohr. For instance, his use of those terribly trite and to me totally unacceptable words "natural" and "unnatural," and "normal" and "abnormal." How can anything in nature be capable of being unnatural? Harmful perhaps, but scarcely unnatural. Then to his use of that demeaning word "deviate." Technically correct, yes, but emotionally destructive. The word connotes something bad. If you call me a deviate, I am offended; but if you call me a variant, which really means the same thing, I am complimented—since the essence of life is to vary rather than to conform.

Still another bit of nit-picking: I don't feel that von Rohr goes deep enough into the matter of homosexual relationships. Honesty should have compelled him to emphasize more the deep trouble that heterosexual relationships are experiencing in our culture and this when they have all the social pressures going for them, whereas homosexual relationships have just about everything going against them, except love. And even so, there are far more successful and meaningful and fulfilling homosexual relationships than von Rohr seems to be aware of. Also the point ought to have been made, it seems to me, that theologically there should be no difference in the premises upon which the two different kinds of relationships are built. In other words, whatever theological basis one uses to validate a heterosexual relationship, I believe must also be adequate for a homosexual relationship—indeed, for any relationship.

Von Rohr's references to the "fall of man" are, of course, as indicated at the outset, totally unacceptable to me. Once again this is an instance of von Rohr allowing the Bible to be a millstone about his neck. And, if I may mix my metaphors, it really hangs him. I can fully appreciate primitive man's originating such a doctrine—so enmeshed in fear was his life—but in this day I can accept no doctrine or theological position except that which is predicated, not upon the "fall of man" but, rather, upon the "rise of Life." How can anyone look at the magnificent revelation contained in evolution and fail to see that the fundamental fact so beautifully portrayed there is that all Life is rising! Physically it began with the simple one-celled amoeba and has progressed to the multicelled human. Spiritually—at least for the human—it began with the caveman clubbing not only his enemy but even his desired mate only to progress to the law-based Hebraic society and then on to the love-premised Christian concept. Where in that story is there a fall? Life—and I spell that with a capital L—is rising! And it's rising because it's shot through with what I call God, or what Tillich called Being. It's rising because that God or Being, that is the Essence of our existence, is not a failure (as the "fall of man" doctrine implies) but rather a success, an inevitable and irrepressible success.

Is it not possible that this is why Jesus talked of his mission as one, not of saving man, but rather of enabling man to achieve abundance in the experience of living? Essentially that demands, not denial and restraint, but competence and proficiency.

Perhaps what disappoints me most about von Rohr's treatment of the theology of sex is that he seems to abandon the basic stance of a Christian. At least it seems to me that there is implicit in his entire paper the question of whether Christians ought to judge homosexuals adversely. Surely it is neither a Christian's responsibility nor prerogative to judge other people's life-style. Our sole responsibility as Christians, it seems to me, is to accept people whether or not we approve of them.

In conclusion, I would again stress my own deep conviction that any answers for the present must be generated in the present. For instance, von Rohr's final paragraph would perhaps have been venturesome twenty-five years ago—but scarcely today. The fact of the matter is that once again the church is getting to where the action is too late and with too little (with a few fortunate exceptions). But the homosexual is no longer waiting for the church to get around to redeem the sinful relationship it has developed with the homosexual or for the church to suggest or even allow male or female couples to dance or to adopt children or to have homosexual relationships. Homosexuals *are* doing all these things and many more that are within their rights as full citizens.

But more important, some homosexuals are developing new life-styles—creative life-styles—that don't require their imitating present heterosexual life-styles. It just could be that the homosexual will end up redeeming the heterosexual far more than the reverse—as implied by von Rohr.

Having written this criticism, I have just once again reread von Rohr's paper. I find it so reprehensible that I don't feel I've done justice to it in my comments. I'm staggered to realize that in the year 1970 a professor of theology in a supposedly progressive seminary would write this kind of paper. Von Rohr's naïveté and insistence upon hanging on to traditional theology is amazing. And his repeated insults to the thousands of his Christian brothers and sisters who are homosexual is appalling. I can only conclude by asking, Why is anyone bothering to publish this paper?

3

In and Out of the Gay World

CARL F. H. HENRY

The New Society is reinstating many ancient pagan perspectives which Christianity has long viewed in sharper moral focus and regarded as beyond the pale of decency and ethical sensitivity.

The new moderator of the Free Church of Scotland, the Reverend Clement Graham, recently noted, for example, that the God of Christianity casts the mantle of his protection around the weak and defenseless, whereas the new god "Society" exposes to the knife the unborn child, the misshapen, the deformed, the old, the incurably sick, in fact, precisely those who in other times and under another rule had evoked compassion.

To this complaint one may add still another, the erosion of the severe condemnation which Christianity attached to certain moral evils, particularly in the realm of sexual immorality. Jesus of Nazareth, and the New Testament as a whole, reserves some of the most stringent moral condemnations for sexual infractions. Yet it is precisely in this area that many churchmen today plead for a more "compassionate" view. The gospel of Christ is given a sympathetic stance that virtually erases the sinfulness of much that Christianity has long deplored as wicked. In the name of Christian love we hear louder and louder pleas for a new attitude toward divorce and remarriage, toward adultery, toward premarital intercourse, and toward homosexuality.

Many of these new proposals follow a quite predictable line. The first point to be established is that the Christian church has taken a stern, hard, legalistic line. Then it is noted that in our time especially a deeper interest in the realm of the personal has resulted in a discovery in depth of what love is. On the edge of this profounder knowledge the sympathetic exploration of all manner of moral deviation becomes a central interest of religious ethics. The Biblical data are then introduced mainly to destroy the force of the Scriptural tradition itself, usually by a selective and arbitrary use of texts. So, for example, in the Sodom narrative in Gen., ch. 19, one can exclude the intention of sexual abuse from ch. 19:5 only by overlooking Lot's offer in ch. 19:7 f. of his virgin daughters to the Sodomites rather than that the law of hospitality be breached by the homosexual violation of strangers. The usual conclusion is that, by setting aside what the Bible teaches and by substituting what the moderns prefer, one can best preserve the Scriptural concern for personal values.

Seldom is the question raised whether the values specially cherished by the unregenerate worldling of the twentieth century are precisely the values that need most to be questioned. If Jesus of Nazareth is God's perfect Son, to whose likeness all men are ideally to be conformed, much that today passes as authentically personal may in truth be strikingly antipersonal. The very understanding of personality flourished first in the context of

Christianity; it would be ironic indeed were that understanding now to be subverted by a pagan transvaluation of Biblical values.

One need not, for all this, defend as authentically Scriptural whatever the church has ardently espoused in every age. The tradition of the elders, be it Victorian or contemporary, can have a stiffling effect on spiritual vitality, and nullify the very Word of God. Moreover, the reliance of some branches of the church on the legal force of civil government to impose spiritual ideals upon society in general has inevitably fallen on hard days. Where the church no longer informs the consciences of men, eliciting from them an open acknowledgment of ethical standards that ideally shape community life, it is fruitless to impose legal restraints which a majority of citizens no longer consider to be binding. The people of God will of course want to see a society in which the commandments of God hold full sway. But they will seek it first of all in the church, which is a miniature concentration of the Kingdom of God, and then by example and persuasion will seek to extend its ideals and influence in the world at large. Yet a generation that lacks the vitalities of a personal relationship to God will soon find the personal values of the church of Christ abrasive. The church's task is to see that this abrasion is due not to its espousal of traditional taboos rather than of the Word of God and his revealed commandments, and to offer good news whereby broken lives may be mended anew. The apostles enunciated the revealed commands of God, and they proclaimed the gospel of forgiveness and new life in Christ. Twentieth-century Christianity can do no better.

In his book *Into the World,*[1] Professor J. N. D. Anderson, director of the Institute of Advanced Legal Studies in London University, sides with Lord Devlin against Professor Hart in holding that the state may use the criminal law to uphold moral standards *provided* the relevant legislation does not involve an unacceptable invasion of privacy, is broadly acceptable to public opinion, is of a sort that the police can properly enforce, and would not involve side effects (e.g., blackmail) that might cause even more harm than good.

What does this imply for homosexuality? No longer can it be said that the Christian church universally manipulates the social scene to preserve a special condemnatory attitude toward homosexuality. The Wolfenden Report declared it odd and inconsistent that male homosexual behavior should be singled out in Britain for special handling as a criminal offense, while adultery, fornication, and lesbianism, which are no less reprehensible from the standpoint of danger to the family, should not be so regarded. Adultery would seem not only to be damaging to national morale and well-being, as well as hurtful to its children, but to involve a breach of contractual commitment. Recent British legislation exempts from criminal sanctions homosexual acts in private between two consenting male adults, and in the United States a federal task force has recently recommended the repeal of laws against homosexual activities between consenting adults.

But that is hardly to say—as newspapers frequently do—that England has "legalized" homosexual acts. Nor would the removal from the crime roster of homosexuality in private by consenting adults provide a precedent for the similar removal of overt aggressions such as assault, rape, and seduction. Benjamin Karpman rightly contends that certain homosexual offenses ought also always to be considered illegal. He points to a survey in 1954 that showed that some 58 percent of 1,022 male prisoners were involved in offenses against boys under sixteen.[2]

The Wolfenden Report did not imply that society should condone or approve homosexual behavior, but rather that criminal sanctions are not the way to confront and meet it at certain levels. The Christian community proclaims a higher solution than the terror and penalty of the law. The Anglican bishops reiterated that homosexual relations between consenting adults are sinful. While the Christian community insists that God's purpose in and through civil government includes a coercive restraint of disorder and of crime, it recognizes that spiritual resources alone can give the offender a mind and will to do the right.

Yet the church is now offered contemporary psychological and sociological insights which—it is argued—require a modification of the Biblical norms and a new evaluation of homosexual activity. These are: (1) the presence in some persons of a homosexual "condition" underlying homosexual acts as a dominantly present inclination; (2) clinical studies reporting a rather substantial incidence of homosexual behavior in modern society; and (3) reports that homosexuals are not more criminally inclined than are heterosexual persons.

The use that is now frequently made of these observations deserves special scrutiny. Some champions of a new "morality" imply that homosexuality is therefore not to be deplored either as a crime or as a sin because (1) genetic or endocrine factors are *causative;* (2) the phenomenon of homosexuality is virtually *normal;* (3) homosexuality is frequently a feature of seemingly stable lives and hence *irrelevant* to considerations of character. Sometimes more weight is assigned to one than to another of these contentions. But the outcome is a view in which homosexuality is considered an entirely natural life pattern for many persons, not to be deplored but rather to be welcomed. So, in John von Rohr's words, it emerges as "an avenue for the approximation of one of the intentions of God's creation, self-giving and faithful love between persons."

What happens theologically through this inversion is clear: what belongs actually to the realm of the fall and sin, and stands in dire need of redemption, is assimilated instead to the divine order of creation. The result is that Biblical condemnations of homosexuality become a jungle of nonsense. If von Rohr really thinks that the homosexual would be vouchsafed a "wholesome restoration" to the life of the redemptive community were the church to encourage dancing by male couples, or to hold marriage ceremonies for homosexuals, and to permit such married homosexual partners to adopt children, he fails to understand that the Spirit of God transforms all men into the moral image of Jesus Christ and not the church into the image of the gay world.

That the church of Jesus Christ is to view all men with compassion, that its heart must go out in a special way to those who are trapped in the borderlands and wilderness of life, that it must face the gay world with the proffer of a new song in its soul and not alone with a determination to wipe the grin off its face, is beyond dispute. But what the gay world needs is redemption, not reinforcement.

From the Genesis creation narrative, which Jesus made part of his own teaching, we know that God ordained a heterosexual life for mankind, and that the monogamous union of Adam and Eve as "one flesh" is the pattern of God's intention for the whole human family. In this framework of relationships both the procreation of the race and the sexual fulfillment of the individual were ideally and naturally to be found.

To be sure, the fall of man involved the common sinfulness of all persons in their sexuality, and marred the ideal expression of all love—matrimonial love included. But if one speaks within Scriptural perspectives, one can hardly on this account contend that heterosexuality is as totally exposed to divine condemnation as is homosexuality. Beyond doubt, some forms of heterosexual behavior are in principle condemned no less than homosexuality. But monogamous marriage is principally approved as the divine order of sexual life. And what is in principle divinely approved, even though in practice it be sometimes turned into a mockery of its intended reality, cannot be leveled to what is in principle divinely disapproved. Von Rohr has neither Scripture nor reason on his side when he contends, therefore, that homosexuality is sinful only because all *sexuality* in man's present disordered state becomes an instrument of lust, but not sinful because it is homo rather than hetero.

It is true indeed that divine redemption alone can lift the universally broken life of sex to an approximation of the ideal. But in the one case, that of heterosexuality and marriage, redemption renews and perfects human sexual relationships, while in the other instance, that of homosexuality, it brings such relationships to a halt and shapes a kind of interest in the divine order of creation and in the expression of deep and abiding personal love in ways the Scriptures encourage.

This does not mean that the devout Christian is lightly to dismiss his homosexual neighbor with scornful pride. Every twice-born man or woman must die to the old self, and new life in Christ can help the homosexual find release from a past no less sorry than that of the heterosexual. For one thing, the heterosexual can only be grateful that Divine Providence has spared him horrific experiences of babyhood and childhood whose lingering influences often have a deforming effect upon sexual attitudes. For another, the statistics of sexual deviation are staggering enough to remind us all that the wild winds of lust have left a mark on every life, and one can be thankful that the power of Christ came in good time to contain his own moral compromises. Then too, he will know that if the homosexual is a stranger to the world of heterosexuality, even the realm of sex and marriage has but a temporary role in the created order of God and is not the ultimate value in life. The apostle Paul could implore, "Let those who have wives live as though they had none" (I Cor. 7:29). For some homosexuals, not marriage but celibacy may be the path of spiritual service through which immorality is conquered. As Frank Lake discerningly put it: "The aim of pastoral therapy is sanctity, not matrimony. The soul is delivered first from its failure of commitment to God, not to the woman."[3] Moreover, the Christian must be constantly aware of how fully the love life of marriage and the home falls short of the ideal of Christ's love for the church; the sting of this contrast will serve to narrow the severity of unloving judgment upon those whose homosexuality marks them off from the realm of heterosexuality. The church of Christ must never forget that the homosexual has little disposition to seek help while he associates only with his "queer" cohorts. Only the opening of new avenues of acquaintance and fellowship initiated from the side of the heterosexual world can be the first introduction to a therapeutic community.

There is insufficient evidence that homosexuality has a genetic or endocrinic basis. Many human habits take on a compulsive character, so that it is risky to leap from fixity of behavior to hereditary or constitutional variants, thereby disregarding psychogenic and personal-dynamic factors. A hurried reference to inborn or genetic factors to explain sexual behavior proves too much, since it presumably would have to account for heterosexuality in the same way; this would strip all sexual behavior of moral significance as well. Clifford Allen, who considers the theories of hormonal or endocrine causation to be unsubstantiated, expressly states: "I do not believe that there is such a thing as inborn homosexuality." [4] If that reflects the actual situation, no basis remains for distinguishing congenital or constitutional homosexuality from an acquired homosexuality that attaches to normal persons who subsequently fall into perversion.

On the basis of extensive investigation, Lake contends that one root of homosexuality is psychogenic, that is, rests on a schizoid detachment from the mother and a hysterical attachment to a man through an emotional conflict in the first half-year of life.[5] Some studies suggest also a possible correlation between birth trauma and later male homosexuality, particularly when subsequent mother love does not heal an early deterioration of the infant's relation to the mother, in which relation the breakdown of maternal trust issued in a hysterical relationship to the father. Other studies relate patterns of homosexual deviation to hysterical and schizoid reactions to one or another parent during childhood. The point at which theological analysis and moral judgment must enter is the attempt to remedy an early shattering experience of panic and dread through homosexual expression. If, as must be insisted, alongside all factors of heredity and environment there survives a range of responsible personal decision that shapes sexual commitments, then homosexual behavior cannot be considered irresistible. The Wolfenden Committee, in fact, found "no *prima facie* grounds for supposing that a particular person's sexual propensity . . . is any less controllable" in the case of homosexuals than in the case of heterosexuals. Lake writes with great insight that "the remedy for dread is not genital intimacy but spiritual intimacy. . . . Experience both of hysterical women and homosexual men in therapy shows that the problem of dread may be effectively met without recourse to genital intimacy."[6]

The authentic role of psychiatric analysis is to prepare the way for the gospel, not to dissolve the need for spiritual healing. While Christian redemption does not depend on any specific formulation of all the factors contributory to man's deviant behavior, an informed awareness will prevent hasty oversimplifications and enlist compassionate sympathy. But that is hardly to say that all homosexual behavior is referable to a propensity acquired during a painful period in birth, and purely improved obstetrics can do much to eliminate even such occasions. Sympathy must not be exported from such instances to homosexual practices in adult life whose psychodynamic roots are rather to be found in lust and perversion. The victim who realizes that he or she is not the pawn of a genetic defect, that commitment anxieties can in fact be coped with, and that one can find new and higher resources to master sexual propensities, has taken the first necessary steps to a new way of life.

Now often forgotten in the evaluation of sexual ethics in respect to interpersonal values is the fact of divine personality and the expressed will of the Creator for man's life in society. Once the commandments of God are dropped from view, and divine consent and faithfulness to God's purpose are demoted to irrelevance, it is easy enough to discuss sex relationships only in terms of consent versus seduction and faithfulness versus promiscuity, and thus to arrive at commendations of both homosexual and heterosexual relationships simply because they avoid aggression.

Man's life of love has a dual dimension, one that towers above considerations of statistical averaging both in respect to frequency of deviation and depth of deviation. Paul did not distill his moral judgments on the sexual aberrations of Corinth from a statistical survey of the extent of homosexuality or its crime-relatedness. He did not derive the direction and content of God's moral norms by an examination of the capacity for wickedness in human life. He set the sexual life of man, and the totality of his life, in the context of love of God and love of neighbor—and precisely in that order. When God's commandments are scouted, what passes for love—both in respect of self-fulfillment and of self-giving—tends quickly to become a mere shadow of the real thing.

The Christian community has no calling to dignify homosexuality as a way of life equivalent to heterosexuality. It remained for Plato and other pagans to view homosexuality as a higher way of life than heterosexuality; the sons of Christianity have no excuse for going even half this distance, and putting them on a par.

The healing of homosexuality is possible by the same method whereby Christ makes all men whole who come to him, by opening their beggarly lives to the realities of the spiritual world. The new birth inaugurates a new series of relationships with God and man, one in which we are fully accepted in Christ as we are, while we are on the way to a wholly new selfhood. The Holy Spirit then triggers the human ego with a new sensitivity to the possibilities of decision for good and evil, enhances the sense of responsibility and love for other persons, and undergirds the determination to do the right. Lively communion with the Risen Lord quickens the awareness of the invisible spiritual world and its moral claims.

For the homosexual the critical moment on the way to a decisive turn is the fleeting feeling of aversion—sometimes through an awareness of inordinate lust, or a halting sense of the devaluation or exploitation of a sexual partner, of a despairing longing for death, or the search for an alternative way to drown one's sorrow. That is the moment when the Holy Spirit is calling, and blessed is he who reaches upward for a new and higher fellowship of love.

Notes

1. J. N. D. Anderson, *Into the World* (London: Church Pastoral Aid Society, 1968).
2. Benjamin Karpman, *The Sexual Offender and His Offenses* (The Julian Press, Inc., 1954).
3. Frank Lake, *Clinical Theology* (London: Darton, Longman & Todd, Ltd., 1966), p. 926.
4. Clifford Allen, *A Textbook of Psychosexual Disorders* (London: Oxford University Press, 1962), p. 179.
5. Lake, *op. cit.*, p. 926.
6. *Ibid.*, p. 931.

4

God Loves Me Too

TROY PERRY

Homosexuality is condemned in the Old Testament book of Leviticus (Lev. 20:13), along with the sins of adultery (Lev. 20:10), incest (Lev. 20:11–12), bestiality (Lev. 20:15–16), sorcery or witchcraft (Lev. 20:27), eating such foods as rabbit (Lev. 11:6), oysters, clams, shrimp, lobster (Lev. 11:10–12), or your steak too rare (Lev. 17:10). This book in the Bible also prohibits men from becoming priests if they are blind, lame, humpbacked, short, or flat-nosed (Lev. 21:17–24). Christian theology for centuries has based its condemnation of the homosexual more or less on one story in the book of Genesis (Gen., chs. 18 to 19), four verses of Scripture in the Old Testament (Lev. 20:13–16), and three verses in the New Testament (Rom. 1:26-27; I Tim. 1:9-10; I Cor. 6:9).

The story of Sodom and Gomorrah is a strange one indeed. God comes in the form of three messengers to the patriarch Abraham, and tells him that his aged wife Sarah is going to have a son. After this message is delivered, the messengers start to leave, and God asks himself the question, "Shall I hide from Abraham that thing which I do?" With this, the Lord tells Abraham, "Because the cry of Sodom and Gomorrah is great, and because their sin is very grievous, I will go down now, and see whether they have done altogether according to the cry of it, which is come unto me; and if not, I will know." In other words, God is going to destroy the city. Abraham recognizes this and starts pleading for the inhabitants of Sodom and Gomorrah. He asks God the question, "Wilt thou also destroy the righteous with the wicked?" And then asks, "Peradventure there be fifty righteous within the city: wilt thou also destroy and not spare the place?" God readily agrees and this agreement seems to frighten Abraham. Afraid that there might not be fifty righteous, he bargains with God until he gets God down to the sum of ten righteous in the city, asking him to spare the city if he finds that amount. At this point God and Abraham part company.

The scene changes to the city of Sodom. Two angels enter the city and are met by Lot, the nephew of Abraham. Lot invites the two visitors to his home. After a nice meal, before the visitors can go to bed "all the people from every quarter" come and ask Lot to send the two men out to them, "that they may know him."

Lot now pleads with the people of the city to leave the two strangers alone. He even goes so far as to offer his two daughters to the crowd. This offer is rejected and the multitude threatens the life of Lot. Lot is pulled back into the house, out of danger, and the two angels cause blindness to fall upon the mob outside the doors.

At this point, the angel warns Lot of the impending disaster and tells him to flee the city with his family. Lot agrees to leave Sodom and tries the persuade his entire family to leave with him. Only his wife and two daughters agree to accompany him out of the city. As the family is leaving the city, Lot's wife turns back to take one last look and is turned into a pillar of salt. Lot and the two girls flee into another city, and not feeling safe there, they rush to the countryside and into a cave.

According to most fundamentalist theologians, this is where the story stops. But it doesn't. For some reason, the Christian church remembers only the so-called homosexual side of the story. Most of us seem to forget that Lot's two daughters decide that they, with their father, constitute the only people on earth, and in order to preserve the human race, they would have intercourse with their father and become pregnant. This they do. Not once do we read where God condemns the girls for committing incest, which along with homosexuality is punishable by death in the Old Testament. Not once do we hear Abraham mention this to his nephew. Even the Christian church seems to have forgotten this part of the story. For some reason when we remember the story of Sodom and Gomorrah, we quote that as being the gospel from the Old Testament concerning homosexuality. And yet, as I stated, we forget about the other sins that are mentioned. For this reason I would like to leave the Old Testament and go to the New Testament, where supposedly the Christian church finds its theology.

Of the three direct Scripture references to homosexuality in the New Testament, the most widely quoted is the one damning overt homosexual expression, Rom. 1:26-27 (KJV): "For this cause God gave them up unto vile affections: for even their women did change the natural use into that which is against nature; and likewise also the men, leaving the natural use of the woman, burned in their lust one toward another." Note the key words of the apostle Paul: "changing" and "leaving."

In order to change from or to leave heterosexuality, one must first be a heterosexual.

What we have is an account of lust, and Paul does say lust, placing this behavior out of the higher realm of love and devotion. It is interesting to note that this is the only Old or New Testament Scripture in reference to sexual relations between females.

In I Timothy 1:9-10 (KJV) Paul places them together with those who "defiled themselves with mankind," under the same condemnation given murders. Whether the word "defiled" is used also in deploring lustful heterosexual and beastial acts is open to question. So, does one defile himself through the actual act, or through the motivation of lusting desire, separating from the higher emotional plane? Note that Paul does not clarify the gender of "them" or the usage of "mankind" as meaning man, or the totality of human beings, thus leaving this often-quoted condemnation of homosexuality quite open to interpretation.

Christian theology has changed in the last nineteen hundred years. Let's look at some of the things forbidden in the New Testament church that are practiced widely or sanctioned by our churches at the present time. I quote from the King James Version of the Scriptures. We read in I Timothy 2:11-12, "Let the woman learn in silence with all subjection." Also, a woman is "not to teach, nor to usurp authority over the man, but to be in silence." If the church began a crusade against women teachers based on this Scripture, what would happen? How many female Sunday school teachers and missionaries, women preachers and evangelists, would the church lose if it followed I Cor. 14:34-35? Will the church turn away hatless women from its doors, following I Cor.

11:13? Should the church reconsider its position on slavery, remembering that the apostle Paul commanded servants to "obey in all things your masters" (Col. 3:22).

My list could go on and on, and few of us would disagree with the church's lack of strict interpretation of the Scriptures in such incidents. Yet, I wonder how theologians can overlook entire passages, passages that pertain to the majority, while seizing upon a few verses in the Bible that condemn the homosexual minority. I am not trying to berate the Bible with this analysis, but I am trying to point out that it was originally written by men, translated and interpreted by men, and its doctrines supplemented by men into a broad-faced Christian theology. And man is fallible. Even Paul, recognizing this, often states that he is giving his own views, rather than commandments of God.

We need the Bible as the source for understanding Christ. But we need to spend more time observing his Spirit as related there and less time following the letter of the law given by his followers while attempting to spread his message.

It is interesting that Christ never specifically mentioned homosexuality in any of his teachings. In fact, if Christ lived in our day and age, he would have probably been labeled a homosexual. Let me say now I am not calling Christ a homosexual. I am merely stating a fact. When you have a man in our society who is raised by a mother with no father (Mary's husband, Joseph, is last heard of in the Scriptures when Jesus was twelve years old), who never marries, who is constantly in the company of twelve men, who allows one of them to have bodily contact with him (John 13:21-26), and who is taken into custody by the police after another male kisses him—you would have, according to so many Christians, a homosexual on your hands. Again, let me state that *I* am not calling Christ a homosexual; many others would.

According to Christian theology, Christ "came unto his own, and his own received him not. But as many as received him, to them gave he power to become the sons of God, even to them that believe on his name." I believe in the personal commitment to Christ, as Savior, Lord, and Master. I believe that Jesus died upon Calvary for all the people of the world and that he was the one supreme sacrifice for all sins.

I believe in the fundamentalist doctrine of being "born again" of the Spirit and the water. I know that I am a "born again" child of God. I also know that I am a homosexual. Can this change my relationship with my Lord? No, never! Jesus said: "Come unto me, all ye that labor and are heavy laden, and I will give you rest. Take my yoke upon you, and learn of me; for I am meek and lowly in heart; and ye shall find rest unto your souls." And, again, "For God so loved the world, that he gave his only begotten Son, that whosoever believeth in him should not perish, but have everlasting life."

Not once do I read Jesus saying in the Gospels, "Come unto me, all you heterosexuals who, if you have sex or intercourse, must have it in the missionary position with another heterosexual, and I will accept you as the only true believers." No, Jesus, my Lord, sent the invitation to all, whosoever will.

It is up to the Christian church to reevaluate its theology concerning the homosexual. The church has all but closed its doors to millions of people in America whose only difference from the majority is their sexual orientation. Homosexuals want to be a part of the church of the Lord Jesus Christ, as happy individuals, as "born again" believers, and as individuals who can hold their heads high without shame. The church only can make that possible!

5

Pastoral Responses to Gay World Questions

JOHN F. HARVEY

I agree with Professor John von Rohr that we need to rehabilitate not only the homosexual but also our Christian thinking about inversion. But the way in which we would achieve these objectives would be different. First allow me to affirm a point of fundamental agreement. All who are truly interested in the homosexual as a person must try to break away from the stereotyping tendency so prevalent because of popular treatments of the subject. Homosexuals are as different from one another as heterosexuals. While homosexuals share some traits, they possess all the individuality of persons who happen to be heterosexual.

Professor von Rohr begins with the premise that the grace of God works in corrupt man (*simul justus et peccator*) whether he be heterosexual or homosexual and compensates for the inevitable effects of carnal tendencies. As he sees it, the real issue is not whether the homosexual acts according to nature or against it—that problem remains unresolved—but whether by the grace of Christ the homosexual can find a partner to whom he will be faithful like a husband or wife. Even the love of spouses in heterosexual marriage is not without tarnish, because all acts of sexuality are tainted by lust despite the undoubted presence of motives of true affection.

Accordingly, a person convinced that he is homosexual should be allowed to seek a stable partner with whom to live in as close an approximation to Christian marriage as possible. In this way he can reduce the probability of promiscuity with its impersonal lust.

However plausible this argument may be, it leaves unanswered questions. The first is whether homosexual tendencies *merely* are contrary to the prevalent sexual conventions of society, or are contrary to human nature. Homosexual practices are not a matter of convention for the vast majority of humans—not even for many homosexually inclined—who feel guilty upon their discovery that they possess this drive.

These feelings of guilt, it is argued, are really the result of the homosexual's absorbing the attitude of heterosexual society. While it may be granted that society's critical viewpoint does *increase* the feelings of guilt in the homosexual, it does not account for the origin of these feelings of both guilt and fear. There is a deeper disorientation within such a person which goes back to the very early years of life. The so closely woven skein of factors makes it practically impossible to say which was primary in the genesis of homosexual inclinations in this person. But no matter which factor is stressed, it is a disorder in the due psychological relationship of the child to some significant person or group. Many homosexuals, for example, have possessive mothers who, allegedly, made them afraid of all physical intimacy with women; others possess fathers who were *psychologically* absent at that period in their sons' lives when they should have identified with their fathers. Still others feel that inability to communicate with other children in the pre-school scrambling age contributed to the growth of homosexual tendencies. No doubt there is clinical evidence to support each of these and other theories, but one must be careful not to overstress any one factor so as to avoid oversimplification. (Mart Crowley's *The Boys in the Band* pokes fun at simplistic theories of the etiology of homosexuality. The text is available in both London and New York.)

In any case homosexual inclinations are the result of any one or all of the above-mentioned disorientations. It is difficult to see how one can call an inclination "natural" which originates in a series of psychological privations. To say that the homosexual inclination is "natural" is to destroy the meaning of the term "natural," which denotes a quality of perfection shared by all humans. Something "natural" makes one a better man. It follows, then, that if the homosexual tendency is natural to certain persons, they find in its expression a way of becoming more human and more perfect. But the characters in *The Boys in the Band* hardly regard their overt practice of homosexuality as a perfection. It is something to which some have resigned themselves, while one character, Michael, does not want to admit that he is so miserable in his way of life.

The psychological argument found in this play, namely, the internal hopelessness and misery of the homosexual way, adds a dimension to the contention of many moralists that homosexual acts are completely contrary to the principal natural purpose of sexual intercourse, namely, the hope of children.

Von Rohr does not support the argument that homosexual acts are "natural" when he writes that "it is doubtful whether homosexual tendency can be designated as a part of one's biological inheritance and therefore as physiologically 'natural.' " Nevertheless, because a man may be preconditioned by his early life to homosexual practices, von Rohr sees some reason for regarding such actions as "natural": "Thus the significance of the 'natural' in homosexuality is that it is an avenue for the approximation of one of the intentions of God's creation, self-giving and faithful love between persons, even though the mode of expression is also 'unnatural' when seen against the pristine and prevailing patterns of that creation."

At this point von Rohr terminates discussion of the "natural" and "supernatural" to take up two other categories of moral action: "sin" and "redemption."

Working from a Lutheran premise, von Rohr affirms that "there is no sanctuary of the untouched natural which can be either an epistemological or ethical haven from the ravages of sin."

This transition to a concentration on the subjective sinfulness of man is significant, because it implies that any discussion of *peccatum contra naturam* (sin against nature) must ignore the objective aspects of moral acts, or what has been known as traditional natural moral law morality. The argument moves to new ground in that it focuses on the ravages of original sin and man's need for redemption. Yet it is also old, because von Rohr follows the concept of Luther, who held to man's corruption by original sin. This corruption is so deep that all men sin in their expression of sexuality. Even in marriage, man gathers within himself the impulses of both lust and love. Since all humans have a common ground of sinfulness, there is no need for the heterosexuals to cast stones at the homosexuals. In this way von Rohr disengages the "sin of homosexuality" from its relationship to natural moral law. But the disengagement is not convincing.

Ethical norms discovered by reason or given to mankind by revelation are concerned with man's person and nature. The concept of sin must likewise be understood in terms of man's person and nature, that is, what is contrary to his human perfection is sinful and what is in accord with it is good. Human nature in all its essential relationships is normative of human conduct. The wondrous fact of God's graciousness in providing us with a Redeemer should not obscure the basic norms of human acts but should help us to live up to them.

Von Rohr says that his purpose in disengaging the discussion of the sexual acts of the homosexual as *contra naturam* from the question of sin and redemption is to root the sinfulness of some homosexual acts in their inordinate lust, a characteristic also found in many heterosexual acts. Man is in a disordered state "where all sexuality becomes an instrument of his lust as well as of his love."

In this perspective, acts of sexuality will be morally good if they help the person to achieve personal fulfillment in some form of permanent relationship. As already indicated, the difficulty with this position is its removal of any objective norm of judgment of either heterosexual or homosexual acts.

There is no clear way to determine what acts of marriage come from lust and what from love, because all sexual acts partake of lust and love; then, there is no basis for distinction between sexual acts of unmarried men and women and those of the married; or between stable homosexual unions and stable heterosexual unions. (In *The Boys in the Band,* the idea of stable homosexual union is mocked.) Unnecessarily, von Rohr separates the personal order of individuality from the basic norms applicable to all persons sharing a common human nature. Consequently, he reduces moral judgments to an almost exclusively subjective basis, although he does consider the sinfulness in the "violation of the personal order through aggression and exploitation."

Von Rohr and I hold different positions on the effects of original sin and the effects of redemption. I believe that after the guilt of original sin has been removed by Baptism and grace, a man is able to overcome the effects of original sin by cooperating with grace. He is capable of overcoming lust through divine love infused in him by the Holy Spirit. The struggle to win out over unruly movements of our human nature is proximately possible provided one prays constantly and performs or accepts works of penance in his daily life. A homosexual who has followed the plan of life outlined in this article said that prayer without penance is like eating food without salt. Von Rohr, however, holds that the effects of original sin are so great that the interior life of any man contains elements of sinfulness together with the grace of Christ. Man is at one and the same time both just and sinful.

Our different theologies will lead us to different conclusions concerning the pastoral care of the homosexual, as will be seen. Even our conception of redemption is different. Von Rohr seems to identify redemption with the possible redirection of instincts of the homosexual (cure), or his discovery of a deep and abiding love relationship. I see redemption as an act wrought by Christ's sufferings and death by means of which I can live in his friendship while avoiding any free and serious violation of his law. I believe that the graces of redemption can work in the soul of a homosexual whose instinctual life is unruly and rebellious. Whatever therapeutic effects take place through psychotherapy are on the *natural* plane of men's existence; that is to say, the grace of God is not necessary for them.

Von Rohr also refers to "redemptive possibilities" for the homosexual. These can be actualized only if others genuinely accept homosexuals. With this position I agree, but I do not agree with some of the means suggested by von Rohr. *Tentatively* he suggests three means of rehabilitating the homosexual with the life of the community, both civil and Christian: (1) dancing at church or community functions by male couples; (2) a marriage ceremony for homosexuals; (3) adoption of children by married homosexual couples.

The assumption upon which these suggestions are made is that a homosexual marriage is just as natural and normal for some people as a heterosexual union is for others. Many homosexuals would not agree with this position despite their overt practices.

They do not want to be known as homosexuals; for this reason they will not attend even private meetings of homophile societies, let alone dance together in public. Only other homosexuals are aware of their "marriages." Many dangers lurk in their adoption of children, because homosexual men find it difficult to relate to women, and very probably would impart this fear to a male child; that male homosexuals could rear a little girl seems equally improbable. Many lesbians, moreover, find the thought of rearing children terribly restrictive; they do not want to be mothers.

Besides these specific comments on von Rohr's position, I should like to add several other points. Von Rohr assumes that the sexual orientation of the homosexual must be expressed in some permanent love relationship if he is going to find personal fulfillment; implicitly, permanent abstention from sexual acts is ruled out as a practical impossibility. Again, it is assumed that the principal way in which the homosexual is going to find happiness is in an abiding, marriagelike, love relationship.

The first assumption is familiar to Christians who believe in and practice lifelong chastity out of love for God.[1] Such a belief and practice presupposes a view of man's redeemed nature radically different from Luther's and von Rohr's.

The Catholic conception is that all forms of chastity (that of the unmarried or widowed; that of the married: conjugal fidelity; and that of the vowed person in the religious life or priesthood) are possible to those praying for the gift. Chastity is a gift to those who seek it. But its constant practice (by unaided humans) is not possible. By the grace of Christ, man is able, not to rid himself of the tendency to lust, but to control it—in the sense that lust does not determine our free human acts. Those who abstain from all sexual acts out of love for Christ are able to sublimate the sexual tendency into channels of fruitful apostolic work without harmful psychological effects. To be sure, the intention to remain chaste must be wholehearted; halfhearted attempts usually involve a sexual neurosis. In brief, sexual abstinence for love of God is possible for all, including the homosexual.

Von Rohr also assumes that a marriagelike relationship

is the best way for a confirmed homosexual to achieve fulfillment. Apart from moral considerations concerning homosexual unions, I would question this assumption for several other reasons. One is the fact that the homosexual already has a sexual neurosis by his attitude toward the opposite sex, a neurosis that is intrapsychic as well as social. In many homosexuals, moreover, the attitude toward the opposite sex is only a symptom of other psychic disorders. The literature of both the Mattachine Society and the Daughters of Bilitis asserts that there are just as many heterosexual neurotics as there are homosexual, proportionately speaking; and the psychiatrist sees only the neurotic and not the normal homosexual. But it has been my pastoral experience in helping homosexuals of both sexes to observe that in the vast majority homosexual tendencies are associated with other symptoms as well. Generally speaking, the *internal* difficulties that both members of the union suffer are not eliminated by the marriagelike union. For this reason so many homosexual unions are short-lived. The individuals involved bring to their union a host of past unresolved personal conflicts, which are not resolved by the union. For a time the welcome experience of the friendship palliates internal conflicts, but gradually the problems that existed before the union reassert themselves in various ways, often leading to a dissolution of the union. The homosexual male seems more prone to infidelity and promiscuity than the homosexual female, but she also has tendencies of this sort, which are counterbalanced to some degree by her greater desire for stability and emotional security. In either case, lack of children makes separation easier. While some form of permanent homosexual relationship carries with it elements of true love, and psychologically is better than impersonal promiscuity, it is no solution of the homosexual's problem. On the psychological level there is no complete remedy short of extended therapy which might transform homosexual tendencies into heterosexual. Usually such a radical reorientation is possible only in a young person who is willing and can afford to pay the price. Some succeed in this difficult venture according to the clinical experience of Dr. Samuel Hadden and others.[2]

Group therapy methods give interested homosexuals cause to hope. Beginning with a series of private interviews with the homosexual, Dr. Hadden places him then in a group who are similar in age and life situation to the newcomer. If he comes twice a week for ninety-minute sessions over several years, he has a good chance of developing heterosexual tendencies, or at least of reducing the homosexual tendency and other neurotic traits. Dr. Hadden reports that twelve out of thirty-two patients had achieved an exclusively heterosexual pattern of adjustment, and also showed significant improvement in other respects. Still others showed signs of a reversal in sexual tendency. Most benefited from association with other homosexuals in therapy.[3]

Some Alternative Proposals

Since I have criticized von Rohr's position, it is time that I develop some alternative proposals. My suggestions are conditioned by the disposition and the age of the homosexual who is seeking counsel. If a young man or woman wants help to redirect his or her sexual instincts, I endeavor to get psychiatric aid for this person, either through a clinic or through private practice. Oftentimes all that is available for the poor are long lines before clinical therapy; and while some wait for clinical therapy, I render as much supportive therapy as possible. Experience has taught me to fulfill the role of the counselor and priest and not that of the psychiatrist. In this way the influence of the priest or any other clergyman is significant. But he must not underestimate his influence in helping the homosexual to understand his condition and to learn to live with it, presupposing psychological change is morally impossible, as so often it is.

With the adolescent or young adult, however, it is important to determine the degree of homosexual interest and activity already present. While some young men and women are already firmly orientated toward a homosexual way of living, particularly if they were seduced at an early age in boarding school or in prison, others are in a state of sexual confusion. They are physically attracted to both sexes; but they find the attraction to their own sex frightening and incomprehensible; generally, they do not want to speak about it for fear of being branded "queer." If they reveal these inner ambivalen*cies* to anyone, it must be someone whom they trust; consequently, much depends upon how the counselor treats the *person* who trusts him with this secret.

In such situations the clerical counselor should encourage the person to associate with members of the opposite sex in various group activities, including dating situations, but not necessarily immediately in the case of the very shy individual. In many instances a deep fear of the opposite sex is present, and very probably only psychotherapy will resolve this fear; but in every situation the counselor should treat the person with just as much respect as if he were unaware of the difficulty. This is a general principle: In working with homosexuals relate to them as you would to heterosexual humans; such is not unrealistic or dishonest; it is acknowledgment of our common humanity, in which we are all united far more than we are separated by heterosexuality or homosexuality.

One of the most harmful myths eradicated by counselor and psychiatrist is that the homosexual is a different and special kind of person. He is neither superior nor inferior to the heterosexual; if one were to consider the homosexual's total personality and character, one would discover that he is more like a given group of heterosexuals than other homosexuals—Mattachine and Daughters of Bilitis literature to the contrary notwithstanding! The only important thing that homosexuals share is a sexual orientation, which many psychiatrists regard as a neurosis—to be eliminated or controlled. Those who consider homosexuality a form of normality should not exaggerate the difference between the homosexual and the heterosexual, because this contributes to the alienation of the homosexual into a subculture full of defensive postures.

Accordingly, the adolescent or young adult should seek the heterosexual company of both sexes by breaking away from the frequentation of exclusively homosexual groups. Let him not experiment in overt sexual acts of any kind on the futile pretense that in this way he will discover his sexual orientation. Psychiatric case histories indicate that individuals only deepen their confusion by such experimentation. Sometimes failures in heterosexual relationships drive persons to take refuge in a homosexual way of life.

On the positive side, both those homosexuals who are under therapy with the hope of change and those who feel they are too old to change the direction of their instincts need an ascetical plan of life if they desire to be fully human and Christian. It is important that a young person formulate a plan of life. This involves a radical rethinking of one's philosophy of life, coupled with deep determination to redirect the will to truly Christian values; it also includes the gradual formation of systematic practices designed to help the homosexual in leading a virtuous life. More than a rule of thumb, this plan must be specific enough to include certain systematic practices every day, yet sufficiently pliable to allow for daily exigencies. The details of this plan will vary according to the religious commitment and state of life of the person. As illustrative I set down the outline of a Catholic plan of life:

1. Some form of meditation for at least twenty minutes a day.
2. Mass and Communion as often as possible during the week.
3. Daily examination of conscience with stress on the purification of motives.
4. Systematic reading of Holy Scripture and practical ascetical works, such as Guardini's *Meditatations Before Mass*. At the beginning of spiritual direction I have found very helpful a kind of paperback bibliotherapy, including inspirational works such as Viktor Frankl's *Man's Search for Meaning* and William F. Lynch's *Images of Hope*.
5. A carefully chosen confessor and guide.
6. Habitual involvement in works of charity.

An element of proven worth within the plan of life is the actual performance of apostolic and charitable works. Usually fully aware of the frustration of homosexual liaisons, the invert seeks some means of serving God which will prove to himself that he is making some contribution to life. Just as parents experience a sense of genuine achievement and peace in the thought of children reared and given back to God, just as priest or nun or any person dedicated to some service finds joy in his work, so also the invert can find the place willed for him by God if he learns to view his condition within the perspective of faith. Some inverts have enriched their lives by such faith.[4]

What the homosexual needs more than the achievement of satisfactory sexual relationships is an inner sense of personal dignity and worth and the feeling of fulfilling a purpose in life. A plan of life helps to create this sense.

All that has been said about a plan of life for the young homosexual applies also to older homosexuals. Usually, however, older homosexuals cannot afford extended private psychiatric treatment which would probably have benefits in other ways distinct from the redirection of the sexual instincts. Tempted as he may be to bitterness, the adult homosexual finds it difficult to accept his condition in a spirit of faith. For this grace he must pray. He will come to accept himself more easily if his counselors treat him like a person. As I have already said, "I am most helpful to the homosexual when I forget that he is a homosexual, and remember that he is human, fully human."[5]

Anomaly, author of *The Invert,* advocates that other inverts make it known in their old age that they led chaste lives in spite of their condition.[6]

The homosexual needs constant spiritual guidance to realize that he is just as pleasing to God as a heterosexual. "Since he did not *will* to be this way, he should not hate himself for an *involuntary* development within his own person." [7] But since human emotions are not completely subject to reasoning, feelings of self-hatred and depression will not depart readily. Found in all humans, loneliness is more acute in the homosexual. If he is going to lead a life of service to God and country, he needs some form of chaste companionship. I propose therefore that homosexuals who desire to live chastely form Homosexuals Anonymous.

Some will ridicule this suggestion as antisexual and beyond human capabilities. They assume that chastity is impossible for the homosexual. But their assumption runs contrary to pastoral experience. A creative spirit finds ways of living chastely with the support of spiritual direction and prayer. But these creative persons should be able to communicate their way of living to other homosexuals—some of whom want to be chaste but are afraid of the allegedly deeper loneliness of the chaste, and some of whom are chaste but are tempted constantly to join others in overt practices.

So far as I know, such a Homosexuals Anonymous has not been tried on any large scale. It will be worth the effort. It will appeal to many homosexuals who live lonely lives in the company of heterosexuals who are continually trying to marry them off. It will appeal to homosexuals who do not share all the tenets of the Mattachine Society or of the Daughters of Bilitis while respecting their opinions.

The motivation of desiring to lead a life of more spiritual communication with other Christians and non-Christians who have suffered in the same way should offset whatever moral dangers may exist in such a community. Surely the dangers faced by most isolated, or noncommunicating, homosexuals are greater: "cruising" in homosexual bars—really a form of voyeurism; reading homosexual erotica, usually followed by self-abuse or blind pickups in lavatories; and so on. Through spiritual guidance these dangers could be reduced.

While I do not expect everyone to agree with my proposals, I ask of them the same respect that I give their opinions. In October, 1964, I was impressed by the respect accorded to my notion of a life of *chastity* by members of the East Coast Homophile Organization meeting in Washington, D.C.

Conclusions

I have four conclusions: (1) I believe in psychotherapy for the homosexual so that he may understand the unconscious sources of his difficulty. I believe in close cooperation between clergymen and psychiatrists in helping the same person. (2) Just as important, I believe in spiritual direction for the homosexual, achieved either in private direction or in conferences to groups of homosexuals, such as the proposed Homosexuals Anonymous. (3) I believe that female homosexuals are receptive to spiritual direction, like the males, but on the whole have been neglected by the clergy. It would be a mistake to transfer all the research made on the male homosexual to the female. She is different, but relatively unknown by both the clergy and the medical profession. I propose therefore that all interested parties do basic research on the etiology and nature of female homosexuality. (4) The most basic reality in the life of any human is his love of God. The homosexual, therefore, will find fulfillment "not in a catalogue of things to be done or avoided, but in the love of God. All the details of a plan of life become expressions of that love, his love for God and the realization of

God's love for him. Beginning with charity, one increases in love by more acts of charity. Love of God and neighbor must become the driving force in the life of the homosexual who, otherwise, will grow restless for an alienated way of life in which he had been formerly immersed, to which he is still attracted, and in place of which divine love must be found."[8]

Notes

1. Cf. Pius XII, March, 1954, "On Holy Virginity," where objections to chastity are well treated, and suggestions for the celibate are found.
2. Samuel B. Hadden, "Treatment of Male Homosexuals in Groups," *International Journal of Group Psychotherapy,* 16:13–22 (Jan., 1966); "A Way Out for Homosexuals," *Harper's,* March, 1967, pp. 107–120.
3. "Newer Treatment Techniques for Homosexuality," American Academy of Occupational Medicine, *Arc. Environ. Health,* 13:284–288 (Sept., 1966).
4. J. F. Harvey, "Morality and Pastoral Treatment of Homosexuality," *Continuum,* 5:296, n. 40 (Summer, 1967).
5. Harvey, *loc. cit.,* 296.
6. Anomaly, *The Invert and His Social Adjustment* (The Williams & Wilkins Company, 1948), pp. 245–246.
7. Harvey, *loc. cit.,* 296.
8. *Ibid.*

6

Homosexuality—A Provisional Christian Stance

H. KIMBALL JONES

In reading John von Rohr's essay "Toward a Theology of Homosexuality," I found myself agreeing initially with much that he has to say. His essay could be commended on many points: it reflects an enlightened understanding of much of the recent theory on homosexuality; it is a very thorough treatment of the topic; the theology is quite sound. But I somehow find myself dissatisfied with the overall impression that the essay leaves upon me. It is "liberal" and yet somehow sterile, "relevant" yet off the mark, "thorough" yet insufficient.

In terms of the theological/ethical stance he takes, I find him to be both logical and consistent. Basically, this is a stance which says that though the homosexual is crippled by virtue of his sexual anomaly—which deviates both from the Christian norm for human sexuality and from the predominant norms in Western society—he should not be seen as a particularly reprehensible individual, since all forms of sexual expression contain elements of sin. Like all men, he is a victim of the Fall; and in his fallen state he can experience redemption either by changing his sexual orientation or by living creatively and responsibly within the confines of his situation (which, nevertheless, is an undesirable one).

I sympathize a great deal with this view.[1] However, I am increasingly coming to feel that it is an insufficient one. The intentions behind such a view are quite commendable, reflecting both a desire to atone for the ignorance and injustice that have marked the attitudes and actions of the church concerning the homosexual over the ages, and an attempt to achieve a new and enlightened understanding. Certainly a view such as that presented by von Rohr goes a long way toward achieving this. However, it falls short of the mark. While picking the homosexual up with one hand, it knocks him down with the other; for regardless of what acceptance is offered him within this stance, it remains implicit that he is out of tune with the universe, less than whole by virtue of his sexual anomaly.

I am sure that von Rohr does not wish to emphasize this. Indeed, he is very careful to point out (and with good reason) that the categories of "natural" and "unnatural" are incapable of conveying an adequate theological appraisal of homosexuality. However, he falls back into the same trap when he chooses to appraise homosexuality within categories of "sin" and "redemption." At root, these terms have connotations that are similar to those of "natural" and "unnatural." "Sin" connotes a deviation from God's intended creation, a brokenness of that which was once whole, while "redemption" connotes a restoring of that which has been broken. Redemption is always redemption *from* a less desirable state *to* a more desirable one.

When speaking of the redemption of the homosexual, one must raise the question, "Redemption from what?"

Is it the homosexual predisposition itself from which the homosexual need be redeemed? Von Rohr would appear to be saying no in suggesting that one possible avenue for redemption is in becoming a "different kind of homosexual." However, he has defined redemption as a "new and better life," and this implies that life for the homosexual is not happy or satisfying as normally structured.

This may be true; but again it may not be true, and this is the primary difficulty in such a stance. Biblically and theologically it is sound, but in terms of what we know about homosexuality, it is based on insufficient evidence. As von Rohr points out early in his essay, a responsible Christian stance must take into consideration the discoveries of the social sciences. At present, the information which the social sciences offer us concerning homosexuality is so conflicting that we simply do not have any degree of certainty about the "facts"—a situation which, in my mind, prevents us from being able to adopt a definitive ethical stance at this time.

This may appear as a "cop-out" to those who are anxious to arrive at a definitive Christian view of homosexuality; but given the present degree of conflicting evidence and theory concerning homosexuality, I do not think that we can arrive at a responsible ethical judgment at this time. We have been premature (and this applies to me as well as to others) in our attempts to arrive at an ethical stance which appraises homosexuality in terms such as illness and health, natural and unnatural, sin and redemption. We would do well to steer clear of pronouncements along these lines for the time being, seeking simply to learn as much as we can about homosexuality in a spirit of openness.[2] Indeed, one of the major responsibilities of the church in this matter should be to encourage the kind of unbiased research and dialogue that alone can give us more factual information.

One might ask to what extent such information is essential to a Christian theology of homosexuality. In my mind, it is crucial. Information, or lack thereof, influences considerably the kinds of ethical pronouncements we arrive at. The following two experiences are illustrative of this.

A clergyman has been invited by a group of homosexuals to meet with them in order to help them set up a "responsible, Christian homophile organization." At the meeting he is struck by the hostility and apparent immaturity displayed by many of the homosexuals who are present. He finds them extremely defensive and not at all open to discussing the very topic they have invited him to explore with them. When he suggests that it is possible for two homosexuals to form a lasting and binding relationship founded on mutual love and concern, he is literally hooted down by several members of the group, one of whom exclaims: "Get off it, man. I like my loving free and easy." Throughout the meeting a sizable segment of the group displays rude, immature behavior, and it soon becomes apparent that they are less concerned with having an open discussion than with harrassing their guest. Try as he may, he is unable to involve them in any serious, responsible discussion. Thus, he leaves the meeting both angry and discouraged.

The following experience stands in stark contrast to this.

A clergyman (the same man) has been invited by a homophile organization to speak to them on a book he has written about homosexuality. Throughout the talk he is struck by the level of concern among the members of the audience. A long period of discussion ensues during which it becomes apparent that most of those present are deeply concerned about coming to terms with their homosexuality in a responsible manner. The speaker is struck by the maturity and apparent emotional stability of those who are present. They seem to be quite open to listening to his point of view, even when he expresses thoughts that raise some question as to the naturalness or desirability of homosexuality. He leaves the meeting with a feeling of warmth and admiration for the group; and as a result, he begins to question and reexamine his own previous stance.

Both of these situations are typical of what a clergyman might encounter in meeting with a group of homosexuals (though my own experience would indicate that the latter is more representative than the former). If a clergyman were to meet just once with a group of homosexuals, he would certainly form strong impressions as a result of that meeting, and these impressions would tend to color whatever "ethical stance" he might try to achieve concerning homosexuality. Yet, as the above situations illustrate, the nature of these impressions would depend very much upon the makeup of the particular group with whom he was meeting, and would not necessarily be representative of the homosexual community at large.

This has quite serious implications for the modern theologian who wishes to arrive at a responsible ethical stance not only regarding homosexuality but regarding any contemporary social issue. In the first place, it should be apparent that in order to arrive at a responsible stance on any issue about which the social sciences can offer useful information, a person has the responsibility of acquainting himself with as much of this information as he possibly can. This is no easy task in an area such as homosexuality, where a great deal of new relevant material is being published every year. Yet, it is a task that must be undertaken with some degree of thoroughness if one is to begin to get a balanced picture of the present level of knowledge and the myriad conflicting opinions surrounding the various aspects of the subject. Too many supposedly "enlightened" theological statements about homosexuality have been based on a minimum and biased segment of the resources available.

Von Rohr seems to be well read in this area. Yet, in the short period that has transpired since he first wrote his essay, a number of significant studies have appeared that have a direct bearing on many of the issues he discusses (e.g., Marmor, Cappon, Pomeroy, Hoffman, etc.). Thus, we see the need to keep abreast of new studies (as considerable a task as this may be) if one is not to base one's opinions on obsolescent data.

Equally significant is the need for direct confrontation between theorist and those about whom he is theorizing. As useful as book research may be (and I don't want to underrate its significance), it cannot serve as the sole basis for responsible theological or ethical pronouncements on a problem such as homosexuality. If recent studies on "contextual" or "situational" ethics have taught us one thing, it is that as theologians we can no longer be content to sit in our cloistered offices writing theological pronouncements about human problems from which we remain experientially aloof. Just as it is inconceivable that one who has never met a black person could begin to write responsibly about the racial situation, it is inconceivable that one who has never participated in dialogue with homosexuals could write knowledgeably about homosexuality. Yet I would venture to guess that few of those who have offered theological pronouncements about homosexuality have engaged in much, if any, dialogue with homosexuals.

Unfortunately, a little experience can sometimes be worse than none at all. Too often one feels that he has "done his duty" by meeting once or twice with homosexuals; yet, as our examples above illustrate, such isolated meetings can be misleading in that they may be misrepresentative of the larger homosexual community.

I realize that these implications would tend to place a great burden upon those in the church who wish to write theological critiques of social issues and whose time commitments are already overextended, but I can see no way out of this dilemma. If one is to begin to write knowledgeably about homosexuality as it exists in our society today, then one must be willing to do a great deal of research in the area and to spend a considerable amount of time in dialogue with both individual homosexuals and groups of homosexuals.

Perhaps this means that the theologian who is concerned with contemporary social problems is going to have to narrow down his field of concern to one or two areas rather than offering ethical pronouncements on several unrelated areas as so many have done in the past, for any ethical stance that is based on half-knowledge and half-truth runs the risk of being mistaken and misleading, and in the long run may do more harm than good.

This is not intended as an indictment of those like von Rohr who have attempted to offer enlightened Christian statements on subjects such as homosexuality. Rather, it is simply a warning to move more cautiously in the future. Much of what has been written by those in the church in the last few years on homosexuality has done a great deal to dispel some of the ignorance and prejudice which have characterized Christian attitudes toward the homosexual, and as such it has served a worthy purpose. However, in our desire to make amends for the past we have often been too hasty in trying to arrive at a definitive theological/ethical stance when the level of information that is available simply does not permit enough certainty upon which to base such a stance.

As an example of the degree of uncertainty and disagreement that exists among professionals concerning homosexuality, let us look for a moment at the question of promiscuity among homosexuals—a question that is central to arriving at a Christian ethic. Many of those who have worked with homosexuals and who have studied homosexuality agree that, in general, sexual promiscuity is much more widespread among the overt homosexual population [3] of our country than among heterosexuals. While this would appear to have definite implications for a Christian ethic, it is misleading in that there is much conflicting evidence and theory as to why homosexuals should tend toward more promiscuity.

This can be seen in looking at the views of two professionals who have worked closely with members of the gay subculture in America: Martin Hoffman (a psychiatrist) and Evelyn Hooker (a research psychologist). Hoffman,[4] as a result of his clinical experience, suggests that male homosexual alliances are by and large more fragile and transitory, marked more by a pervading promiscuity, than are either heterosexual or female homosexual alliances.[5] The reason for this, says Hoffman, is not that these men are *homosexuals,* but that they are *men;* and men, by nature, tend to be more promiscuous than women. "Without the stabilizing female the dyad tends to break up. When two females interact, as in Lesbian relationships, the dyad tends to be more stable." [6]

One might seriously question Hoffman's assumption that men by nature are more promiscuous than women. However, we must remain open to the possibility that this is an accurate observation. What's more, we must take seriously his observation, based on clinical experience, that lesbian relationships tend to be more stable than male homosexual alliances. If this is true, we need to ask "Why?", and Hoffman has offered one possible explanation.

Evelyn Hooker places her emphasis elsewhere, suggesting that the high incidence of promiscuity among male homosexuals is due to the "system effects of a market economy" in which sex becomes a commodity subjected to the values of the market—values that give priority to appearance and superficial attractiveness.[7] She further suggests that promiscuity in our society is more marked among males than females (heterosexual as well as homosexual) because:

> women have more to lose by divesting sexuality of rights, obligations, and commitments. . . . Their value in the competitive marriage market depends on them as bargaining power. . . . Their role as child-bearers and child rearers requires psychological and economic support. The relative absence of women in the homosexual world, the negative sanctions of society against homosexual relationships, the pressures toward secrecy and the risks of revealing one's own personal identity as a homosexual, and the market character of the bar setting in which

> meetings occur, combine to produce the kind of sexual exchange which [is] a stable feature of the gay world.[8]

These are only two of several possible explanations of the high incidence of promiscuity among male homosexuals in our society. These two views are not necessarily contradictory, but reflect quite different emphases: Hoffman emphasizing more the sexual nature of the human male, Hooker emphasizing the influence of a society in which a "market mentality" is pervasive. In addition to these two emphases, one could list several additional factors that probably play a part in male homosexual promiscuity, factors such as psychodynamics, early family constellations, changing mores within the society, etc.

The point that I wish to make is that with this question, as with every question concerning the homosexual in our society, the determinative factors are multidimensional and exist in varying ratios which, at this point, remain obscure.

The implications of this for Christian ethics are clear. Many of the facts concerning homosexuality which at this point remain elusive are essential to a definitive ethical stance. For example, if Hoffman's observations are correct, then the question concerning promiscuity among homosexuals would broaden to include the larger and more basic issue of the sexual nature of man (whether or not man is, by nature, more promiscuous than woman).

Similarly, if Hooker's observations are accurate, then to get at the root of homosexual promiscuity we need to look carefully at the prevailing values in the society, which may be merely reflected rather than created in the homosexual community.

Thus, each of these theories has its own implications as

to where the focus ought to occur in an ethical approach to the problem. In both instances we see a good reason for basing a Christian stance upon a broad framework that deals with the homosexual not as an isolated entity, but rather as a *man,* a member of a society whose values are reflected in his behavior and self-understanding. Only when this broader approach is kept in mind can we begin to get a balanced idea of which characteristics are inherent in homosexuality and which are merely by-products of other influencing factors.

Too often those who have written theological appraisals of the subject have taken a narrow, unidimensional approach. Consequently, they have often done injustice to the homosexual (however liberal or enlightened their theology) by seeing his sexual proclivity as an entity that could be discussed and analyzed in isolation. As one observer has justly pointed out, such an approach "violates the humanity of the homosexual by equating him totally with [his sexual] identity." [9]

It is a well-known fact that when an identity is imposed upon a minority group, that identity will eventually become incorporated into the self-image of the members of that group. When we see the homosexual only in terms of his sexual identity, we indirectly encourage him to adopt a distorted self-image within which his sexual identity assumes a disproportionately dominant place. Thus, ironically, those within the church who have been most anxious to help the homosexual and to make amends for the past have often contributed to the very situation that they wished to help alleviate.

Von Rohr has avoided this pitfall somewhat by taking a multidimensional approach to homosexuality and by centering his critique in the position that "the sinfulness of homosexuality is not to be found in the fact that it is *homo*-sexuality, but rather in the fact that it is homo-*sexuality* in the midst of man's disordered state."

However, in assuming this position, he falls into a trap almost as great as that which he has so carefully avoided. If he is convinced that the question is one of homo-*sexuality* rather than of *homo*-sexuality, then why does he bother to speak at all of the "sinfulness of homosexuality" and the "redemption of the homosexual"? Why does he not simply speak of the "sinfulness of sexuality" and the "redemption of sexuality?" Because the question at hand is that of *homo*-sexuality!

While von Rohr is wise to avoid identifying the homosexual too closely with his sexual proclivity, he sidesteps the issue when he moves the focus from *homo*-sexuality to homo-*sexuality*. The fact is that there may well be something inherently sinful about *homo*-sexuality. It may well be that when all the various contributing factors are better understood we will discover that there is something inherently exploitative about the homosexual alliance. While I don't personally feel that this will prove to be the case, I think that at this point we must be open to it as a possibility. On the other hand, we must remain equally open to the possibility that, as the studies of Hooker, Pomeroy, and Simon and Gagnon indicate, there is nothing inherently sick or sinful about homosexuality per se and that therefore the apparently sinful aspects of homosexuality are chiefly attributable to other contributing factors and may well lie in the fact that it is homo-*sexuality* rather than in the fact that it is *homo*-sexuality. We simply do not know; and given our present level of knowledge, we are not in a position to arrive at a responsible judgment on this question.

What, then, are we to say both *to* the homosexual and *about* him if we wish neither to ignore him entirely (which would be irresponsible, given the serious problems that surround homosexuality in our society) nor to achieve a definitive stance concerning the nature and desirability of his sexual identity (which would be equally irresponsible, given our present inadequate knowledge about homosexuality)?

This is a dilemma which needs to be worked through carefully and which may require at times that we follow a path that is ill-defined. However, it is not insoluble, and I think that we have a clue as to what a responsible Christian approach might be in the suggestions that von Rohr offers in the latter part of his essay under the unfortunate rubric of "redemption for the homosexual."

The fact is that many homosexuals in our society are unhappy, whatever the reason, and are seeking help from various types of agencies. The church is certainly one place where the troubled homosexual ought to feel that he can receive help. Unfortunately, in the past the church has, by and large, been more detrimental than helpful to him. Thus, one of the main thrusts in the church's concern with homosexuality today should be in trying to discover new and viable ways of helping the homosexual.[10]

Von Rohr suggests three ways in which the homosexual might be helped: (1) through encouragement to seek a "cure," a transition from homosexuality to heterosexuality via psychotherapy; (2) through encouragement to become a "different kind of homosexual" who seeks to form a responsible and lasting alliance with one homosexual partner; and (3) through the creation of a more accepting attitude toward the homosexual among the people in the church and in the total society. Let's look carefully at each of these suggestions.

It is interesting that von Rohr gives more space to his discussion of the first of these suggestions—that of "cure" —than to either of the other two. This is the one that I would emphasize least. Too often, those who have counseled homosexuals have seen this as the only desirable goal and have used every possible means to try to coerce their clients into seeking a "cure." Given the present level of confusion among professionals concerning this question, it is not at all clear whether a change to heterosexuality is either possible or desirable for most homosexuals.

It is true, as von Rohr says, that "all other things (i.e., sexual impulses) being equal, it is a lot better to live in our world as a heterosexual than as a homosexual." However, we must be very careful here. It is too easy to say simply that since the homosexual is unhappy, whatever the reason, the best thing would be for him to change. In the first place, it is not at all certain that it is possible for many homosexuals to change (though many recent studies are claiming success in this area).[11] Secondly and more significantly, it remains an open question whether homosexuality is inherently either an immoral or a pathological condition from which one need seek to change.

Current research indicates pretty conclusively that there are cases in which one's homosexual proclivity is closely tied up with psychodynamic pathology. Where this is the case, it would appear that psychotherapy, with an aim toward transition to heterosexuality, should be recommended. However, one must be careful to distinguish between pathology which has its etiology in the psychodynamics which led to the formation of the homosexuality and that which may have its source in external pressures from the society.

There is a great deal of evidence which suggests that the source of the pathology in many disturbed homosexuals lies in attitudes and pressures manifest in the society rather than in the psycho/biological makeup of the homosexual (though these are not unrelated and cannot be seen as operating separately). If this is true, then perhaps our first responsibility toward the homosexual should be to work toward the redemption of the society in terms of its distorted sexual values while helping the homosexual who is the victim of these values to adjust to his homosexuality. Indeed, if research should show that pathology among homosexuals is chiefly the result of societal pressures, then the most responsible advice that we could offer the homosexual who is the victim of these pressures would be to encourage him to adjust as well as possible to his condition and suffer the abuse, if necessary, with the broader aim of working toward the redemption of the society.

Such a stance may appear to invite the kind of "martyr complex" that many observers have already pointed out as a characteristic of many neurotic homosexuals. Nevertheless, this is a risk that we may have to be willing to take if we are to adopt a responsible Christian attitude. However, this question must be held in abeyance until we have a clearer picture of the etiology of pathology among homosexuals, and those who counsel homosexuals should be extremely cautious in encouraging a "cure" through transition to heterosexuality.

I find von Rohr's second suggestion to be much more helpful and practicable. In stressing to the homosexual the possibility and desirability of establishing a permanent relationship with one partner grounded in mutual love and commitment, we can offer him a viable Christian alternative to the depersonalizing cruising and one-night stands that appear to be characteristic of the observable gay community. What's more, this norm applies equally to all men and to all areas of sexuality and does not single out the homosexual as being particularly needful of moral guidance.

Unlike the suggestion of "cure," that of "commitment" would appear to be a viable possibility for most healthy homosexuals. However, we need to be careful how we communicate this to the homosexual (who may be suspicious of any "advice" offered by the church, given what the church has had to say to him in the past!). We need to make it clear that he has not been singled out as being particularly needful of a norm more than any other group in our society, but that the same norms which apply to heterosexual alliances (love, commitment, stability) are equally applicable to his situation.

For this reason I find the term "a different kind of homosexual" somewhat offensive, even though it was apparently a homosexual who first coined the phrase. It is true that for the homosexual who is caught up in the life-style of the "cruiser" or "oncer,"[12] such a norm would imply becoming a "different kind of homosexual." But we have no assurance that the "cruisers" and "oncers" make up a majority, or even a large minority of the homosexuals in our society, particularly when we consider those who are not involved in the activities of the more readily observable gay subculture and whose homosexuality remains covert to all but those who are closest to them. It may well be that a large number of these homosexuals are already expressing their sexuality within a responsible framework of love and commitment. We simply do not know. Therefore we should not assume that what is more readily observable is necessarily more representative.

Having said this, however, I do not want to diminish the importance of encouraging homosexuals (as, indeed, one should encourage all men!) to express their sexuality within a context of mutual love and commitment.

It is von Rohr's third suggestion which I find to be most significant, and it is here that I would place the greatest emphasis—in educating the public about homosexuality and creating a greater atmosphere of acceptance and understanding of the homosexual. This, in my mind, is where the primary thrust of the church should be in dealing with homosexuality.

Many within the church have written of the need for a "greater acceptance" of the homosexual, but few have taken the time or trouble to offer any guidelines as to just how this might be accomplished. While the concrete details must be worked out differently in each church and in each community, I would like to suggest some general guidelines, which I would see in terms of three categories: (1) discussion, (2) education, and (3) action.[13]

The most fundamental need at present is to expose those within the church—both clergy and laity—to open discussion on the question of homosexuality. Such discussion should be encouraged by national church bodies and might assume various forms in local churches: forums, panel discussions, small study groups, etc. In each instance homosexuals should be invited to participate in the discussions. Open confrontation with homosexuals would, in itself, go a long way toward dispelling many of the myths that so many Christians harbor concerning homosexuality.

Education will result from discussion insofar as discussion is informed by fact. But discussion will not lead automatically to enlightenment. Too often it merely creates the opportunity for the rephrasing of old prejudices and the reaffirmation of false stereotypes. Thus, we see the need for consulting both homosexuals and professionals who work with them in planning effective educational programs. Such programs might center upon relevant and informative study materials that could be published by national denominational publishing houses and might be initiated at the local level in any number of ways (e.g., through a sermon or an article in the church newsletter, through the formation of a study group, through the calling of a congregational meeting to discuss a crisis situation involving homosexuals in the congregation, etc.). The forms that educational programs might take are limitless and would depend upon the ability of individual pastors to respond creatively to the needs in their own congregations.

Discussion and education are both essential, but they fall short of the mark if they do not lead ultimately to concerned Christian action. Both clergy and laity should examine the various ways in which their concrete actions might help to alleviate the ignorance and hatred, prejudice and injustice, to which the homosexual is subjected in our society. The more pressing needs will vary from one community to another and will involve questions such as the following: biased reporting on homosexuality by mass media, antiquated laws that offer heavy penalties for homosexual relations among consenting adults, unethical entrapment tactics of law enforcement agencies in apprehending homosexuals, employment practices (particularly in Government-related agencies) which discriminate against homosexuals, discrimination against homosexuals in the Armed Forces resulting in dishonorable discharges, etc. The church should seek to play a major role in combating these injustices. Indeed, if we would spend more time spelling out our responsibility along these lines and less time trying to define a "theological stance" toward homosexuality, we might act much more responsibly toward the homosexuals in our society than we have up to the present time.

Finally, I should like to add one further dimension to the question. As I said earlier, it is not at all clear to what extent the pathology demonstrated by disturbed homosexuals is derived from the psychodynamic and/or biological basis of their homosexuality and to what extent it may merely reflect a deeper pathology in the sexual attitudes and mores of the society. Few studies on homosexuality have given even fleeting consideration to this question, and yet it is a question that must be dealt with thoroughly before we can even begin to have an objective understanding of homosexuality.

One need not look far to see evidence of the fact that Americans today are both confused and disturbed (in the clinical sense of the word) concerning questions of sexual identity and mores—and this applies as much to the heterosexuals in our society as it does to the homosexuals or to any other group that has been labeled "deviate." Indeed, many of the prevailing sexual attitudes in our society engender the very kind of compulsive behavior, confused role identity, exploitation, and depersonalization that are so often seen to be the earmarks of sexual deviation.

The epitome of this can be seen in the *Playboy* philosophy in which persons are seen as little more than consumer goods with a sexual product to sell. As Harvey Cox has pointed out, such a philosophy is not only deviate, it is antisexual.

> *Playboy* and its less successful imitators are not "sex magazines" at all. They are basically antisexual. They dilute and dissipate authentic sexuality by reducing it to an accessory, by keeping it at a safe distance.[14]

What is most often seen to be pathological or deviate in homosexual behavior is precisely that which is emphasized within the *Playboy* philosophy—preoccupation with the sexual partner as an object to be used and then discarded. Yet somehow we fail to label this "deviate" when we see it in a heterosexual framework. It is time that we begin gaining a clearer perspective here and begin asking to what extent such an attitude among homosexuals may be reflecting a prevailing attitude within the society.

Von Rohr discusses this question of depersonalized sex in terms of *eros* vs. *agape,* "I-it" relationships vs. more fulfilling "I-thou" relationships. Certainly this is central to the problem. However, in terms of contemporary American society, as Rollo May has observed, it may also be a question of "*eros* in conflict with sex." [15] Not only have we placed too much emphasis upon *eros* in our society (at the expense of *agape*), but we have also stripped *eros* of its true meaning, labeling as "erotic" that which is essentially anti-erotic. In its truest and noblest sense, "*eros* seeks union in delight and passion, and procreating of new dimensions of experience that broaden and deepen the being of both persons." [16] However, in modern American society *eros* has become "a synonym for eroticism, sexual titillation, the name given to a journal of sexual arcana."[17] "*Eros* has lost passion, and has become insipid, childish, banal."[18]

It is precisely this anti-erotic, antisexual atmosphere prevalent in current American sexual attitudes which is characteristic of what we tend to label "deviate." It is, indeed, "deviate" from a Christian point of view, but it is by no means to be found only among those who are labeled "deviate" by the society. It is an atmosphere that pervades the entire society—heterosexual as well as homosexual—and it should be dealt with as such. Consequently, I would stress at all costs the need to study homosexual behavior within the framework of the prevailing sexual attitudes and behavior within our society as a whole. Any assessment of homosexuality that sees it as an isolated phenomenon is bound to go astray at some point. Only when we study it within a broader social framework will we begin to achieve a balanced objective view.

This applies as much to a "theological" approach to homosexuality as it does to any other kind of approach. Only when we have a broader picture of homosexuality and begin to understand how the various factors that fill this multidimensional picture are interrelated will we be in the position to arrive responsibly at a definitive "theology of homosexuality." Meanwhile, we must take a provisional stance, pushing on in those areas where we stand on safer ground: toward greater research in all areas of human sexuality, toward a greater understanding and acceptance in the name of Jesus Christ of those who have been labeled "deviate," and toward more enlightened and responsible sexual norms and mores in a society in which the prevailing attitudes toward sex could only be described as "deviate" when seen from the perspective of the Christian gospel.

Notes

1. Indeed, I take a very similar stance in my book. See H. Kimball Jones, *Toward a Christian Understanding of the Homosexual* (Association Press, 1966), Part III.

2. I should like to express my indebtedness to a colleague whose thoughtful criticisms have helped me to arrive at this position. See Neale A. Secor, "A Brief for a New Homosexual Ethic," in Ralph W. Weltge (ed.), *The Same Sex: An Appraisal of Homosexuality* (The Pilgrim Press, 1969), pp. 67–79.

3. By this I mean the more readily observable gay subculture. This may not apply to those homosexuals whose sexual identity remains hidden from public scrutiny.

4. Martin Hoffman, "Homosexual," *Psychology Today,* 3:43 ff. (July, 1969). Also see Martin Hoffman, *The Gay World: Male Homosexuality and the Social Creation of Evil* (Basic Books, Inc., 1968).

5. In the light of this, it is interesting that the statement chosen by von Rohr to illustrate the position that homosexuals are not necessarily more promiscuous than heterosexuals was written by a woman, Iris Murdoch.

6. Hoffman, *loc. cit.,* p. 70.

7. Evelyn Hooker, "The Homosexual Community," in Weltge (ed.), *op. cit.,* p. 32. Dr. Hooker spells this out in terms of the "market mentality," a term that was coined by Karl Polanyi and has been used extensively by David Riesman.

8. *Ibid.,* p. 33.

9. Ralph W. Weltge, "The Paradox of Man and Woman," in Weltge (ed.), *op. cit.,* p. 62.

10. This does not assume that all, or even most, homosexuals are in need of help or that the cause of disturbance in those who manifest pathology lies in the na-

ture of homosexuality. The emphasis I am making here is the need to deal with a blatant and extensive social problem, whatever its cause and however representative or unrepresentative it may be of the total homosexual population in our society.

11. For a thorough discussion of this, see Jones, *op. cit.*, pp. 54–63.

12. This term is often used by homosexuals to describe the homophile who never has sexual relations more than once with the same partner.

13. For a more thorough discussion of guidelines, see "Suggestions for Future Action," in Jones, *op. cit.*, pp. 129–134. Also see Lewis I. Maddocks, "The Law and the Church vs. the Homosexual," in Weltge (ed.), *op. cit.*, pp. 95–96, 110.

14. Harvey Cox, *The Secular City* (The Macmillan Company, 1965), p. 204.

15. Rollo May, "Love and Will," *Psychology Today*, 3:30–35 (August, 1969).

16. *Ibid.*, p. 31.

17. *Ibid.*

18. *Ibid.*, p. 33.

7

Walls of Ice—Theology and Social Policy

LEWIS WILLIAMS

Theology may claim to be the most important of all the sciences, since it is, by definition, the science that purports to show mankind the way to godhead. But it has, on occasion, badly mistaken its destination. Indeed, for centuries it put on the throne of heaven a kingly monarch who was conceived as torturing men, not for years (as we do in our prisons) but for all eternity, and not to reform or change them but merely to impress them with his might and moral superiority. All thoughtful and humane men now repudiate such a conception as being, not godly, but, in the exact sense of the word, diabolical.

Having blundered so badly in its special domain, that of divinity, it is not surprising to find that theology has on occasion erred disastrously in matters of social policy. Usually it has done this by rigidly upholding some position on faith or morals and refusing to look at the human consequences. The birth control controversy is one example. A hundred years ago, proponents of contraception were hotly vilified, as much by Protestant as by Catholic theologians, and the English judge who deprived a mother of the custody of her daughter on the grounds that the former, because she had publicly advocated birth control, could not possibly be a fit parent, undoubtedly felt he had the religious sentiment of the nation behind him. At other times, religion has actively promoted the oppression of minorities, as in the case of Luther's violent denunciation of the Jews, the burning of witches, and the persecution of heretics. On all these historic issues, the Christian churches have finally, to their credit, reversed themselves. But we tend to forget how strange it must have seemed, to theologians and laymen alike, that Christians should stop killing heretics and witches and proselytizing Jews, after the church had sanctioned such actions for more than a millennium, and what anxieties these changes in policy must have aroused about the imminent dissolution of society.

Surely it is now time for the churches to admit that, just as they were wrong about witchcraft, about the Jews, about the treatment of heretics, and about contraception, so they have been wrong about homosexuality. What I miss in Dr. von Rohr's kindly and well-intentioned essay is a clear call to our national churches to speak out as institutions and repudiate a tradition of antihomosexualism that has endured in Christianity since its origins. That, and any direct and immediate sense of the human suffering involved as a result of church attitudes. But perhaps the last lack is not too surprising. A wall of ice has existed between the homosexual and the church: in the Midwestern city where I live I have talked to several dozen clergy and only a tiny handful have ever directly communicated with a homosexual parishioner, though all of them presumably have homosexuals in their congregations. And the speculative theologian is even less likely to encounter the homosexual in a crisis than the pastor.

The use of laws by Christian states to persecute homosexuals goes back to the fourth century, the century in which Christianity became the dominant religion of the Roman Empire. Until this time the Greco-Roman world had generally treated the homosexual with tolerance, though occasionally interfering where minors were involved. The Christianization of Rome seems to have ushered in a radically different feeling. Twenty-nine years after the Edict of Milan, Constantine's sons Constantius and Constans ordained that "the laws be armed with an avenging sword, that these infamous persons who are now, or hereafter may be, guilty [of homosexual acts] may be subject to exquisite punishment." [1] In 390 another law commanded that men "shall expiate a crime of this kind in avenging flames in the sight of the people." Both of these statutes, which are cryptically and obliquely worded, were incorporated into the great compendium of Roman law made under the emperor Theodosius II. But though they belong to Rome's first Christian century, they do not make a clear appeal to theology for their sanctions. It is only when we turn to the Code of Justinian that the religious bias of the law becomes unmistakably evident. Title VI of the *Novellae,* issued in 538, lumps homosexuality together with blasphemy in one statute, which reads:

> Therefore, as certain persons, instigated by the devil, devote themselves to the most reprehensible vices, and commit crimes contrary to nature, We hereby enjoin them to fear God and the judgement to come, to avoid diabolical and illicit sensuality of this kind; in order that, through such acts, they may

> not incur the just anger of God, and bring about the destruction of cities along with their inhabitants; for We learn from the Holy Scriptures that both cities as well as men have perished because of wicked acts of this kind.[2]

The reference to the destruction of cities is, of course, to the Sodom and Gomorrah story of Gen., ch. 19. Its introduction here is of crucial significance for Western law codes when they touch on homosexuality, for the Code of Justinian was the model that legal students at Bologna studied when Roman law was revived in Europe in the eleventh century. It is thus the progenitor of a legal tradition reaching back continuously for nine hundred years. Our own American statutes attest to this influence and preserve the Biblical reference by calling homosexual acts "sodomy," though the offense itself has been redefined to include all oral and anal intercourse, marital as well as homosexual, a use of the word which, if Kinsey is to be believed, makes a large minority, if not a majority, of state legislators technically "sodomites," on the basis of their heterosexual relations. The English legal term "buggery" also has a religious significance, "bougre" or "bugger" (Bulgar) being the epithet bestowed on the Albigensian heretics, who were accused of homosexual practices as well as false doctrine in orthodox propaganda.

Because of the close connection between church and state in early Christian and medieval times it is perhaps not surprising to find such explicit links between religion and law in these periods. After the Reformation, the law tended to be largely secularized, especially in Protestant countries. But laws on homosexuality seem to have been the notable exception. In Blackstone's *Commentaries,* published in England in 1769, the sense of a specifically religious sanction is still very much alive. After calling sodomy the crime "not fit to be mentioned among Christians," Blackstone continues:

> This the voice of nature and of reason, and the express law of God, determine to be capital. Of which we have a signal instance, long before the Jewish dispensation, by the destruction of two cities by fire from heaven: so that this is an universal, not merely a provincial precept. And our ancient law in some measure imitated this punishment by commanding such miscreants to be burnt to death. . . .[3]

But surely, the reader will protest, all this is merely part of our past, of our verbal heritage, but not present reality. Alas, this is not so. Far more than the educated and sophisticated reader supposes, repressive social policy on homosexuality is justified, on the popular level, in religious terms. The Congressional Record recounts how, when he was opposing the Washington Mattachine Society, Congressman Dowdy of Texas thought it sufficient, in making his case against civil rights organizations for homosexuals, to quote Paul. And in Florida in 1964, the notorious Johns' committee's inflammatory antihomosexual pamphlet, *Homosexuality and Citizenship in Florida,* after what purported to be a survey of modern scientific opinion, tartly concluded, "We would, however, suggest that the Biblical description of homosexuality as an 'abomination' has well stood the test of time." I have myself been told on educational television by a fellow panelist that homosexuality was the only sin for which God destroyed an entire city. Moreover, lest the reader should think this outlook is uniquely a Bible belt phenomenon, there is the famous case of the officer in San Francisco who indignantly told a group of ministers who had come to him to protest the harassment of homosexuals that if they weren't prepared to enforce God's law, the police were. Sometimes such responses come close to pure fanaticism. In her book *The Puritan Jungle,* Sara Harris shows how a former Miami vice-squad head based his personal conviction that "homosexuals would be better off dead" on his interpretation of Leviticus and First Corinthians.[4] And on campuses members of student Christian groups have been known to approach students at homophile league booths with the query, "Are you a blankety-blank homosexual?" or a "blankety-blank lesbian?" using expressions until recently unprintable, and feeling justified in their self-righteousness by their religious faith.

What I am saying is that theologians must turn from a preoccupation with *henosis,* with personal morality, and with whether "love is the only norm," and take a steady look at the consequences of traditional theological teaching, as a result of which homosexuals are being treated in a way that is very unlovely. First of all, this means laying the ghost of biblicism. The man in the street does not go to the Bible for his biology or astronomy. That is, he does not regard the Bible as an infallible treatise on science. But he does, more often than is realized, unreflectingly take it as an infallible treatise on morals, largely because he has not read it and does not know at how many places his own moral convictions differ from it. And in an area where he is confused or fearful, such as sexual ethics, he may fall back on it in desperation, or at least give way to people who quote it with conviction. He does not know that for hundreds of years young girls were led to the stake in accordance with the command in Exodus, "Thou shalt not suffer a witch to live," or that the use of anesthetics in childbirth was at first passionately opposed because of a text that makes labor pains a divine punishment for Eve's eating the forbidden fruit in Eden. Thus, if he hears men make heated appeals to Genesis or Leviticus or Paul to oppose homosexuality, he is uncertain what to reply. He knows what is in fact the truth, that the Bible is an ancient religious book containing much that is wise and noble, but he does not know how to discriminate between Biblical wisdom and Biblical deadwood or folly. And not only laymen are discomfited in this way. As I write these lines the papers are full of the news that the General Assembly of a large liberal Protestant denomination has added to an otherwise enlightened draft of a study report on sex a paragraph condemning America's 15,000,000 homosexuals as sinners, on the motion of a delegate who used a string of Biblical quotations as his argument.

So men of goodwill who have been bypassing the Biblical issues on the grounds that they are dead ones must now face up to them and be prepared to meet them head on. They must explain to people that the Sodom and Gomorrah story, an incidental detail of which is a threat of rape by the men of Sodom to Lot's two angelic visitors, is a fantastic mixture of folklore, legend, and perhaps some true history. In it women are turned into salt, angels strike men blind, and two cities of Palestine are destroyed by what seems to be a volcanic eruption of the sort that destroyed Pompeii and Herculaneum, though there have in fact never been volcanoes in the Holy Land, and the myth is obviously fanciful. They must also explain that when Old Testament writers such as Isaiah, Jeremiah,

Ezekiel, Amos, and Zephaniah speak of Sodom, as they frequently do, they make no reference at all to homosexuality. (Indeed, Ezekiel writes more like a modern socialist than a fundamentalist moralist, making the sin of Sodom luxury and idleness and a failure to take care of the poor.) Not until about two thousand years after the events that are supposed to have taken place, at the beginning of the Christian era, did the story become the vehicle for antihomosexual propaganda in the hands of Jewish philosophers and historians who were in revolt against Hellenic manners.

The reader will note that I do not here follow Sherwin Bailey's *Homosexuality and the Western Christian Tradition* as Dr. von Rohr does. With the amiable intention of lessening Christian bias against homosexuals, Dr. Bailey reads homosexual interpretations out of Scripture at every possibility. In some instances he seems to me right in being skeptical—the debated question of the Temple prostitutes in The Books of the Kings is one—but that the "knowledge" of Gen., ch. 19, is carnal knowledge seems to me clear enough from the parallel story in Judg., ch. 19, where a substitute heterosexual rape does take place. Probably the Judges story is the older one and the same tale was merely adapted at a later date as a preamble to the Sodom legend. This might help explain the prophets' silence on the matter. But the more likely explanation is that the strong wave of antihomosexual feeling that arose at about the time of Christ simply seized on this dramatic fable as available for its purposes. One can compare the use rabid antimasturbationists made in the eighteenth and nineteenth century of the story of Onan.

In short, the Sodom and Gomorrah story is a fanciful medley of fact and fiction, the moral import of which is hopelessly obscure. On the other hand, the Levitican code is, in a literal sense, deadly clear. Chapter 18 prohibits homosexual acts and ch. 20 makes them capital crimes. But Leviticus is a book largely devoted to ancient Jewish dietary and sanitary law, and ceremonial ritual. It also prohibits the eating of blood sausage and rare beef, camels, hares, lobsters, turtles, owls, and vultures, but allows the Jews to eat grasshoppers and beetles. It forbids witchcraft, tattooing the body, shaving the beard, child sacrifice, and sowing mixed crops. The book is an extreme mixture of the barbaric and the humane. Between the passage condemning homosexuals and the one ordering them killed, there is a chapter admonishing us to be kind to deaf and blind people and to love our neighbors. Obviously, among these precepts we must discriminate carefully.

When we come to Paul the problem is of a totally different sort. Paul is neither obscure (at least not on sex) nor barbaric. He is, by contrast, subtle, sophisticated, and civilized, often poetic and, occasionally, intellectually brilliant. But he is not only antihomosexual, he is also antisexual in a more general sense. Sexuality is his great aversion. He thinks the best and most Christian society would be one in which men abstained from sexual relations entirely: "It is good for a man not to touch a woman." [5] He thinks it would be better if all men remained bachelors as he himself did. He grudgingly allows marriage, but only, he makes it clear, because the alternative is fornication and hellfire. Only a step seems to separate Paul from sects such as the Albigensians or the Shakers, or from thinkers such as Schopenhauer and Tolstoy, who recommended that men give up sexuality entirely, even at the risk of the extinction of the race. He obviously would have sympathized with Jerome's remark that the best thing about marriage was that it produced virgins. This antisexualism of Paul's has colored Christian thought for two thousand years. But nowhere has it acted with such devastating effect as in the case of the homosexual. Not having grasped the fact that homosexuality is a psychological condition and not a willful perversion of nature, Paul makes no concession to the homosexual comparable to heterosexual marriage.

The theological influence on our legal tradition is bad enough, but the public climate it has created has also led to serious difficulties in employment. While American society, including the churches, is now showing a concern about job discrimination against the Negro, the Indian, and the Mexican American, it still actively supports discrimination against the homosexual. If he is a churchman, it says, "You are a sinner: get out"; if he is a member of the legal profession, it says, "You are a felon: get out"; if he is a teacher, it says, "You are a seducer of the young: get out"; if he works for the civil service, it says, "You are an immoral person and a menace to your fellow employees: get out"; if he is a serviceman or an officer, no matter how distinguished, it says, "You are a threat to discipline and morale: get out," and attaches a lifelong stigma in the form of a less-than-honorable discharge; if, on the other hand, he identifies himself to his draft board and is exempted from service, it keeps the record on file and later refuses him a security clearance on the ground that he is open to blackmail.

Thus does our society treat its 15,000,000 homosexual citizens—the nation's second largest minority—despite the fact that the vast majority of them serve faithfully and well as clergy, church organists, choir leaders, lawyers, judges, professors, elementary teachers, and civil servants at every level, and pursue military careers with sufficient success that the services are sometimes embarrassed to find themselves revoking the pensions of retired officers of the highest rank who are found to belong to an unexceptable sexual minority. When one thinks of the homosexuals who have served and now serve the church conscientiously as pastors to heterosexuals and homosexuals alike, one might be tempted to weep at the ignominiousness of their treatment if the situation did not simply make one angry. And where the Negro, for instance, used to be confined to jobs such as scrubbing floors, our official Government policy bars the homosexual from such work in a public building on the alleged grounds that the public would be shocked beyond endurance if it discovered it was being served by a homosexual even in the capacity of a janitor. How insane our national policy is will occur to anyone who reflects that, if America's 15,000,000 homosexuals really were the unemployables the Government declares them to be, we would have an economic crisis on our hands. Yet, so far no national church group has raised its voice against the civil service discrimination that sets the pattern for the country.

But there is also the problem of youth. It is not only in official attitudes to employment that the homosexual is worse off than other minorities. A child that is born into a Jewish, Negro, or Chicano family will ordinarily be loved and cherished, perhaps all the more tenderly for his parents' knowledge that he will share with them an outcast status. But the church does not teach parents to accept their homosexual children at all, so that when boys and girls in their teens discover their sexual orientation they face a hostile world in isolation, fearing even to reveal themselves to their parents. Indeed, the Dade County policeman we have already met explicitly declared that his faith taught him that he should wish any homosexual child of his dead. In the light of these facts it is interesting to note that in the last two years teen-agers in colleges and high schools have been forming themselves in Gay Liberation Fronts or Student Homophile Leagues, partly as an expression of youthful radicalism, but more out of a dire need for a sense of community, since older homophile civil rights organizations have feared to admit minors. Among other places, such groups have appeared in New York, Boston, Ithaca, Pittsburgh, Detroit, Ann Arbor, Kalamazoo, De Kalb, Champaign-Urbana, Normal, Chicago, Evanston, Madison, Minneapolis, Fort Worth, Austin, Billings, Seattle, Portland, Sacramento, Berkeley, San Jose, Los Angeles, and San Diego. Since the most notorious antisexual witch-hunts in the United States—those in Boise and Florida, for instance—were organized ostensibly to protect the young, it is interesting to see the young organizing to protect themselves, not against older homosexuals, whose aid they seek out, but against what we may call society's "homophobes," a fanatical and unreasonable hatred of homosexuals being quite as specific a mania in our society as racism. At the moment, congregations are being treated to the spectacle of young men unexpectedly lecturing them on antihomosexual prejudice from the pulpits of our metropolitan cathedrals or demonstrating in the company of young women at the church door. What this Youth Movement bodes for the future will be interesting to see. The churches have so little educated themselves as to be totally unprepared for the crisis. But after two millennia the walls of ice are toppling down.

Yet when we turn from our children to their elders and betters in the persons of twentieth-century theologians, the spectacle, to put the matter frankly, is depressing. Karl Barth is more hostile in the page he devotes to homosexuals in *Church Dogmatics* even than Paul.[6] Helmut Thielicke takes Barth to task for his lack of charity and human understanding, and makes a valiant plea for law reform, but after nearly sanctioning homosexual love, he ends up counseling sublimation.[7] Even when the writer comes to the question with a much broader knowledge of the social situation and a genuine sympathetic desire to be humane, as is the case with Kimball Jones, old prejudices can trip him up. Jones's *Toward a Christian Understanding of the Homosexual* is a valuable textbook for the bewildered pastor, well worth study. But unless he gets beyond Jones's final moral position, he will strike any genuinely self-respecting homosexual as hopelessly patronizing. Though Jones recognizes clearly that any realistic Christian ethic must reject sublimation as impracticable, the best he can bring himself to do is to argue for the acceptance of the homosexual as a kind of sexual cripple whose relations will always fall short of the heterosexual ideal.[8] Perhaps the most refreshingly sane view of the matter still remains that of the so-called Quaker report of 1963. Its authors maintain that "one should no more deplore homosexuality than left-handedness." "It is the nature and quality of a relationship that matters; one must judge it not by its outward appearance but by its inner worth. Homosexual affection can be as selfless as heterosexual affection, and therefore we cannot see that it is in some way morally worse."[9] It may be significant that the authors of this pamphlet are laymen and not theologians.

What vitiates the positions of such men as Barth, Piper, Thielicke, and Jones is the doctrine of heterosexual superiority which underlies them. This comes through strongly also in Ralph Weltge's often admirable essay in *The Same Sex*. According to Weltge, "It is the relationship to woman that makes a man a man, and vice versa."[10] It would be interesting to see Mr. Weltge defend this proposition before a Women's Liberation group. Mr. Weltge has a vivid sense of the need for the church to "become the homosexual's advocate in fighting for civil liberties" that one can applaud, but he just cannot bring himself to regard a homosexual as his equal. The latter fails the crucial bedroom test. Then again, through all these essays runs the common assumption that God's "intention" for the race was universal heterosexuality. Generally the writers appeal to the Genesis creation myth and the "one flesh" conception of the Old Testament and the Gospels. But this is as absurd as to use Genesis to refute Darwin, or to condemn Negroes as the descendants of Cain or Noah's wicked son Ham. The homosexual is granted a place in the church if he will sit in the back pew and acknowledge the superiority of his heterosexual betters, much like the Negro in a Mormon congregation. Dr. von Rohr is not totally free from this attitude when he says: "God's primary order of nature would seem to lay an expectation upon men for a heterosexual life. This is the pristine order of creation, even as it is the means of that order's extension through procreation." Later, Dr. von Rohr seems to draw back from that position and argues that "unnatural love" is at least love and hence good. But why not drop the opprobrious epithet? Kinsey and the biologists have demonstrated beyond a doubt that homosexuality is inescapably part of nature. One recalls that Dante (on good Biblical authority, be it said), included usury along with homosexuality in the seventh circle of the *Inferno* as a typical "crime against nature," a judgment that would in modern terms make loan company presidents the compeers of gay men and women. So does our conception of what is "natural" undergo historical change.

There is another difficulty here that American liberal theologians have not come to terms with. This is dramatized in the analysis of the morality of homosexuality that Sherwin Bailey gives at the end of *Sexual Offenders and Social Punishment*.[11] Bailey himself condemns all extramarital sexual acts as "materially" sinful, but notes that the writers of the Bible and the theologians of the middle ages were simply ignorant of homosexuality as a psychological state. Further, the fact that some men and women have no heterosexual responses does indeed, he admits, pose problems for the moralist. Celibacy is a special vocation one cannot demand of all homosexuals any more than of all heterosexuals, but homosexual acts are themselves sinful: how are we to escape from the dilemma? Bailey's solution is ingenious. Homosexual acts are materially sinful, but they do not have the "form" of sin, since the homosexual knows no better—i.e., he is, in theological jargon, "invincibly ignorant." But since he acts with a clear conscience in believing what he does is right, we must respect his conscience even though it is in error. Hence, he is not morally blameworthy. (The parallel here with the Catholic Church's attitudes toward Protestant heretics is obvious.)

Bailey's Anglo-Catholic casuistry will strike most American Protestants as a mere academic curiosity, but in fact it is perfectly logical, if one accepts his initial premises. The real difficulty is the difficulty that besets Thielicke and Jones and Dr. von Rohr; the belief that sexual acts are intrinsically bad. Whereas in America this assumption is buried under facile ecclesiastical rhetoric about sex being God-given and good, Bailey has the candor to make it explicit. The notion that sex is basically wicked and can be condoned only if blessed by marriage, or at least a continuing sentimental relation between the couple (whatever their sex) lies at the root of nearly all theological writing on the subject, in the twentieth century as much as the first, among liberals as much as conservatives. The sane, sensible, and finally unavoidable position that sex acts are in and of themselves morally neutral is still astonishingly rare in theological circles, though Neale Secor, to his credit, puts it forth in a companion piece to Weltge's as the only reasonable working hypothesis.[12]

At this point it is appropriate to turn from individuals to the churches. In England the Anglican Church and Canon Bailey deserve the highest praise for taking the initiative that led to the setting up of the Wolfenden Committee and for strongly supporting the recommendations that brought about law reform in 1967. Reform was also endorsed by the Roman Catholic Church, by the Methodists, and by the Presbyterian Church in Scotland. The Swedish Lutheran bishops gave their approval to legal changes in Sweden. In all those cases known to me,[13] however, advocacy of statutory reform has been accompanied by formal statements damning homosexuals unequivocally as sinners, which have undoubtedly helped to reinforce traditional prejudices. There has been no evidence that the change of law in England has improved the employment situation. Entrapment still goes on. Minors are still being jailed, incredibly enough for offenses that adults would not be punished for, and the morale of the English homosexual community remains low.

In the United States, the picture is quite different. As I write, no church has as yet gone on record nationally in favor of legislative changes.[14] One important Protestant denomination has issued a statement on homosexuals in a general pamphlet on the church and sex; the paragraph, which makes no reference to any social problems, reads in its entirety as follows:

> Medical and psychiatric advice leads us to view homosexuality as an immaturity or an illness which can be treated and sometimes cured. We reaffirm our belief that homosexuality is contrary to God's will for the proper use of sex drives. Nevertheless, we agree that the homosexual should be regarded as a person in need of help and healing for his warped sexuality. He may find in the redeeming strengths and influence of Christian fellowship, fed by the Means of Grace, the power for a changed way of life. We do not condemn him, but we do not condone his behavior.[15]

One wonders if, apart from homosexuals, there is any group in America that a church could call "warped" and ungodly without feeling condemnatory! Fortunately, other national churches are at present considering statements that are miles distant from this one both in substance and in tone. One pioneering group, the Council for Christian Social Action of the United Church of Christ, has drawn up an exemplary statement on "Homosexuals and the Law," which covers a wide range of civil liberties questions, and avoids moral censoriousness. What has redeemed the record of the churches in the United States, however, has been the work of individual pastors and their staffs. These men and women have often cooperated in a heartwarming way with the national homophile movement, which has no real counterpart abroad. They have opened their churches for meetings of homosexual organizations and for social gatherings and dances. They have worked, at hazard to their own careers, to found councils on religion and the homosexual, preached sermons, joined homosexuals in demonstrations, and spoken out publicly in opposition to police harassment and entrapment. For this, they deserve the fullest credit for their courage and humanity.

I have left till now Father John Harvey's article on homosexuality in the *New Catholic Encyclopedia,* because, though the work of an individual rather than a church body, its position in this ambitious work of scholarship gives it at least quasi-official authority. Clearly, Father Harvey was chosen by the editors as the leading Catholic scholar on the subject in America, a position to which his earlier essays no doubt entitle him. But what are his views? First, he thinks that all homosexuals are neurotics. Secondly, he thinks all homosexual acts are objectively sinful. But, though tortured by an "obsessive compulsion," the homosexual can, by the grace of God, achieve absolute continence. Father Harvey will have nothing to do with those who think homosexuals may express their love by overt acts. Anyone who believes this "must logically condone any form of sexual irresponsibility"—for instance, birth control. Indeed, for Father Harvey, all homosexual love is a "sterile love of self, disguised in apparent love for another. What seems like ideal love to the homosexual must be shown [to him] to be narcissism." The homosexual must work out a systematic regimen in which the love of God replaces any sexual experience. "This plan must be practical enough to include certain ascetical activities of daily life. Included in this plan would be some form of meditation for at least twenty minutes a day, Mass and Communion as often as possible during the week, daily examinations of conscience, a carefully chosen confessor, and habitual works of charity." [16]

Speaking personally, I find this carefully thought out document astonishing. Despite its length, there is nowhere any mention of the fact that homosexuals are subject to the law or to police action. There is no mention of the Archbishop Griffin Report in England,[17] in which the Roman Catholic Church spoke out unequivocally for the repeal of laws against private acts by consenting adults as ineffectual, inequitable, inordinately severe, and an incitement to blackmail. This being the case, it is not surprising that there is no reference to civil service discrimination, or military witch-hunts, or the draft, or questionable police tactics. On the moral side, the life that Father Harvey prescribes for the homosexual is that of an ascetic priest, despite the fact that the church at no point in history has ever regarded priestly celibacy as the vocation of more than a highly select few, and that many priests and even some bishops are now questioning it as an ideal even for the clergy. Father Harvey does not tell us that some distinguished Catholic theologians have publicly raised the question as to whether all homosexual acts can be called sinful, nor that there is a growing number of humane priests who simply tell homosexual parishioners in the confessional that they do not regard them as sinners, or that Masses of reconciliation have been openly held for homosexuals in some cities. In the light of this inflexibility it is not surprising that unhappy Catholics frequently turn up at homosexual meetings in Protestant churches, since they feel cut off from their own church because of official attitudes. There is even a certain irony that this article should have appeared in the *New Catholic Encyclopedia,* since this reference work, far from being a hidebound captive of the past, notes in its essay on "Nativism" that Catholics, themselves a minority group in America which in former days suffered much pointless discrimination, have often been insensitive to the plight of other minorities.

By now it should be evident that what American churches need is a new theology—a "theology of engagement," aimed at undoing the effects of two thousand years of religious antihomosexualism. They need not only to inaugurate more pastoral programs of the sort Dr. von Rohr has recommended but also to issue, as national bodies, clear and emphatic statements opposing our present laws, discrimination against homosexuals by the Government, by the military, and by private employers, and harassment by local police. There is also need for a revocation of the calumny, which Christianity has promulgated from its beginning, that homosexual acts are always intrinsically sinful. We need, in short, an American counterpoint, for homosexuals, of the historical Vatican statement on the Jews. Other minorities have asked the churches for billions in reparations. America's homophile community is more modest. It asks only for words, which means, of course, finding the courage to speak them. But can anyone who values the good name, not just of theology, but of religion itself, find it in his heart to keep silent?

NOTES

1. The *Theodosian Code,* tr. by Clyde Pharr (Princeton University Press, 1952), p. 232.
2. *The Civil Law* (*Corpus Juris Civilis*), ed. by S. P. Scott, Vol. XVI (Cincinnati, 1932), p. 288.
3. Sir William Blackstone, *Commentaries on the Laws of England* (London: Dawson's of Pall Mall, 1966), Vol. IV, Ch. 15, p. 216.
4. Sara Harris, *The Puritan Jungle* (Pocket Books, Inc., 1970), p. 119.
5. I Cor. 7:1.
6. Karl Barth, *Church Dogmatics,* Vol. III, Part 4 (Edinburgh: T. & T. Clark, 1961), p. 166.
7. Helmut Thielicke, *The Ethics of Sex,* tr. by John W. Doberstein (Harper & Row, Publishers, Inc., 1964), pp. 269–294.
8. H. Kimball Jones, *Toward a Christian Understanding of the Homosexual* (London: SCM Press, Ltd., 1967), p. 110.
9. *Towards a Quaker View of Sex,* rev. ed. (London, 1964), pp. 26, 41.
10. Ralph W. Weltge, "The Paradox of Man and Woman," in Ralph W. Weltge (ed.), *The Same Sex: An Appraisal of Homosexuality* (The Pilgrim Press, 1969), p. 58.
11. Derrick Sherwin Bailey, *Sexual Offenders and Social Punishment* (Church of England Moral Welfare Council, 1956), "Appendix I: The Homosexual and Christian Morals," pp. 65–81.
12. Neale A. Secor, "A Brief for a New Homosexual Ethic," in Weltge (ed.), *op. cit.,* pp. 67–79.

13. I have not seen the Methodist or Presbyterian statements.

14. June, 1970. (On July 4, the General Assembly of the Unitarian Universalist Association, meeting at Seattle, after a dramatic debate, passed a historic resolution favoring law reform and an end to government discrimination in all fields.)

15. I have forborne identifying the church, since I am told by a representative that this statement does not preclude their taking a positive public stand on civil liberties. It was issued in 1966. In August, 1969, the annual meeting of the North American Conference of Homophile Organizations protested the statement as "inhumane, unchristian, and derogatory" (Report of the NACHO Religious Committee, December, 1969).

16. J. F. Harvey, "Homosexuality," in *New Catholic Encyclopedia,* Vol. VII (McGraw-Hill Book Company, Inc., 1967), p. 119.

17. The Report was published under the title "Homosexuality, Prostitution and the Law," in the *Dublin Review* for Summer, 1956. As far as I know, it has not been republished in the United States, though its views on the law would seem to apply equally to American jurisdictions.

8

Changing the Law — The English Experience

P. E. COLEMAN

The problem of homosexuality has been an important topic for moral theologians and law reformers in England in the past thirty years. Von Rohr's admirable paper shows that the debate among moral theologians is following very similar lines on both sides of the Atlantic. His careful presentation of the Christian traditional teaching, and of the new knowledge about human sexuality which demands a fresh appraisal of this teaching, would be recognized as accurately describing the problem as it is thought about in England and in Europe generally. Where the English experience seems to have made a distinct step forward is by their removal of legal penalties for homosexual acts between consenting male adults by the passing of the Sexual Offences Act of 1967. It is too early to say, at the time of this writing, what effects on the general social problem this act has had, except in the direct ways of ending police prosecutions and lessening the opportunities for blackmail, but the publicity that accompanied the parliamentary debates has clearly increased public tolerance and helped toward a wider understanding of the problems that homosexuals face.

Until the passing of the 1967 act the law in England relating to homosexual practices was similar to that which still exists in many American states.[1] Three categories of homosexual behavior were punishable. These were sodomy (anal intercourse), indecent assault on a male, and gross indecency between males. The third category from the Criminal Law Amendment Act of 1885, was the most recent to be included, and it has also been the most criticized because it covered both private and public behavior, and made the participants liable to prosecution even when they had mutually consented to what was done between them. Before we consider the Act of 1885 and its recent repeal, it is useful to set the whole matter in perspective by tracing briefly how the English law about homosexual practices in general has evolved from its roots in the ancient Jewish-Christian tradition. Although much English common law is of indigenous origin, rather than an adaptation of the Roman Code usually found in other European countries, the law of sexual relations was originally a matter dealt with by church courts which applied the regulations laid down by the Roman Church.

As von Rohr has shown, this tradition was condemnatory, and the teaching of the Bible and the early church fathers was reiterated by popes, bishops' councils, and theologians throughout the first thousand years of the history of the Western Catholic Church. It is sometimes falsely assumed that this teaching was in direct opposition to that of the Greek and Roman culture which Christianity displaced. This is an oversimplification, based on the supposition that everyday life in Greece and Rome was a sensualized version of life in Plato's academy or Nero's court. In fact, the laws of Athens contained strict penalties against those who seduced boys, and equally,

Roman law in the third century, before the Empire became Christian, had begun to extend its protection of minors from homosexual assault toward a general condemnation of all male homosexual practices.

After Constantine had made the Empire Christian, stricter laws were passed, and Valentinian, in A.D. 390, ordered that those convicted of sodomy should be burned. The great legal reformer, Justinian, issued two edicts, in 538 and 544, concerning homosexuality. Neither of these edicts changed the law or the severe punishments associated with it, but concentrated chiefly on exhorting those guilty of these offenses to repentance and forgiveness as a better way than risking conviction. Justinian clearly accepts the interpretation of the Sodom story that explains its destruction as an act of divine vengeance for homosexual practices, and is anxious to preserve his own Empire from a similar fate.

In the medieval period, Western canon law developed systemized regulations to govern all aspects of sexual morality. A wide range of homosexual offenses was recognized, with appropriate penances according to the gravity of the act. Sodomy was, of course, the most serious, kissing among men a slight offense, though licentious kissing was distinguished as graver. Undoubtedly, the temptations of the monastic and celibate life contributed to the necessity of these regulations, though such practices were also well known in secular life. Lesbianism was punished with a three-year penance or with seven years for nuns. Boys under twenty were treated more leniently, according to their age. The penalty for sodomy could be death, but this had to be carried out by secular authorities and apparently seldom was. It is difficult to establish how widespread homosexual offenses were, for few records are extant. There seemed to have been periodic outbursts of scandal and indignation when a notable ecclesiastical or civil personality was convicted, and this would be followed by a reissue of the regulations and solemn exhortations to discourage future offenders.[2]

The Norman conquest of Britain brought with it the beginnings of a secular legal system, because William I's policy was to establish his own separate courts for common law. Matrimonial causes and offenses against sexual morality continued, however, to be within the jurisdiction of the ecclesiastical courts. In early English legal treatises there are references to burning or burying alive as the proper punishment for homosexuals, but there is no evidence that this was ever done.

As part of Henry VIII's policy of asserting royal supremacy over ecclesiastical matters, he caused an act to be passed in 1553 which transferred jurisdiction "for the detestable and abominable vice of buggery committed with mankind or beast" to the royal courts. The act's preamble complained that "there was not yet sufficient punishment" for the crime, and this suggests that the church courts were very reluctant to pass a death penalty. The act, however, only related to sodomy, jurisdiction in other homosexual offenses remaining with the church. This new law was only occasionally enforced in the next two hundred and seventy-five years. Among those convicted were the Earl of Castlehaven in 1631, the Bishop of Waterford in 1640, an Oxford clergyman in 1739, an actor in 1742, and a woman, Mistress Clap, who kept a sodomitical house in London in 1742. The death penalty was still being exacted in the nineteenth century, of which examples were an army trooper, caught with the Irish Bishop of Clogher (1822), and two laborers in Bristol whose execution the local newspaper reported in 1860 without further comment. Henry's act had made sodomy a felony, as theft also was, and felons were usually hung or deported.[3]

The death penalty was finally removed in 1861, when the punishment of penal servitude for life was substituted. To establish the crime, it was necessary to prove only anal penetration and not seminal emission. At this time the jurisdiction of the ecclesiastical courts was substantially curtailed. All matrimonial causes were transferred to a division of the High Court, and church courts ceased to be concerned with sexual offenses except where clergymen were involved, and not always then. The civil courts had meanwhile come to deal with indecent assault as one of the types of "offenses against the person," and, under this heading, homosexual practices other than sodomy could be included where a complaint was made. The 1861 act laid down a maximum sentence of ten years for attempts to commit sodomy or indecent assault, and thus the viciousness of the old law was ameliorated.

This might have meant that homosexuals who kept their physical activities private among themselves could remain tolerably free from legal prosecution, but in 1885 a bill was introduced into Parliament "to make further provision for the protection of women and girls, the suppression of brothels and other purposes." At a late stage of the bill's passage through Parliament an extra clause was added which provided that "any male person who in public, or private, commits or is a party to the commission of, or procures or attempts to procure the commission by any male person of any act of gross indecency with another male person, shall be guilty of a misdemeanour." The punishment was to be a maximum of two years' imprisonment. The briefly stated reason for adding the extra clause [4] was that it would provide for the protection of boys as well as girls, the main object of the act, and this reasoning may well have been justifiable, since there were numbers of male prostitutes and boy catamites to be found in the parks of London at this time. If that was the intention, it was a great pity that the clause was a late addition and so escaped any serious exmination, for it apparently unintentionally made a much wider change in the law.

Ten years later the implications of this ill-considered and loosely worded extra clause were fully exploited in the trial of the famous playwright and novelist, Oscar Wilde. Wilde was a married man with two children, the son of a famous Irish surgeon, and notable for his wit as well as his aesthetic style of life. This was sharply satirized in an operetta, *Patience,* by Gilbert and Sullivan, which played to packed houses in London and New York in 1881. Wilde formed a close friendship and strong passion for Lord Alfred Douglas, a son of the Marquess of Queensberry. The Marquess accused Wilde of posing as a sodomite, and Wilde prosecuted him for criminal libel. In the trial, the defending lawyers produced sufficient evidence of Wilde's relationship with other men to defeat the prosecution and make it inevitable that Wilde himself would be charged with indecent behavior.

This later trial took place in 1895, and, although the integrity of those who gave testimony against Wilde was dubious and the evidence in some ways unsatisfactory, he was convicted of indecent behavior and sent to prison for eighteen months. He died, penniless and friendless, five years later in Paris, shortly after being received into the Roman Catholic Church. Some people thought at the time that the conviction was unjust, but it is now known that Wilde was, in fact, a practicing homosexual, although he probably avoided sodomy. He grew up as a normal heterosexual, contracted syphilis as an undergraduate from a prostitute, and abandoned heterosexual intercourse with his wife when the supposedly cured disease reappeared two years after his marriage. His homosexual interests were at first intellectual, but he probably began to express them physically some years before he met Lord Douglas, and he continued homosexual practices in Paris after his release from prison.[5]

Scandals and occasional prosecutions continued in England for the first half of the twentieth century, and, from 1950 onward, a number of thoughtful people began to think seriously about changing the law. An Anglican clergyman, Dr. Sherwin Bailey, was appointed at that time to the Church of England Moral Welfare Council and was asked to write an article on the subject for a leading theological journal under the title "The Problem of Sexual Inversion."[6] He began this article by asking what is meant by "homosexuality" and distinguished the different types—the natural inverts, those who have acquired homosexual characteristics or have become addicted to homosexual practices, the bisexuals, the perverts, and those temporarily driven toward homosexuality by abnormal conditions of life. After pointing out that lesbianism was ignored by the law, he argued that, by its intrusion into the privacy of the male invert's private life, the law was grossly unfair and conducive to crime. He concluded: "It is, without doubt, a Christian duty to press for the removal of this anomalous and shameful injustice, which has done untold harm and has achieved no good whatever, and it is to be hoped that those who look to the Church for a lead in this matter will not be disappointed."

In the next few years, Bailey was himself to take the initiative and to work with a group of doctors and clergy on a report that was privately published and circulated to selected members of Parliament and others in authority. This report reiterated the basic objection to the law as it then was: it discriminated against homosexuals in that, while ignoring fornication and adultery among heterosexuals, it punished private homosexual acts. On what basis, the report asked, can it be possibly held that such activities have a more harmful effect on the life of the community than do these other two offenses? The effect of this private report was considerable, not least because of its Christian origination, and other groups were pressing the same point. Public interest, however, was chiefly awakened by the trial and conviction in 1954, under the same act, of Lord Montague of Beaulieu and a journalist friend of his, Peter Wildeblood.[7] Again, as with Wilde, the evidence brought against them was circumstantial and the witnesses of uncertain character, and there was also a suggestion that the prosecution was deliberately brought against a public figure as something of an example to others.

The widespread disquiet and feeling that prison sentences were inappropriate led to a parliamentary debate and the setting up of a parliamentary committee under Sir John Wolfenden to examine the whole problem. The Committee's terms of reference were "to consider the law and practice relating to homosexual offences and the treatment of persons convicted of such offences by the courts, and to report what changes if any were in the Committee's opinion desirable."

The Committee deliberated for two years and received evidence from public and professional bodies of all kinds, from government departments, from individual witnesses, and from a number of written memorandums. Among those giving written and oral evidence were the Roman Catholic Advisory Committee and the Church of England Moral Welfare Council.[8] Both bodies recommended to the Committee that homosexual acts between consenting adults in private should no longer be criminal offenses and that the state should restrict penal sanctions for homosexual offenses to prevent the corruption of youth, offenses against public decency, and the exploitation of vice.

In considering the workings of the present law, the Committee noticed that between 1931 and 1955 prosecutions for homosexual offenses increased from 390 to 2,504. The police claimed to know of about double this number of offenses, and their policy varied from force to force: some were zealous in seeking out and prosecuting all practicing homosexuals they could find irrespective of whether their acts were committed in public or in private, while other forces took action only when a complaint was made to them.[9]

When the Committee finally reported in 1957, it dealt, as the church's memorandums had done, with the function of the criminal law in relation to matters of private moral conduct. The Committee concluded that the function of the criminal law in this field "is to preserve public order and decency, to protect the citizen from what is offensive and injurious, and to provide safeguards against exploitation of others, particularly those who are specially vulnerable. It is not the function of the law to intervene in the private lives of citizens, or to seek to enforce any particular pattern of behaviour, further than is necessary to carry out the purposes we have outlined." The Committee further observed that "it is important to make a clear distinction between 'homosexual offences' and 'homosexuality' " and stressed that " 'homosexuality' is a state or condition, and as such does not, and cannot, come within the purview of the criminal law." [10]

The chief recommendation of the Wolfenden Committee was "that homosexual behaviour between consenting adults in private be no longer a criminal offence." [11] Ten years were to elapse before this recommendation became law, thus bringing England into line with the majority of other European countries, including Belgium, Holland, France, Italy, Spain, Greece, and Norway, Denmark, and Sweden. In the intervening years several parliamentary debates dealt with the subject and the voting figures show how opinion was steadily swinging toward the Wolfenden Committee's view. To some extent, these widely reported debates reflected public opinion, and to some extent they led it. Christian spokesmen on the whole consistently pressed for the law to be changed, while asserting, against the accusations of their critics, that the Christian moral attitude to homosexual practices remained unchanged. Typical of the Christian position in the debates was that taken by the Archbishop of Canterbury in the House of Lords on May 12, 1965:

> I want to make clear the moral standpoint from which I approach this question. I believe that homosexual acts are always wrong in the sense that they use in a wrong way human organs for which the right use is intercourse between men and women within marriage. Amidst the modern talk about the "new morality" I would uphold the belief that just

> as fornication is always wrong, so homosexual acts are always wrong. At the same time, wrong acts in this case as in others can have various degrees of culpability attached to them. In this case there are not only degrees of culpability, but also varieties of causes of the trouble and categories of the trouble, psychological and sociological. . . . The case for altering the law in respect of homosexual acts between consenting adults in private rests, I believe, on reason and justice and on considerations of the good of the community. I think there is a real cogency in the plea of the Wolfenden Report that not all sins are properly given the status of crimes, not even such sins as the adulterous conduct of a man or a woman, which can smash up the life of a family and bring misery to a whole family of children. If a line can reasonably be drawn anywhere, homosexual acts in private between consenting adults fall properly on the same side of the line as fornication.[12]

This speech, and others like it, were politically wise because they reassured the more conservatively-minded members of Parliament that by passing the bill they were not at the same time deciding the moral issue. There was, however, some criticism by those who thought that the Archbishop's reiteration of the traditional condemnation showed that homosexuals would still not find real acceptance within the church.

How far, it may be asked, does the Archbishop's attitude reflect the contemporary mind of Christians in England? An attempt to find out has recently been made, as far as the leaders of the Church of England are concerned, by sending all members of the Church Assembly a detailed questionnaire on their attitudes to homosexuality.[13]

The Church Assembly consists of the English diocesan bishops, and elected clergy and lay representatives from each diocese, numbering some seven hundred and fifty people in all. The membership of the Assembly tends to be senior both in age and responsibility, and many of its present members took part in the Assembly debate in 1957 that approved the Wolfenden Committee recommendations.

About a third of the members of the Assembly proved willing to answer the sixty questions in the rather detailed questionnaire and one hundred of these said they were interested in the subject. One hundred and twenty-three agreed that homosexual behavior between consenting adults in private should be no longer a criminal offense, twenty-eight disagreed, twenty-five were undecided. Similar answers were given in approving of the 1967 act. Ninety members of the Assembly thought that homosexual behavior between consenting adult males is always sinful, sixty said no and twenty-six were undecided. There was no significant difference in their attitude to female homosexuality. Nearly all who answered the questionnaire had met people who they thought to be homosexual.

The Bible was thought to give useful guidance about the Christian attitude, and the most frequently referred to text was from Rom., ch. 1.[14] The Sodom and Gomorrah story was seldom referred to and there was hardly any mention of passages on which a "situational" approach could be based. More than half of the members thought that the Church of England's present attitude toward homosexual behavior should change, but there was considerable doubt that a consistent official attitude existed.

A similar survey among junior clergy shows, as might

be expected, that in the younger age group a more permissive attitude is being taken. Unanimity on such a difficult subject at the present time is not to be expected, especially in a church that has never attempted to lay down a specific moral code for the guidance of its members. A similar divergence of views seems to exist in the Catholic and Protestant churches, and certainly the debate will continue.

NOTES

1. The main provisions of English law were codified together in the Sexual Offences Act of 1956, secs. 12–16 and 32. These are summarized in *The Wolfenden Report: Report of the Committee on Homosexual Offenses and Prostitution* (London: Her Majesty's Stationery Office, 1957, Cmnd. 247), pp. 29–30.

2. For the history in detail, see Derrick Sherwin Bailey, *Homosexuality and the Western Christian Tradition* (London: Longmans, Green & Co., Ltd., 1955), Chs. 3, 4, and 5.

3. Judge Tudor Rees wrote in 1955 that he was unable to come across a recorded instance of the extreme penalty of death or life imprisonment being inflicted. See Tudor Rees and Harley V. Usill (eds.), *They Stand Apart: A Critical Survey of the Problems of Homosexuality* (The Macmillan Company, 1955), p. 3. But, in fact, such punishments were inflicted. See Norman St. John-Stevas, *Life, Death and the Law* (Indiana University Press, 1961), p. 208, and also H. Montgomery Hyde (ed.), *Trials of Oscar Wilde* (London: William Hodge and Company, Ltd.), Appendix F, pp. 375–384.

4. John-Stevas, *op. cit.*, p. 210.

5. For the trials of Oscar Wilde, see generally M. Har-

ford Hyde, *op. cit.* and for Wilde's own inversion in particular, see the account based on later evidence in Appendix E of Hyde's book.

6. The journal *Theology,* Feb., 1952, pp. 47–52, published by S.P.C.K., London.

7. Wildeblood describes the sequence of events in his book *Against the Law* (London: George Weidenfeld & Nicholson, 1955; also published in Penguin Books, 1957).

8. Summarized in Stevas, *op. cit.,* pp. 223–224.

9. *Wolfenden Report,* p. 46, paras. 128, 129.

10. *Wolfenden Report,* pp. 9–11, paras. 13, 14, 18.

11. The Anglican Church Assembly approved the Wolfenden Committee's main recommendations in November, 1957, and so did the Methodist Conference in July, 1958.

12. Parliamentary Debates (Hansard), House of Lords Official Report, Wednesday 12th May 1965, pp. 80–84.

13. The questionnaires were sent out to the 741 members in December, 1969, by P. E. Coleman.

14. The Biblical texts most frequently cited were Gen., ch. 19, and Rom. 1:26.

9

The Church's Role After Law Reform

Antony Grey

Ten years of work with the Albany Trust (which began its life as the social service arm of the Homosexual Law Reform Society, and now helps several hundreds of people each year who come to it with a wide range of sexual problems) has convinced me that the debt which society—and more specifically, Christian society—owes to homosexual men and women is a large one. When, two years ago, I was asked to write a short paper for an Anglican study group on this question, my concluding words were: "What is called for in this matter from Christian society is compassion, realism—and, not least, atonement." I stand by those words today.

Books such as Kimball Jones's *Toward a Christian Understanding of the Homosexual* and Norman Pittenger's *Time for Consent?* are a welcome indication that such a process is beginning. But there is still a long way to go. In the paper just referred to I wrote of the homosexual's need of love:

> To many people, the most shocking thing about homosexuality is that it is about love. (This is the

> most shocking thing about Christianity too.) If the realisation can be grasped that even the most degraded, promiscuous homosexual—just like the most degraded, heterosexual—was made to love and is seeking love even in his degradation, it becomes possible to begin helping him towards redemption. Love often means suffering, for the homosexual as well as for the heterosexual. But the love of God cannot be brought nearer through a denial of the right to human love; homosexuals need not only acceptance of their homosexual state, but also acceptance of their capacity to love others and to be loved by them. It is their lack of faith in this possibility—a belief essential to every human being unless he is to become prey to utter despair—that makes so many homosexuals hard (and sometimes impossible) to help. From the Church, above all other sources, the homosexual needs help in finding a renewed belief in the reality of love for himself, as well as for others.

I am glad to see that John von Rohr has emphasized this truth in his interesting essay. But it is a little disappointing—though perhaps at this stage still necessary—that he has devoted quite so much space to those traditional but somewhat irrelevant theological preoccupations with the "naturalness" of homosexuality, its causation, the desirability or otherwise of physical homosexual acts, and whether homosexuals are more promiscuous than heterosexuals. While it may be important to know the facts (or at least to hold well-informed views) about all these questions, there are others which, I venture to suggest, are much more urgent, both morally and socially speaking.

For if we are to evolve a meaningful theology concerning homosexuality, which implies a truly Christian attitude and approach to homosexual people and their problems, we must surely start from the premise that homosexuality exists (or we would not be discussing it), and that, whether heterosexual, homosexual, or bisexual, we are all God's children and equal in his sight. This equality (unless we wish immediately to degrade our homosexual brethren to an inferior ethical plane) extends to the degree of moral responsibility that we each share for our sexual lives; for I am entirely convinced that a homosexual man or woman is just as much (or just as little) "in control" of his or her sexual drives as heterosexuals are. But equal moral responsibility does not, of course, mean that the issues which homosexuals have to face and resolve in their lives are just the same as those confronting heterosexuals, or that the "correct" solutions are identical. They are not, and failure to recognize this surely obvious fact leads much well-intentioned "rethinking" about homosexuality sadly astray. One of the most telling sentences in von Rohr's essay is his comment that "it is a lot better to live in *our* world as a heterosexual than as a homosexual" (my italics). And this, as he rightly says, remains true even when the law has been reformed, as in England, to legitimize the private acts of consenting adults.

It may be useful, at this point, to comment briefly upon the effects (and noneffects) of this change in England. Three years after the event, the limited law reform that was achieved only after fierce parliamentary battles over a ten-year period looks more like the essential first step in public education than the victorious end to a campaign. For the homosexual in Britain, if nowadays regarded slightly more tolerantly and with less alarm than before, remains furtive, unaccepted, and, when recognized, ridiculed or pitied rather than simply accepted. Consequently, while the British tendency (somewhat overrated at the best of times) to mind one's own business about other people's private lives has received some encouragement from the change in the law, there is an unfortunate and quite erroneous belief on the part of those members of the public who consider such matters at all that the 1967 legislation has "solved" the problem.

Nothing could be farther from the truth, of course. Legally speaking, the reform was a limited and negative one —while freeing two consenting adults aged over twenty-one in private from criminal punishment, it increased the penalties for homosexual relations between those over and under twenty-one and did nothing to alter the highly unsatisfactory state of affairs whereby any male homosexual manifestations in public (by which I mean not only soliciting or "picking up" activities, but even single-sex dancing in a private members' club) can be much more heavily penalized than similar heterosexual activities. And it has left the young homosexual in his teens in a much more socially isolated and legally vulnerable situation than before, when all were "in the same boat" from puberty onward. As the excellent Dutch Government recommending reduction of the age of consent to sixteen—now in process of enactment by the Dutch Parliament—points out, it is utterly unrealistic to discriminate in this way against the young male homosexual just at the time when he most needs constructive help and support from responsible older people who share his orientation and understand his problems. For the young homosexual, as for the young heterosexual, the risks and dangers of sexual maturing and self-realization are part of life, and, like other fields of exploration, they belong to the growing-up process. It is surely far better both for the individual and for society that they should be entered upon without the crippling sense of fear and guilt all too commonly experienced by young homosexuals today in an age of so-called sexual emancipation. And if the adolescent is in fact merely passing through a temporary phase of homosexual feeling, this is far less likely to become fixated and obsessive if his fears are removed and his right to associate freely with *all* his fellow human beings in the process of learning to make wise choices is recognized.

Homosexuals, no less than heterosexuals, need love and a framework of stable relationships in their lives if they are not to become neurotically unhappy and a burden to themselves and society. It is in helping and encouraging them to find and give this love that the Christian's mission to the homosexual lies. If some Christians may persist in regarding *all* physical homosexual acts as "sinful," even between partners who love each other, while others take a more charitable view, is this really the main issue? Is that not rather our attitude to homosexual people as whole human beings, and our concern for their well being?

To make anyone feel unwanted and unloved is, in the words of Dr. David Stafford-Clark, "the most destructive wrong that can be inflicted upon a human being." I agree with Canon Douglas Rhymes that we must gear the church's whole responsibility to dealing with the homosexual *in his situation,* and I welcome the approach that is being made to this task by von Rohr in the opening essay of this book. It is high time for all Christians to realize that sexual Pharisaism—the "holier than thou" attitude that looks with smugly exaggerated horror alike upon the heterosexual fornicator and the homosexual "pervert" and says "Thank God I am not like *these*"—is the deadliest sexual sin of all.

10

The Self-availability of the Homosexual

HENRI J. M. NOUWEN

Not too long ago I defended the position that homosexual feelings and acts should be considered in themselves as a sign of immaturity, a result of sexual retardation and an expression more of competition than of real love. I felt that psychotherapy was the ideal way of helping the homosexual, and that toward those who did not desire it or could not afford it an attitude of understanding and sympathy should be taken.[1] Since I wrote that, I have been told by many homosexuals that I was wrong or at least one-sided, since most of my impressions came from my practice as a psychologist and since I had never had real contact with the many homosexuals who never seek or want to seek any professional help. Through many discussions I have become more and more aware of the fact that for the homosexual his sexual feelings are just as real, personal, and intimate as for the heterosexual and that quite often the attitude which suggests that the best thing a homosexual can do is to change his feelings is a direct offense to his most precious self.

I am not speaking about people who have doubts concerning their sexual identity, but about those for whom there is no question at all that their erotic inclination is predominantly homosexual. Therefore I would like to bypass in this article the difficult question about the causality of homosexuality and to start from the simple fact that there is an impressive number of men and women for whom a basic change in personality structure is completely out of the question. The question for the homosexual then is not, How can I become different from who I am? but, How can I meaningfully relate to my own sexual feelings? This question is important for every human being, but especially for the homosexual, since quite often his feelings are already judged and evaluated by his milieu before he is able to make them his own. The strong social pressure that exists in respect to homosexual behavior makes it very difficult for the homosexual to come to terms with his own sexuality and to relate to his own feelings in a realistic way. Still, that is what counts the most. Therefore I would like to focus here on the question, How can the homosexual make his own feelings available to himself so that he can meaningfully relate to them?

I would like to discuss this question under two headings:

1. *Self-availability in General*
2. *The Homosexual and His Self-availability*

1. *Self-availability in General*

In order to relate meaningfully to your own self you have to be, first of all, available to yourself. This, however, is not a very easy task. We are usually only partially available to ourselves. This is very visible in daily life. We tend to look at ourselves in a certain way and to call only those feelings, experiences, and events really our own which best fit our preconceived ideas about ourselves. In this way the perception of our own world is very selective. If you consider yourself to be an optimist, you might go home after a hard day of work allowing only those experiences to come into your consciousness which reinforce your optimistic outlook on life. On the other hand, if you talk about yourself as a pessimist, you will allow only the negative experiences to strike you and strengthen your self-concept. It is difficult to be a realist and to face the wide range of feelings, experiences, and ideas that are a part of your life and consider them all as really your own, and to allow them constantly to alter your perspective on yourself, your world, and your fellowman. It seems as if there is a deep conservatism in man which makes him cling to the self-concept that he has developed. In this way man tends to close himself off from real growth and limit his large range of potentialities. In this way also he becomes easily the subject of the self-fulfilling prophecy, by which he lives in the direction of his own idea about himself. If he says, "I am no sportsman," he will never try any sports and make his own prophecy true. If he says, "I am very unattractive," he will stay away from other people, become shy and jittery, and force people to think about him according to his own "prophecy." If he says, "I always have luck," he will show a lot of self-confidence, people will relate to him more easily and give him more chances than others and therefore make his prophecy true.[2]

All this is to say that it is very difficult for man really to become available to himself and really to claim all his experiences as his own. But how can you relate to a reality that is not available to you? You cannot keep what you do not have, nor can you detach yourself from something you do not own. This is true not only of property but also of feelings and emotions. Man cannot detach himself from a feeling that he never considered his own. Nevertheless this happens quite often. In religious life it sometimes happens that people detach themselves not only from property, while never having understood what it means to own something, but also from sexual experiences without ever having been aware of their own eroticism. Much suffering is the result of detachment from feelings that were never really available.

This general phenomenon is of special importance when we want to speak about homosexual feelings.

2. *The Homosexual and Self-availability*

In a culture in which homosexual behavior is quite easily associated with abnormal behavior, and referred to in terms of pathology, it is quite understandable that a man or a woman who experiences homosexual feelings will be inclined to disown himself or herself from these feelings and put them in the periphery of his experience. The idea of being or becoming "a homosexual" is so loaded with fear that it is really impossible for many to relate realistically to these real feelings as being their own.

The Dutch psychiatrist W. G. Sengers has shown in a very elucidating way how the deep-seated resistance against the existing homosexual feelings in man is one of the main reasons for the great suffering of the homosexual. Only when this resistance is gone and the homosexual feelings can become available to one's self is one able to relate realistically to them.

Dr. Sengers remarks that only the erotic feelings toward another person of the same sex as such can be experienced as positive. Love is a beautiful, enjoyable, pleasant, freeing experience, and the strong attraction between two people cannot be considered otherwise than something valuable and enriching. The fact, however, is that in reality this is not always the case. The growing awareness of erotic feelings toward persons of the same sex creates often strong feelings of shame, low self-esteem, and fear of being "abnormal." Feelings that in themselves are positive are being condemned by many people who experience them. Dr. Sengers writes: "The pressure leading to condemnation must be strong. What is good must be called bad, what is positive must become negative. It amounts to adapting his own feelings to what others say about them." [3]

This situation makes it extremely difficult to make your most intimate feelings of love and attraction your own, and you are forced to deny them and build up a strong wall of resistance which quite often causes the problem with which many psychologists and psychiatrists have to deal. In this perspective, not the homosexual feelings themselves but the strong resistance against them causes the many personal problems with which homosexual people are burdened.

Dr. Sengers distinguishes different levels of resistance. We will discuss the two most important ones.

1. The first level includes a radical resistance in which man completely denies his homosexual inclinations, not only to others but primarily to himself. By doing this, man cuts himself off from his own most personal, intimate, and creative feelings and forces himself to "evacuate" to the safe place of cerebral life. Once man does this, he tends to become a rigid and impersonal man who impresses others as being very distant and who

seems to have everything under control.

It is obvious that this kind of denial does great harm to the personality, easily creates emotional poverty, and makes social life a very "dry" reality.

2. The second, less serious, level of resistance is the resistance by which a person in no way wants to communicate his feelings to anyone else. The homosexual knows and understands his feelings but is tortured by the fear that anyone else should know them. Through this fear the homosexual suffers much from isolation even when he is with many others, since he constantly has to pretend that he is "normal" and is never in a position where he can be himself and express his real feelings.

This can lead to an obsession with the homosexual condition. In that case the homosexual becomes so preoccupied with the fear of becoming known as a homosexual that his sexual feelings are constantly in his mind and become like an isolated power which haunts him day and night and sexualizes his total existence. Every situation becomes filled with dangerous occasions and the homosexual is constantly on his guard to prevent anyone from discovering his condition.

Dr. Sengers clearly shows the danger inherent in these forms of resistance when he writes:

> I have to stress the fact that people whose lives are lived in resistance are convinced of the positive value of this attitude. In conscience they are honest and responsible and can face their fellowman without shame. . . . But the price they pay is high: there is an increasing tension, internal as well as in every relationship to the other; the sexual life cannot form a unity with the rest of the personality, it has become a hostile part which through its increas-

> ing power becomes a disturbing reality. Every form of social life remains superficial, which causes life to become increasingly distorted and narrow.[4]

From all this it becomes clear that man cannot deny without harm his most essential feelings. Homosexual just as heterosexual feelings touch the core of a man's internal life and he who pretends not to have them is like a man who pretends to be able to live without a heart. But when man is able to overcome his resistance and make his homosexual feelings available to himself and recognize them as belonging to the center of his own life, he will be in a situation in which he can relate to them on a realistic basis.

Christian morality in no way advocates the denial of feelings, but only a responsible way of relating to them. Man becomes a moral man only when he is able to face his own real condition and make his decision from there. The homosexual is just as responsible for his way of relating to his sexual feelings as the heterosexual is. But it seems extremely pretentious and even very dangerous to suggest that homosexual feelings are less human, less real, or less authentic than heterosexual feelings. Feelings can never be considered good or bad, moral or immoral, in themselves. Only the way man relates to them can. If a man feels a strong erotic love for another man, he experiences a real deep human feeling which tells him very much about himself. If he thinks, talks, or acts as if this feeling is not there at all, he mutilates his own emotional life and is in danger of a psychological paralysis. But when he makes his real feelings available to himself and recognizes them as his own, he is able to make a moral decision about the way of life he wants to live.

Many choices are open to him and there is not only one choice that is the good one. It is possible to develop a deep personal relationship based on a strong mutual attraction between two men or two women. It is possible to take distance from your own feelings and invest your strong emotions in broader social concerns. It is possible to make your feelings part of a more profound spiritual and contemplative life. It is possible to detect in them a call for celibacy or a bachelor's life, which also may make it possible to develop a larger range of personal friendships.

When the sexual feelings are liberated from their isolation and integrated into the total personality, they can lose their maddening power and their blind energy which can drive man into promiscuous, impersonal behavior, into a lonely and despairing life, or into a behavior dominated by manipulation and prostitution. This is true of homosexual as well as of heterosexual behavior and there is little evidence to show that homosexual feelings are more prone to lead to perversions than heterosexual feelings, although the strong taboos and seemingly insurmountable prejudices seem to make it quite easy to believe the opposite.

Conclusion

The gospel makes it overwhelmingly clear that Christ came to reveal man's real condition in all its greatness as well as misery and to challenge man to face it without fear. Christ invited man to take off the mask of his illusion of self-righteousness.

He in no way judges feelings or emotions. He only asks us not to deny, distort, or prevent them, but to make them available for God's love.

For the homosexual this perhaps is more difficult than for others, but if he can claim his feelings as being his own and liberate himself from the fear of prejudices, taboos, and rejections, he may be a living witness of the necessity to overcome the artificial barriers that separate man from his fellowman.

Notes

1. Henri J. M. Nouwen, *Intimacy: Pastoral Psychological Essays* (Fides, Publishers, 1969).

2. Sometimes it seems that it is more comfortable to people to have a negative self-concept than no self-concept at all. From a negative self-concept you at least can derive the ambiguous satisfaction of pity.

3. W. G. Sengers, *Gewoon hetzelfde?* (Bussum, 1969), p. 23.

4. *Ibid.*, p. 30.

11

A Lesbian Approach to Theology

Del Martin and Phyllis Lyon [1]

The language in the opening sentences of Dr. von Rohr's treatise is significant—that Christian theology has condemned *all* homosexuality as sin, its judgment has been undeviating, and social consequences ranged from ostracism within church and community to criminal legislation.

More significant is the fact that throughout the centuries all the negative sanctions of religious persecution and criminal prosecution have had no effect on the incidence of homosexuality—only upon the consequences of its existence and expression.

But even more significant is the fact that so many homosexuals have been able to survive, with some measure of stability and sanity, the social stigma and strict sanctions against a way of life that is as natural to them as heterosexuality is to the heterosexual. The instinct for self-survival is indeed strong, but some do succumb to their personal conflict with their religion. Church-imposed guilt for a state of being becomes too much to bear and leads to suicide, alcoholism, drug addiction, promiscuity, mental institutions, or prisons—all consequences of a form of self-denial that is in no way inherent in homosexuality itself. This, to us, is a statement of the sin of the church which summarily dismisses homosexuals as something less than human.

Dr. von Rohr rightly raises the question of applying "the Christian norm of concern for the person and the value of personal relationships" to the homosexual—a concept that has been considered, for the most part, as belonging exclusively to the heterosexual.

What condemning Christians have lost sight of is that homosexuals are products of heterosexual parents, reared in a heterosexual environment, and that their values are learned in the home, at school, and from religion. Becoming aware of one's homosexuality and acting upon that self-knowledge is not an automatic rejection of one's sense of values. On the contrary. It has been our observation over a period of twenty years that the lesbian appears to have a definite moral and ethical code that very apparently reflects the mores of society.

Such questions as virginity, the sexual taboos concerning minors, premarital and extramarital intercourse, monogamous "marriage" and fidelity are as important to the lesbian community as to the larger community. While stepping outside the bounds of society in her choice of sex, love and/or life partner, the lesbian still tends to cling to the value system of her heterosexual background and religious conditioning.

To "bring out" or initiate someone in the lesbian relationship is taken quite seriously. While there may be little or no courtship when experienced lesbians get together, there is apt to be much soul-searching before taking such a step with the uninitiated, and this has led to a high incidence of "unrequited love" among lesbians.

And when such a relationship is brought about, the "newcomer" is most often the aggressor. The predatory lesbian makes good fiction, but in reality the gay woman is fearful of rejection, apprehensive about misleading someone into a life she may not be suited for, and concerned about the welfare of the person she loves.

Some of the other taboos in the lesbian subculture include sexual relationships with minors unless such a relationship is within the peer group, making overtures toward someone else's mate, or having any sort of sexual relationship with a heterosexually married woman.

Having been imbued with society's restrictions against girls having sexual relations outside of marriage, lesbians have a tendency to move in together and set up housekeeping. Because of the lack of a courtship period and mistakenly basing "love" on physical attraction or infatuation, one may move out again a short time later, however.

The "one-night stand" among lesbians is more talk than action. While many may seek release from sexual frustration, still the built-in factors of guilt and remorse (even without fear of pregnancy) remain.

The long-term relationship is held in high esteem, and the constant question put to a couple is, How long have you two been together?

Admittedly, this is an oversimplification. There are variations on every theme. And just as society in general is undergoing a change in values, so is this reflected in the lesbian community. The young are now questioning the validity of the one-to-one, long-term relationship and are seeking alternative life-styles in communes and in the extended family.

But whatever the lesbian's values may be, there still

remains a conflict with the arbitrary judgments pronounced against her by society and religion. Judgment is based on the stereotype—a predatory, masculinized woman who spends all her time seducing young girls. It is a judgment that picks out three letters in homo*sex*uality and blocks out the whole person that the homosexual is. It is a judgment based on the Biblical saga of Sodom and Gomorrah which has no relevance to those who must cope with the complications and confusions of the twentieth century.

The lesbian is a woman whose primary erotic and social interest is in a member of the same sex, whether or not this is ever expressed overtly. Lesbians are like other women. They are capable of deep and abiding love. They form lasting relationships, obviously bound by mutual commitment, since there are no laws, no religious rites, no community support or pressure to keep the couple together. Lesbians may also be celibate or frigid or have other sexual hang-ups that women in general suffer in a society that identifies them almost exclusively on the basis of their biological function and assigns their societal roles accordingly.

Dr. von Rohr suggests there is a "growing interest not only in rehabilitation of the homosexual but even more in rehabilitation of Christian thinking itself concerning homosexuality." In the Daughters of Bilitis, a lesbian organization founded in San Francisco in 1955, we have been working to "rehabilitate" the lesbian, but not by changing her sexual orientation. DOB has worked, rather, to give the lesbian a sense of her own worth as a human being, to help her to know and be herself, to learn ways of coping—making her own creative and productive contribution to the larger community despite the repressions of a hostile society and the recriminations of condemnatory religionists.

Through the Council on Religion and the Homosexual, also founded in San Francisco but in 1964, we have made inroads toward rehabilitating Christian thinking about homosexuality by publishing informative materials as well as providing speakers for church groups, high school and college classes, and seminaries. CRH has also been successful in putting on symposiums in which counselors (doctors, psychologists, clergy, social workers, attorneys, etc.) are given the opportunity of talking to homosexuals themselves and of making visitations to the homophile community. In this way they gain firsthand information.

In the name of objectivity churchmen have been all too willing to talk *about* homosexuals, drawing upon the "experts" of academia. This stance may be safer for the apprehensive, but the conclusions they draw are dependent upon the view of those they listen to. Experts are like verses in the Bible. You can select one who will expound the point of view with which you are already in agreement. For no one has yet found *the* single truth about the origin and the development of homosexuality. The experts, as shown in von Rohr's treatise, are as variant in their theories as in their subject matter.

When we have had the opportunity to meet and talk with churchmen openly and honestly as homosexuals, they have found themselves accepting us as persons. We are, you know. But then that always leads to the dilemma: "If we accept homosexuals, then it can be construed that we condone homosexuality. And we can't do that!"

Nonsense. Homosexuality, like heterosexuality or just

plain sex, in and of itself is neither moral nor immoral. However, there may be moral or immoral homosexuals. Christian criteria of love between two persons as encompassing commitment, personal communication, and self-giving can apply to homosexual as well as heterosexual.

Until such time as Christian thinking is indeed rehabilitated in its attitudes toward homosexuality the only salvation for the homosexual is to reject religious orthodoxy and the church as an institution. It is at that point where the homosexual truly can say, "To hell with the great god 'They'—*I* know who I am," that he can come to terms with his inner being and attain self-acceptance. Stability, sanity, spiritual growth, can emerge only when there is self-acceptance—recognition of the worth and dignity and validity of the essence of his being, his spirit.

Homosexuality is but one aspect of the whole person. Its direction, as a constructive or creative power, depends upon the inner strength of that person to rise above the petty, the vicious, and the ignorant who fear and hate him because he is different. Daring to be who you are, risking the consequences, and ultimately finding inner peace with the God of *Love* that has no gender, is the greatest religious experience one can have. It comes from faith that does not require the pronouncements and the papers of religionists, philosophers, or politicians. It cannot be taken away. It simply *is*.

Unfortunately the interpretation of orthodox religion has been too oriented toward negative sanctions and is seldom life-affirming. It is too concerned with homosexuality as a "condition," whether it is natural or a sin or a fixation or pathological, whether the homosexual is promiscuous or lustful or capable of love. Homosexuality, like heterosexuality, can be all those things. It can be positive or negative.

Society and the church, however, must come to recognize their own responsibility in the objectionable manifestations of homosexual behavior. By their rejection they have helped to create the homosexual ghetto, the only basis for which is sexual proclivity, and its only cohesive factor, sex. Is it any wonder then that the practice of it becomes its foremost activity? Are not the "evils" of homosexuality, then, a self-fulfilling prophecy of the church? a projection or an outpicturing of the "teaching"? or lack of it?

But it is not our purpose to heap the blame on the church. Shifting the responsibility leads to self-pity and martyrdom which inhibit spiritual growth. We encourage the homosexual to accept responsibility for himself, not to rely on artificial props, but to establish his own philosophy of life and code of ethics and ultimately to recognize himself not as the problem but as part of the solution to the problems that life presents.

The homophile organizations have always dealt with homosexuals from the stance of their beingness. They *are*. Circumstances in society also being what they are, however, how can we help them to find jobs, homes, financial security? How do we help them to accept themselves so that they can lead creative and responsible lives in the community? How do we change public laws and attitudes that prevent them from attaining self-fulfillment? How do we instill inner strength and hope in the lesbian who has been referred to us by Suicide Prevention? How can we create a wholesome social fabric in the homophile community? How can we convey to the desparing homosexual that he too is a child of God?

These are the questions that self-righteous Christians should be asking. And as they probe for the answers to these problems they may find "redemption" for themselves as well as for the homosexual.

Note

1. An expansion of these remarks can be found in a forthcoming book by Del Martin and Phyllis Lyon on the lesbian in a changing world, to be published by McCall Publishing Company in 1971.

12

The Homosexual Expression of Love

NORMAN PITTENGER

I have read with pleasure and a large measure of agreement Dr. von Rohr's essay "Toward a Theology of Homosexuality." His final conclusions—in respect to matters of "cure," the development of "stable relationships" between homosexuals, and society's acceptance of homosexuals as genuine persons—seem to me balanced and sound. He has covered a vast amount of material in a succinct and interesting way. I welcome his discussion of the attitude in Scripture and in the Christian tradition, so far as homosexuality is concerned—although here I must point out that like so many Protestant critics of Scholastic theology he has made a serious error, when he writes that in that theology the Fall did not include the view that "nature" is "diseased." As a matter of fact, Scholastic theology explicitly asserts that by the Fall man lost the *donum superadditum* (the "Supernature" of which Dr. von Rohr writes) and hence was *privatus boni,* but *also* (because of that "privation") is *vulneratus in naturalibus* ("wounded in what attaches to his 'nature' ") and hence *is* "diseased." One need not agree with this view (I do not), but one ought to get it right—and most critics of Scholastic theology do not do so.

However, this is an academic point, perhaps. What emerges from Dr. von Rohr's paper is a position similar to that taken by Helmut Thielicke in his *Theological Ethics*. That is, all men are "in sin," *all* "have fallen short of the glory of God," in the Pauline phrase. This "fallenness" is manifest in their sexuality and its modes of expression as well as everywhere else. Thus the homosexual is *no more* a sinner than the heterosexual, although *his* way of sinning is different from that followed by the latter. This view naturally follows from the general theological basis that Dr. von Rohr (and Thielicke) adopt, a view that is certainly authentically Protestant, whether found in Lutheran theology or in properly "Reformed" (viz., Calvinistic) theology. An unfriendly commentator might say that what it comes down to is that "people who live in glass houses should not throw stones"—that everybody is "in sin" and nobody can condemn others for being sinners, since we are all precisely that. But this comment would be both unkind and unfair, because it would miss the important point that is being made, namely, the defection of all men from the intended nature or "quality of life" which is proper to man in God's purpose. And with that point I anyway must agree heartily.

But the very phrasing that I have just used to state the point indicates that my own approach to the matter, and in consequence my approach to homosexuality and to homosexuals, differs from that which Dr. von Rohr would seem to take. My approach is basically derived from a combination of what I take to be Biblical insights and the understanding of the nature of man that can be drawn from "process thought." I must assume that the reader is familiar with the latter; if not, I may refer him to my own discussion in *Process Thought and Christian Faith*[1] for an extended summary, and content myself here with saying a very few things.

Men do not *have* a nature, as if it were something they possessed in distinction from themselves; neither are they "souls" who *have* bodies. Man is a process—a serial routing of "occasions" of experience, in which his identity is established by his memory (both conscious and subconscious, and visceral or "bodily"), his relationships with others in the giving-and-receiving of every moment, and his "subjective aim" or human purpose toward which his potentialities (whatever they may be) are actualized. As such a process, with self-identity, man is possessed of a dynamic—he is always moving toward fulfillment, "becoming" what he is to "be." He is an organic complex; bodily and rationally and emotionally he is to greater or less degree an integrated whole. Further, he is a *social* process, in that he exists in and with his fellowmen in what the Old Testament styles "a bundle of life"; his sociality is the condition of and the possibility for his personality. Above all, man is being created *for love;* he finds his true fulfillment only in the mutuality, reciprocity, and participation that love signifies and that love provides. In Christian thinking, this means that man is made for God, who *is* Love.

Man's physiological and psychological equipment is such that his need and desire for love and for loving express themselves through sexual channels, although love and sexuality are not identical terms—the latter is the instrumentality for the former. Thus it is no accident that in the Bible there is much use of sexual imagery, marriage, and "knowing" (as the intimate relationship of sexual union—although I agree with Dr. Sherwin Bailey in thinking that the Sodom story in Genesis does not intend "knowing," in this particular incident, in a sexual sense). Whether we wish to think of marriage as "a sacrament" or prefer some other term to describe it, there is a "sacramental" quality in the marriage union, since it is (for the majority of men) the human physical and psychological condition for their growing in love—and hence, ultimately, growing toward God.

But as a sexual being, man is also able to decide for the proper (that is, the truly fulfilling) exercise of his sexuality or for an improper (that is, finally nonfulfilling) exercise of it. In the latter instance, his sexuality remains more or less on the level of *lust,* although the very dis-ease which lust awakens signifies that there is more to it than that. Yet lust is not a bad thing; sexual drive, sexual emotion, sexual desire, are good things—if lust means those things, it is a good of the created order. On the other hand, the common meaning given to the word "lust" is the *merely* physical gratification of sexuality; and as such, lust is *not* a good thing but a distortion of man's distinctive quality. This is because man's distinctive quality is the utilizing of all his potentialities toward the realizaton or actualization of his aim *to become man*—to become the highly personalized human instrumentality for love in participation, reciprocity, and mutuality.

Thus in his sexual expression, man's total self is to be involved—and the proper or truly fulfilling way of sexual expression is (as Dr. von Rohr rightly says) in "respect, self-giving, and fidelity." I should wish to expand that statement a little and say that true sexual fulfillment is possible only when there is commitment ("fidelity"), giving-*and*-receiving (to be able to receive as well as to give love), hopefulness (eagerly expecting the best from the one loved), establishment of reciprocal or mutual life one with the other—and the whole relationship marked by tenderness, which will include the "respect" about which Dr. von Rohr speaks.

Now very few, if any, human beings realize to the full all these requirements of true love at its best and most fulfilling. That is a measure of the defection of human life from its intentional routing toward its proper goal. *Why* we decide for such less fulfilling ways is a question that cannot be answered—in philosophical idiom, sin is self-posited, like freedom. If we knew *why*, we could not say that man does in fact decide as he does; he would be determined by antecedent or contemporary factors and hence would *not* freely decide. We may have *theories* about this; it is, in my view, part of the wider problem of "evil," which means that it is part of the present and observable fact that in a creation which is not ready-made but is "in the making," there are backwaters, drags, twistings, side attractions, and the like, which militate against true fulfillment. This is why the circumambient grace of God—his love always in action in and upon us—is required for true fulfillment. God lures us by his love; he surrounds us by his love; he provides for us, in his love, the initial aim of self-fulfillment which we may, and should, "decide for" as our chosen "subjective aim." This love from God, this love which is God, is not necessarily consciously known to be such; it may be given only in that "common grace," in Calvinistic terms, found in the world itself, or it may be through those more specifically "gracious" moments which come to each man from time to time, or it may be the very definitely Christian "grace of our Lord Jesus Christ"—but whatever and wherever and however it is, this love makes possible for any man just that self-realization which is his proper aim, for which he is being made, and which is his basic drive.

All this I have treated at much greater length in two books: *The Christian Understanding of Human Nature* [2] and *Love Looks Deep*.[3] It is obvious that my exposition has not been in Biblical language; yet I believe it is an accurate "demythologizing" of the Scriptural view of man. Furthermore, I am convinced that in this respect, as in so many others, we find our greatest assistance in reaching such a "demythologizing" in the conceptuality known as "process philosophy," especially when with this kind of thought we associate the insights of contemporary existentialist analysis of "what it means, and feels like, to be human" and the further contribution of modern psychology (particularly "depth psychology").

Now the question poses itself: What is the relevance of all this to the homosexual condition?

I am glad that Dr. von Rohr lays stress on the homosexual *condition,* rather than on the specific sexual activity of homosexual men and women. For it is the condition—the state of living with homosexual desires and attraction—which is most important, while it is also that condition which is the context for overt homosexual activity. As to what picture may be given of the etiology of the condition, I agree with Dr. von Rohr that the experts do not help us much—their views are very diverse, ranging from the few who still maintain some deep physiological factors to those who speak of strictly psychological or environmental pressures. But whatever may be the origins of the condition, it is plainly *there;* there are millions of men and women who are "in" that condition—in Britain, where I live, it is estimated that "one in twenty" is thus homosexual in the broad definition of the term; in the United States, one writer has spoken of "one in six."

The homosexual, then, is one who through no special choice—above all, no special fault—of his own finds that he is sexually drawn to members of his own sex. For him it is entirely "natural" thus to be drawn; that is the way he *is*. Some homosexuals wish it were otherwise—those are the ones who may be "cured," as the phrase goes, under proper sorts of "treatment"; but in my own experience with homosexuals I should say that they are relatively few in number. Most homosexuals may from time to time be unhappy about their condition, especially in view of current social attitudes, but (as one of them put it), "I wouldn't want to be different—I *like* being what I am." And why not? If such an attraction toward a member of one's own sex is the possibility of true love as well as real sexual satisfaction, there is no reason to wish to kill that best thing in one. This is precisely how most homosexuals feel about the matter. Apart from prejudice and lack of sympathy, who will blame them?

If the homosexual *condition,* whatever may be its etiology, is a given fact for homosexual persons, about which they can do nothing and about which most of them wish (quite rightly) to do nothing, what about the overt expression of this condition in physical sexual acts? Right here there is great disagreement in Christian circles as well as among those who look sympathetically enough at the "condition" but would raise questions about the "acts."

On the one hand, there are those who say that homosexual activity is always of the nature of sin. The condition may not be more sinful than the human condition itself; but to act upon it, by overt contacts, *is* sinful. I confine myself here to the discussion in Christian circles; elsewhere, doubtless, the concept of "sin" does not figure in the picture, but some more or less equivalent idea will be found, such as "socially destructive," "psychologically damaging," "less than truly human," etc. Others, myself among them, would say that such acts are not, in and of themselves, sinful; "it all depends," just as in heterosexual relationships with physical acts of intercourse, the "sinfulness" is determined not by what is done, in and of itself, but by accompanying circumstances, attitudes, situations, and the like.

Here we must do two things: first, we must say something about the nature of those homosexual acts; second, we must try to reach a better understanding of what the term "sin" means in informed Christian circles. The former is important because so many who talk freely on the subject seem to have but the vaguest idea of "what homosexuals do," as Bryan Magee puts it in his *One in Twenty*.[4] The latter is particularly necessary because the word "sin" is so often used to indicate only violation of some imposed moral code or set of commandments external to the supposed "sinner." If some readers are offended by a frank statement of the former, I am sorry; in respect to the latter, I believe "situational" ethics is of great help to us in grasping the Christian use of the word "sin."

The majority of male homosexuals are likely to begin sexual relations with fondling, caressing, and kissing, which may proceed to what is known as "full-body contact" in which the two embrace each other tightly, pressing their bodies together. For a few, such contact of bared bodies is sufficient; but most homosexuals will engage in other more directly genital activity, such as mutual masturbation, the placing of the penis of one between the tightly closed thighs of the other, fellatio (taking the stiffened penis in the mouth and kissing, licking, or sucking it) which is often performed mutually (this is known as "69", an act in which each simultaneously brings his partner to climax), and anal penetration or the insertion of the penis in the rear opening of the partner. There are variations of these acts and there are other combinations, as well as full bodily kissing.

Female homosexuals, or lesbians, act in a similar fashion at the beginning, with caresses and kissing; they may go on to digital or lingual stimulation of each other, centering attention on the clitoris; and in some, perhaps fairly few, instances they may engage in tribadism, or a simulation of the heterosexual act, one placing herself above and on the other and moving as if in male-female intercourse.

Other things being equal, all these physical acts are possible between persons of differing sex; indeed, from recent studies of the behavior patterns of married couples or heterosexual lovers, we know that they are generally practiced. The one sort of activity not possible in homosexual relationships, male or female, is penile-vaginal union—and it is a mistake to think, as do some people, that lesbians frequently use an artificial penis strapped on to one partner and employed in a literal imitation of heterosexual intercourse; this seems to be fairly infrequent, although it is of course sometimes enjoyed.

The point of the above three descriptive paragraphs is simply that there is nothing particularly *odd* about the physical activity of homosexuals of either sex. Especially

I wish to make clear that sadomasochistic behavior, with the purposeful infliction of pain, is not often found among homosexuals. Once again, of course, there *are* sadomasochistic homosexuals, but so are there also sadomasochistic heterosexuals. Sadomasochism is *not* a peculiarly homosexual pattern of behavior; it is very unjust to accuse those who are homosexuals of delighting in inflicting pain or of enjoying pain inflicted by others.

Let us now consider what is meant by the term "sin." I have said that the acts just described are not in and of themselves sinful. What then constitutes a "sinful act"?

If the account given earlier of "human nature" is correct, we can see that sin, which we may call "deviant" or "distorted" human living, is that which interferes with or twists or refuses the right and proper movement of man toward his fulfillment. But since man's true fulfillment is found in a relationship of love—a faithful, committed, tender, mutual, hopeful, giving-and-receiving of personality—then sin is to be defined as a violation or a rejection of love. Traditionally sin has been thought to be the breaking of a moral code or the refusal to obey a moral commandment. But basically, sin is a breaking of an intended relationship—the relationship in which love is given and returned. Thus sin between man and man, between members of the human race, is a refusal to love or a violation of love. And since the love which we know and experience humanly is a reflection of and a participation in (although not identical with) the love that is divine—*God as Love*—sin is a refusal of full and open relationship with God, a violation of a relationship with God such as is the intended end or goal and meaning of human life.

We may explicate this by reference to those ingredients

of love to which reference was made earlier. Sin, then, is refusal or distortion of faithfulness or commitment in relationship; of tenderness and respect; of hopeful expectation in respect to the other; of the giving-*and*-receiving in such relationship—one can give in such a way that the other cannot give in return, one can try to "get" in such a way that the other can receive nothing; of that mutuality or reciprocity or participation which relationship in love at its deepest level would attain and express.

With this in mind, we must agree with Dr. von Rohr that nobody perfectly attains these qualities; hence all of us are "sinners." But the fact is that what counts most is not the perfect attainment, which men do not achieve, but *the direction taken by a man's life*. Is he moving, in his various relationships, *toward* the greater realization of commitment, hopefulness, tenderness, respect, giving-and-receiving, mutuality? Or is he moving *away from* such an increasing realization? We should look at ourselves and others with these questions in mind. Precisely because man is not a static entity but a living process, he is to judge himself and to be judged in terms of his movement and the direction which that movement takes. The degree to which he fails to proceed in the direction of full realization, with his fellows and in and under the Love that is God, is the degree to which he is "in" sin. And his activities, whatever they are, must be judged in the same fashion.

The actions that lead to proper fulfillment are the actions that are good and right; those which lead away from proper fulfillment are the actions that are bad and wrong—they are "sinful." "Circumstances alter cases," it is said; in a sound ethical view, I should insist, this is *always* the point to emphasize. Talk about some supposedly "objective moral standard" that has no regard for the persons involved is talk about an abstraction; what is more, the very standard itself, *when applied,* is almost always nothing but the canonization of conventional moral opinion, a matter of *mores* in the strict sense of the accepted set of ideas entertained in a given society. In one sense, then, Kant was right; insofar as we have in mind an "objective moral standard," it is bound to be *formal,* without content. Such content can only come afterward. So also Thomas Aquinas, defining the "natural law" in its moral sense, said that it reduces to the command, "Do good and avoid evil." Once again, this is lacking in content; it is merely formal until in some other way its detailed application is spelled out for us.

We *should* obey the "categorical imperative," but it can be obeyed only in this or that specific instance. We *should* "do good and avoid evil," but we have to discover *what* is good and *what* is evil, to be done or avoided. One can only agree with those who wish to find the clue to the specific good and the specific evil in the concrete situations in which men and women live. As a friend of mine once put it, "You must keep your eyes open and use your head, if you want to learn God's will for you." This does not imply that the moral tradition which we have inherited is of no value; rather, it is an insistence that the value of that tradition is in providing us with whatever wisdom our ancestors possessed as to how we may most adequately "do good and avoid evil" or obey the "categorical imperative." Our ancestors were not all fools, by any means; the guidelines they laid down should be noted and valued. But it is no false pride to say that in many instances—of which homosexuality is one, since as Dr. von Rohr rightly tells us we have available much information that they did *not* have—we cannot follow those guidelines if we hope to do justice to our fellowmen, and to ourselves, in the particular situations in which we find ourselves.

From this discussion we may return to our question: Are homosexuals committing sin when they engage in physical acts to express their love? As will now be apparent, my own answer is in the negative.

But having given that flat answer, I must qualify it. Homosexual acts are not sinful when they are expressions of love, moving those who engage in them toward faithfulness, tenderness, respect, hopefulness, mutuality. It is not so much a matter of whether or not those qualities are immediately present, as whether or not they are on the way to being realized. Hence we need always to ask ourselves, as we must ask any homosexual, whether the acts we perform, like the thoughts we think, are a mode of increasing within us and between us and among us the development of relationships in which genuine love is more effectively realized and established.

It is at once clear that easy promiscuity, "pickups," "one-night stands," and use of prostitutes will hardly work in that way—among heterosexuals as well as among homosexuals. One can understand perfectly well why resort is had to these expedients. Without concerning ourselves with heterosexuals, we can say that homosexuals are driven by their sexual desires (good in themselves), by their desperate loneliness (a terrible reality for many homosexuals), and by social rejection (felt deeply in the homosexual world), to secure *any* opportunity to find sexual relief, some kind of companionship if only for a few minutes or hours, and acceptance by other human beings. Something of these three may be obtained in the sort of occasional and incidental contacts to which we have referred. But the deep reality genuinely sought for cannot be obtained in this manner—and every homosexual whom I have known has honestly said that this is true. For what the homosexual longs for, with a profound and almost frightening intensity, is a relationship with another person which will have about it the quality of some permanence and thus enable him to know the faithfulness and commitment, tenderness, respect for self and others, hopeful expectation, and mutuality in giving-and-receiving which so frequently I have noted in this essay.

Anybody who says that homosexuals do *not* yearn for this only demonstrates that he has never really known any homosexuals who have opened up to him their deepest selves. The truth is, as Antony Grey (secretary of the Albany Trust, an English society working to help homosexuals) has well said, that homosexuals *want* affection, caring, being together in genuine mutual concern; or, as he goes on to say, "they want *love*." In this respect they are like every other son of man. The tragedy is that so many nonhomosexuals do not, sometimes will not, recognize this patent truth.

As I write these words I think of several couples whom I know, most of them men, some of them women. By good fortune they have "found each other" and have been able to establish what they hope will be and intend to be a permanent relationship; in certain instances, they have found it possible to live together in a shared apartment or house. These people come from diverse backgrounds—one couple is a clergyman and an artist, another two businessmen, still another two research students, a fourth two young women both working as secretaries in city business offices, another two teachers of secondary school level, the last a nurse and an older retired professional woman. The diversity of their backgrounds and their occupations is itself significant; it is an indication of the fact that homosexuals come from all classes of society, with great variety in educational and vocational experience, and with jobs of the most varied sorts.

All these couples, as it happens, are religiously sensitive; it is natural that my own acquaintances should be of that type, although I am also convinced that a very considerable number of homosexuals would very much like to participate in the life of a Christian parish or congregation if they felt that they would be acceptable and accepted. But what most strikes me about these men and women is that they are *real people,* honorable and decent and moral in every sense (excepting that *one* sense which society commonly refuses to allow as moral—their homosexuality—but which they themselves are sure is moral and right for them). In the circles where they can move freely, their homosexual love is taken for granted; it constitutes no problem and hence creates none. When they are permitted to move freely, they are *themselves free*—some of them much freer, in truth, than other acquaintances of mine who in repressing their sexuality, whether homosexual or heterosexual, have become warped personalities and the very opposite of warm and loving people.

Some of these couples I know well enough for them to have spoken frankly of "what they do together." Their physical expression of love includes many if not all the acts described earlier. They find in those acts an inexpressible happiness; through them they are brought close together and by means of them they not only manifest their mutual love but deepen and enrich it. Some of them have experienced misunderstandings, "tiffs," and quarrels; but they have often been able (as one said) to "resolve them in bed." Sometimes there have been occasional acts of "unfaithfulness," but the basic drive toward faithfulness has been great enough to keep the couple together. In other words, they are not unlike the average heterosexual couple.

All this is true despite social pressures, uneasiness about possible discovery and loss of job, a sense of being "unaccepted." Against such obstacles heterosexuals do not have to contend. That so many homosexual couples manage to stick together and make a real thing of their "affair" is a tribute to their integrity, their loyalty, and their affection one for the other. But what should we do to give them help in living their lives in this sort of relationship?

Efforts are being made in Denmark and elsewhere to promote the legality of homosexual "marriages." The problem here is that marriage, through historical development, has become a social pattern of a specific kind, with all the economic factors involved, as well as the legal sanctions, and with children born to the man and wife as a visible expression of their shared love. Homosexual union cannot produce offspring, obviously; while the historical development of the institution of marriage is such that it is difficult, if not impossible, to apply it to those of the same sex. Yet one would think that some method might be found, perhaps one day will be found, to give social recognition and even legal sanction to a homosexual union; one would think that Christian churches might find some way to bless such a couple who genuinely intended permanence and who were seeking that faithfulness (and the other qualities) which such a union might cement.

At the very least, however, one can demand that Christian people should sympathize with, understand, and do all in their power to help men and women like this. Why should they not be welcomed into the life of the Christian congregation? Are we afraid, despite all that the experts now tell us, that they will continually seek to seduce others? Are we unready to take the risk which genuine acceptance of any other person always involves?

I shall end this essay by relating what to some may seem a shocking story—but nonetheless a story that happens to be true. I know two youngish men who have lived together, completely and devotedly, for ten years and who have become so much one that it seems impossible, now, that they can ever separate. Quite literally, they have everything in common. They are both devout Christians. And they told me that their greatest happiness was to "make love passionately on Saturday night," and then go together the next morning to receive the Holy Communion kneeling side by side in a church not far from their home. What did I think of this?—this bringing together of physical sexual communion and communion in the risen life of Jesus Christ in the Sacrament? My answer was that to my mind it was both beautiful and right. I hope that this essay will have done something to make the reader see why I said that, why I believe that, and why I think that anyone who condemns those young men as "dirty," "indecent," or "unchristian," must himself stand under awful condemnation.

Tolstoy entitled one of his stories *Where Love Is, There God Is.* If we believe that—and any Christian surely must, after reading (say) I John 4—how could I have answered otherwise? And how could I, or any other Christian, wish to refuse to such persons the sacrament of love, where the Divine Charity is shared with men precisely in order that human love may reflect something of its loveliness, its wonder, and its splendor?

Notes

1. Norman Pittenger, *Process Thought and Christian Faith* (The Macmillan Company, 1968).

2. Norman Pittenger, *The Christian Understanding of Human Nature* (The Westminster Press, 1964).

3. Norman Pittenger, *Love Looks Deep* (London: A. R. Mowbray & Co., Ltd., 1969).

4. Bryan Magee, *One in Twenty: A Study of Homosexuality in Men and Women,* new ed. (London: Martin Secker & Warburg, Ltd., 1969).

13

A Response to the Reponses

JOHN VON ROHR

If nothing else is made clear by the foregoing responses to this book's initial essay, there stands as evident at least this one fact: the dialogue on homosexuality is characterized, within the Christian community itself, by amazing diversity! Perhaps that should occasion no surprise, for varieties of theology and ethical judgment are surely to be found in many places within the multifariousness of Christian pluralism. But here the spectrum is truly broad indeed, and one becomes aware of the wide range of approaches to and conclusions about this sensitive matter. There is stark and vivid contrast between reaffirmed traditional views and newer perspectives developed in more recent time, while even within the latter added diversity appears. In this final essay, then, it may be useful to attempt to identify some of that variety around major specific issues as well as to continue the dialogue by responding, at least in some measure, to the responses.

A first and basic matter has to do, of course, with the way in which ethical judgments are to be made on patterns of human behavior. The traditional Christian position is represented most strongly by Dr. Henry, who asserts uncompromisingly that the Biblical strictures against homosexuality must be recognized as of divine origin and thus as applicable to life in all ages, including our own. Henry argues against any qualifications of the "stringent moral condemnations for sexual infractions" found in the Bible by those who affirm a position claiming for the gospel of Christ "a more 'compassionate' view." Though the latter is presumably done "in the name of Christian love," it is really, in Henry's judgment, a "setting aside what the Bible teaches and . . . substituting what the moderns prefer."

At the very opposite extreme, of course, is the radical rejection of Biblical legalism, if not Biblical authority itself, in such essays as those of Dr. Williams and the Rev. Mr. Maurer. It is not convincing to me that, as Williams claims, the apostle Paul was fundamentally antisexual in his views, even to the point where sexuality was "his great aversion," for the apostle's brief comments on sex and marriage surely must be read in the light of his apocalypticism, an expectation of the imminent end of the world and its ways and the miraculous beginning of a new spiritual age. But the antihomosexual emphasis was there, as elsewhere in the Scriptures, and this now is rigorously rejected in these essays—and in such manner as to cast doubt on any form of Biblical authority. This is especially true of Maurer's resistance to the Bible as a "taskmaster, a body of writing to which we are enslaved." In this sense the criteria for ethical judgments seem to be entirely extra-Biblical, and Maurer writes about this in terms of the necessity for ideas being "existentially valid." Though the meaning of this latter phrase is not explicitly clarified, the suggestion seems to be that homosexuality carries in experience its own moral justification, as theology itself must "be created out of one's own experience, out of one's own visceral being." And in a way, I suppose, this goes a long step in the direction of simply affirming that what *is* is *good,* especially if it is appealing and satisfying

Neither of these positions, however, seems to me to be adequate. I would want to urge for Christian thinking the continuation of Biblical norms, though in a way that recognizes the cultural conditioning and historical relativity of much of the specific legislation found in the Biblical record. Williams is right in suggesting that the Bible cannot prescribe for us concerning turtles and tatooing—and homosexuality. Perry, of course, despite his Biblical and theological conservatism, suggests the same. Yet it can speak to us about the divine will for love in life and the broad manner of divine expectations for interpersonal and societal relationships. Christian theology and ethics, it seems to me, must be "authoritarian" at that point. There is a way in which the Biblical gospel can talk about both grace and duty. As recipients of divine love, we are under obligation for human love, and Christian norms for this must be attentive to basic Biblical patterns. If Biblical revelation is meaningful, it is surely so here. Yet the contributions of modern understanding concerning the meaning and ways of love must likewise be taken into account, based indeed upon empirical knowledge concerning the human situation.

At this point I find the essay of the Rev. H. Kimball Jones particularly challenging. He has devoted much space to urging the necessity of more complete study and understanding of homosexuality before theological and ethical conclusions with respect to it are reached. And this involves for him not only a comprehensive knowledge of the literature but also a direct confrontation with persons who are homosexuals and a study of their attitudes and experiences. In Dr. Oberholtzer's terms this is a "commitment to the homosexual world." It also means for Jones a more careful scrutiny of the total emphasis upon sexuality in contemporary society so that homosexuality is not seen in isolation, apart from the general values of the culture as a whole. There is thus a multidimensional approach which he commends on this matter and which seems to me to be significant. In a recent essay dealing explicitly with the issue of homosexuality, Dr. Roger Shinn has urged the importance of the empirical along with the more traditionally theological in reaching ethical judgments. He writes: "Meanings, including moral meanings, can never be imposed upon life without regard for the specific facts and circumstances that have meaning for people; hence understanding requires empirical evidence. On the other hand, sheer factual evidence is rarely if ever self-interpreting; it takes on meaning within the experience of persons and communities with their histories, their loyalties, and their purposes. . . . The distinctive quality of Christian ethics is that the experiences, the memories, and the expectations that it brings to all phenomena are related to the experience of Jesus Christ." [1]

Among this book's essays it would appear that the contribution by Dr. Norman Pittenger also complements this general view. The commitment here is clearly to a theology and an ethic based on Biblical foundations, and yet the emphasis is likewise strongly upon the experience of homosexual couples and what this can contribute to moral meaning. So we note that the Biblical and the experiential are both important. It is not enough simply to turn to the Bible. And it is not enough simply to turn to man's experience and desires. A Christian theology and ethic must keep in close relationship both the empirical and the eternal.

A second issue under considerable discussion in these essays concerns the use of the term "sin" in relation to homosexual behavior. At the outset let a word be said to Williams' misunderstanding of my general view of sexuality when he attributes to me the belief "that sexual acts are intrinsically bad." Contrariwise I would want to affirm the goodness of man's sexuality as an aspect of God's creation and as a vehicle for human communication in self-giving and faithful love. The point of the initial essay in this regard was simply to note that man's sex life, like other aspects of his life, is subject to misuse and perversion. Man is a "fallen" creature, though my own understanding sees the Biblical story of the Fall not as historical incident and cause, but as mythical representation of man's condition. There is endemic to our human nature a self-love which both rebels against God and seeks to use and exploit our human companions, even including those to whom we are most tenderly attached. This I take to be man's fallen condition which can then be expressed through his sexuality as likewise through other forms of his behavior—and sexual acts, therefore, be they hetero or homo, can become instruments of lust as well as of love.

In relation to this matter of the "fall" it is interesting to see again in these essays the divergence of views. Maurer, of course, repudiates the idea completely and would prefer to talk about the "rise of Life," a term that emphasizes steady progress both in biological evolution and in human history. Of course evolution is basic to the earth's story, but the fall is of man, not of the amoeba, and human history has a somewhat different tale to tell. At any rate, it is difficult to see much moral ascent from caveman clubbing to modern man napalming. We still live in a fallen condition, though lifted by grace from it time and again and enabled to love. Henry, however, not only affirms the doctrine of the Fall, undoubtedly understood as historic incident, but also sees homosexuality itself as an aspect of man's life belonging to this condition. One might assume that Maurer identifies homosexuality for the homosexual with life's rise, but for Henry it is clearly related to a reverse direction. Yet this as well needs to be protested in the light of the main thesis urged in the initial essay. Homosexuality is a psychological condition, not a moral condition. It may not be in accord with the presumed intentions of creation and is thus deviant—or variant, as Maurer urges—but it still is not of itself a part of man's rebellion against God and his exploitation of his fellows. It can indeed be used in that latter way, with aggressiveness, promiscuity, and lack of faithful love. But so can heterosexuality. Thus the point needs to be affirmed again that homosexual behavior is not of itself sin, though it can indeed become the occasion for sin. And this means that it is not to be seen as part of man's fallen condition. Gay is Good—if it is used in a good way.

The "good way" is in this portrait, of course, the way of a love characterized by respect, self-giving, and fidelity. I fully accept Pittenger's expansion of that description to include tenderness, hopefulness, and the receiving of love in its mutual exchange. These are indeed further characteristics of the love that is respecting of persons rather than exploitative of them. Altogether the emphasis here is upon the commitment of one person to another, a matter that is deeply personal and that perhaps reaches its culmination in not only the protestations but the practice of fidelity.

Thus it is interesting and highly significant to read the essay by Miss Martin and Miss Lyon concerning this matter among lesbian couples. Their emphasis is upon the "deep and abiding love, . . . [the] lasting relationships, . . . [the] mutual commitment" that so often characterizes the female homosexual. Whether or not there is the one-night stand, which they say is "more talk than action," the long-term relationship is affirmed to be of high esteem in the lesbian community and, as they say, "the constant question put to a couple is, How long have you two been together?" We know that male homosexual behavior tends toward a somewhat greater promiscuity, as Jones has indeed indicated in his essay. But here as well love can be characterized by faithfulness. Pittenger's references to the homosexual couples whom he has known and counseled are evidences of this, a fact borne out, of course, in many other studies. And Jones likewise urges in counseling with homosexuals "the possibility and desirability of establishing a permanent relationship with one partner grounded in mutual love and commitment," seeing this as "a viable Christian alternative to the depersonalizing cruising" which so often on the surface at least seems characteristic of the homosexual community. I take this to be a major emphasis in the rehabilitated Christian thinking on homosexuality. Heterosexual cruising can be protested as much as homosexual cruising. But homosexual fidelity can be lauded as much as heterosexual fidelity. The important thing from the moral standpoint is the genuineness and faithfulness of love.

At this point, moreover, a demurrer must be entered to a view expressed particularly in the essay by Dr. Harvey. There it is suggested that this general approach to an ethic of homosexuality amounts to a subjectivizing of ethical judgment and thus to a rejection of any objective norm for the evaluation of either homosexual or heterosexual behavior. But love itself can be objective norm, even though it is comprised substantially of subjective attitudes. Objectivity does not require criteria drawn exclusively from the realm of external act. There are characteristics testifying to the validity of human love, such as those proposed earlier—respect, self-giving, and fidelity—and these can be objective ground for ethical evaluation in interpersonal relationships. This is not to argue for the type of subjectivism in ethics that leads to relativism. But it is to urge that objective ethical norms can exist for man's subjective life as well as for its outward expression. We do not need to turn to "nature" and its presumed indication of what is "natural," as Harvey would have us do, in order to have criteria for speaking about man's sexual life.

Yet this now leads to a third matter. Somehow the question of the "natural" and/or the "unnatural" character of homosexual activity is not easily put down. Antony Grey regrets in his essay that time needs to be given to this kind of discussion, including exploration of the causes of homosexuality. It would be better, he feels, to begin simply by acknowledging that homosexuality exists and by recognizing that all persons, whatever their sexual propensities, are God's children and equal in his sight. One can appreciate the intentions behind such a proposal. And yet not only does the theological task necessitate such exploration, but also the psychological relation of the heterosexual to the homosexual world is contingent to some degree upon it and its conclusions. Some understanding in this area must underlie and contribute to that acceptance of the latter by the former which, as seen in several essays, is earnestly desired.

Once again, of course, differences abound. Traditional views, both Protestant and Catholic, reject the idea of naturalness for homosexual behavior. Henry and Harvey represent those views here. Henry finds the natural mode of sexual fulfillment to be heterosexual as represented in the Genesis creation story. Harvey, supplementing such a view, also argues that homosexuality cannot be termed natural, since it is a form of psychological disorder. Moreover, his conviction that homosexuals have simply resigned themselves to this pathological condition and are indeed miserable in it leads him further to see such life as unnatural, since "the term 'natural' . . . denotes a quality of perfection . . . [and] something 'natural' makes one a better man." Williams, on the other hand, argues for homosexuality as a "part of nature," feeling there is biological justification for this stand. Indeed, he also repudiates the idea that the Genesis story can be used to urge universal heterosexuality as the divine intention in creation. So there is nothing unnatural or pathological about homosexuality. In the terms of the Quaker report of a few years ago, one should no more deplore it than one would deplore left-handedness. As to the matter of misery or self-acceptance, Pittenger sees homosexuals generally satisfied with their condition, unhappiness being created more by society's attitudes than by manner of sexual life. And certainly this testimony emerges strongly from within the homosexual community itself. Martin and Lyon write about the way of life that is as natural to the homosexual as heterosexuality is to the heterosexual. And in this way they find a stability, sanity, and spiritual growth which emerge through self-acceptance. In all of this and much else, homosexuality is appreciated from within as a wholesome and natural condition. Pittenger's quotation from a homosexual friend says it emphatically: "I wouldn't want to be different—I *like* being what I am."

It is here, however, that this particular heterosexual, writing this essay, experiences his greatest difficulty in coming to a theological understanding and ethical appraisal of homosexuality. The initial essay made a double affirmation, that homosexuality could be considered as both unnatural and natural, and I find now that that mixed characterization must continue to be made. At the worst, of course, this is simply an intellectual "cop-out." At the best, it is an essential way of dealing with a complex phenomenon. Readers will need to judge for themselves. But there remains, in this writer's view, both the fact of a total world created for heterosexual living and the fact of individual lives for whom such sexual behavior is simply contrary to all impulse and desire. What is natural—the divine plan of heterosexuality for all persons (yes, I say it), or the demands for homosexuality which are most real, precious, and irreversible for individual persons? The conclusion reached here is that both are natural—and that homosexuality, therefore, is both out of accord with the pristine purposes of creation and fully in accord with what can be called truly natural for many people.

This view obviously will not be satisfying to members of the homosexual community. When Williams accuses

Jones in his book on this matter [2] as being patronizing and seeing the homosexual as a "sexual cripple," he is voicing the kind of criticism that also applies to the view which I have set forth. The charge against Barth, Piper, Thielicke, and Jones is that of affirming "heterosexual superiority," and without question it could be leveled against this writer as well, despite all attempts to be understanding, empathetic, and concerned. The acceptance of the homosexual as a genuine and valued member of the human community cannot, under these considerations, be exactly the same as the kind of self-acceptance and mutuality of acceptance that prevails within the homosexual circle itself. And yet hopefully it is significant acceptance—though it is acceptance of the homosexual as a person or as a faithful lover rather than as a homosexual. Perhaps this is a heterosexual "hang-up" with respect to homosexuality that cannot be overcome. But at least I confess it to be recognized as a final point of difficulty in achieving full intellectual and emotional identity with homosexuality. Let it be noted again, however, that the problem is not one of homosexual sin. Man's sin is a common possession shared by all, with no special sexual form for it! And conversely, homosexuality, like heterosexuality, can be a channel of genuine love. The psychic distance has to do with the degree to which the homosexual form of love can itself be seen to be part of the intended order, rather than simply the developed order, of man's existence.

Now, we are led, however, to a fourth and final matter. Even though homosexuality might fail of acceptance as a part of God's design, the life of the homosexual with its fidelity in love cannot similarly be repudiated. There is a naturalness in this for those who know its compulsions. There is a tenderness. There is an affection. And there is a faithfulness, as we have been reminded time and again. How can one from the outside say this in a nonpatronizing way? Perhaps one cannot. Perhaps that kind of gulf cannot be fully bridged when life-styles, and interpretations of them, are so different. But the word of understanding and acceptance of persons must be continuously spoken. And actions must be in accord with words.

Thus I must personally reject the proposals of both Dr. Henry and Dr. Harvey that the answer to homosexuality is necessarily to be found in the practice of chastity—or further, in religious factors, meditation, discipline, and conversion, which provide the amelioration necessary for what is adjudged to be both evil and distress. Dr. Nouwen seems sounder in stressing the acceptance of one's homosexual feelings and then the responsible handling of them. Vocational sublimation is, of course, a possibility, as it is also for the heterosexual. But this discussion has argued for the validity of homosexual behavior as expressed in mutual faithfulness, and it is to that again that we return. The testimony, if I hear it aright, tells us emphatically of the meaningfulness of such homosexual love. Let us then recognize it and dignify it. Let us change restrictive American legislation concerning it with an eye to the more enlightened British precedents that Coleman has described. Let us find ways, as Jones has suggested, for discussion, education, and action within the church on this entire matter. Let us recognize that Crompton is right in alleging that a "wall of ice" has existed between the church and the homosexual and that this surely now needs to be melted away. Let us begin acting in a more Christian way toward those of our brothers and sisters whose sex style is different but who share our common hopes and aspirations and values and feelings of love.

Notes

1. Ralph W. Weltge (ed.), *The Same Sex: An Appraisal of Homosexuality* (The Pilgrim Press, 1969), p. 45.
2. H. Kimball Jones, *Toward a Christian Understanding of the Homosexual* (Association Press, 1966).

Contributors

P. E. Coleman is both a lawyer and Anglican Chaplain to Bristol University, Bristol, England. He also has been Chaplain and Lecturer in Ethics at King's College, London University.

Lewis Williams, Ph.D., is a literary scholar and award-winning critic. He is also Chairman of the North American Conference of Homophile Organizations.

Joseph Fletcher, Ph.D., is Visiting Professor of Medical Ethics at the Medical School of the University of Virginia and author of *Situation Ethics* and *Moral Responsibility*.

Antony Grey was Director of the Albany Trust and Secretary of the Homosexual Law Reform Society, London, from 1962 until 1970. He conducted the Society's successful campaign for the enactment of the Wolfenden Committee's proposals into English Law.

John F. Harvey, Ph.D., is President of DeSales Hall of Theology, Hyattsville, Maryland, and author of numerous essays on homosexuality, including "Homosexuality" in the *New Catholic Encyclopedia*.

CARL F. H. HENRY, PH.,D., is Professor of Theology at The Eastern Baptist Theological Seminary, Philadelphia, founding editor of *Christianity Today,* and author of numerous books and articles, including *Christian Personal Ethics.*

H. KIMBALL JONES is an ordained Methodist minister, Tutor at Union Seminary, New York, while working toward a Th.D. in Psychiatry and Religion at Union Seminary, and author of *Toward a Christian Understanding of the Homosexual.*

PHYLLIS LYON is Assistant Director of the National Sex and Drug Forum, San Francisco; a founder of the Daughters of Bilitis, an international lesbian organization; and co-author with Del Martin of a book on lesbianism for McCall Publishing Company.

DEL MARTIN is a member of the Board of Directors of The Council on Religion and the Homosexual, San Francisco; co-author with Phyllis Lyon of a book on lesbianism; and was a member of the Joint Committee on Homosexuality appointed by the late Bishop James Pike.

THOMAS MAURER is Associate Director of the National Sex and Drug Forum, San Francisco; President of the Society for Individual Rights; an ordained United Church of Christ minister; and was Field Director for the Institute for Sex Research's study of homosexuality in the Bay Area.

HENRI J. M. NOUWEN is an ordained Roman Catholic priest, author of *Intimacy,* and was both a former fellow at the Menninger Foundation and a Visiting Professor of Psychology at the University of Notre Dame. He received the Doctorandus degree in psychology from the University of Nijmegen, Holland.

W. Dwight Oberholtzer, Ph.D., is Assistant Professor of Sociology, Pacific Lutheran University, Tacoma, Washington; has studied at the Graduate Theological Union and the University of California, Berkeley; and has been a Night Minister for the San Francisco Council of Churches.

Troy Perry is the ordained pastor of the Metropolitan Community Church, Los Angeles, the first congregation of predominantly homosexuals in the United States, having graduated from Moody Bible Institute and the Midwest Bible College.

Norman Pittenger, S.T.D., formerly on the Divinity Faculty of Cambridge University, England, is now senior resident member at King's College there. He is the author of numerous books and articles, including *Process Thought and Christian Faith* and *Time for Consent?*

John von Rohr, Ph.D., is Professor of Historical Theology and History of Christianity at the Pacific School of Religion and the Graduate Theological Union, Berkeley, and is author of *Profile of Protestantism*.

Appendix

Homophile Organizations

This is a partial list of established organizations. Information of this kind changes rapidly, however. The present list is compiled from the mailing list (Nov. 18, 1969) of the North American Conference of Homophile Organizations Committee on Credentials. For a succinct, informed introduction to the homophile movement in this country, see Foster Gunnison, Jr., "The Homophile Movement in America," in Weltge (ed.), *The Same Sex*, pp. 113–128.

The Los Angeles ADVOCATE (ADVOCATE)—Dick Michaels, Ed., Box 74695, Los Angeles, Calif. 90004.
Circle of Friends (COF)—Box 9737, Dallas, Tex. 75214.
Committee for Homosexual Freedom (CHF)—Gale Whittington, Chmn., Box 26496, San Francisco, Calif. 94126.
Committee to Fight Exclusion of Homosexuals from the Armed Services—Don Slater, Chmn., 3473½ Cahuenga Blvd., Hollywood, Calif. 90028.
Corinthian Foundation—83 Sixth St., San Francisco, Calif. 94103.
Council on Equality for Homosexuals (CEH)—Foster Gunnison, Jr., Chmn., Box 535, Peter Stuyvesant Sta-

tion, New York, N.Y. 10009.

Council on Religion and the Homophile of Southern California (SCCRH)—3330 West Adams Blvd., Los Angeles, Calif. 90018.

Council on Religion and the Homosexual (CRH)—330 Ellis St., San Francisco, Calif. 94102.

Daughters of Bilitis (DOB)—Rita LaPorte, Pres., Room 208, 1000 Market St., San Francisco, Calif. 94103.

Dorian Society of Seattle—320 Malden Ave. East, Seattle, Wash. 98102.

H.E.L.P.—1725 N. Ivar, Hollywood, Calif. 90028.

Homophile Action League (HAL)—Room 803, 1321 Arch St., Philadelphia, Pa. 19107.

Homophile League of Richmond (HLR)—Box 12342, Central Station, Richmond, Va. 23219.

Institute for Social Ethics (ISE)—Foster Gunnison, Jr., Adm., Box 3417, Central Station, Hartford, Conn. 06103.

Mattachine Midwest (MM)—Jim Bradford, Pres., Box 924, Chicago, Ill. 60690.

Mattachine Society, Inc.—Hal Call, Pres., 348 Ellis St., San Francisco, Calif. 94102.

Mattachine Society of New York, Inc. (MSNY)—Dick Leitsch, Exec. Dir., 243 West End Ave., New York, N.Y. 10023.

Mattachine Society of Washington (MSW)—Franklin E. Kameny, Pres., Box 1032, Washington, D.C. 20013.

Metropolitan Community Church—Rev. Troy D. Perry, Pastor, Box 1154, Huntington Park, Calif. 90255.

ONE, Inc.—2256 Venice Blvd., Los Angeles, Calif. 90006.

Prosperos—731 N. La Brea, Los Angeles, Calif. 90038.

Society for Individual Rights (SIR)—Tom Maurer, Pres., 83 Sixth St., San Francisco, Calif. 94102.

Student Homophile League (SHL)—Bob Martin, Chmn., 109 Earl Hall, Columbia University, New York, N.Y. 10027.

Student Homophile League of Columbia University (SHL/CU)–Nino Romano, Chmn., 109 Earl Hall, Columbia University, New York, N.Y. 10027.

Tangents Group–Don Slater, Chmn., 3473½ Cahuenga Blvd., Hollywood, Calif. 90028.

Tavern Guild of San Francisco (TGSF)–83 Sixth St., San Francisco, Calif. 94103.

West Side Discussion Group (WSDG)–Box 502, Cathedral Station, New York, N.Y. 10025.

Bibliography

William Parker

MATERIALS OF A GENERAL NATURE

Books

1. Anomaly, *The Invert and His Social Adjustment.* London: Baillière, Tindall & Cox, Ltd., 1927; rev. ed. Baltimore: The Williams & Wilkins Company, 1948.
2. Asprey, Robert B., *The Panther's Feast.* G. P. Putnam's Sons, 1959. (Paperback—Bantam N4473)
3. Bailey, Derrick Sherwin (ed.), *Sexual Offenders and Social Punishment.* London: Church Information Board, 1956.
4. Becker, Raymond de, *The Other Face of Love,* tr. from the French by Margaret Crosland and Alan Daventry. Grove Press, Inc., 1969. (Paperback—Sphere 28770)
5. Benson, R. O. D., *In Defense of Homosexuality, Male and Female.* The Julian Press, Inc., 1965.
6. Cory, Donald Webster, *The Homosexual in America: A Subjective Approach.* Greenberg, Publisher, 1951. (Paperback—Paperback Library 54-207). 2d ed. Castle Books, 1960.

7. ——— *Homosexuality: A Cross-Cultural Approach.* The Julian Press, Inc., 1956.
8. ——— *The Lesbian in America.* Citadel Press, 1964. (Paperback–Macfadden MB75-160)
9. ——— and LeRoy, John P., *The Homosexual and His Society: A View from Within.* Citadel Press, 1963.
10. Garde, Noel I., *Jonathan to Gide: The Homosexual in History.* Vantage Press, Inc., 1964.
11. Gerassi, John, *The Boys of Boise: Furor, Vice, and Folly in an American City.* The Macmillan Company, 1966. (Paperback–Collier 07341)
12. Gide, André, *Corydon,* tr. from the French by Hugh Gibb. Farrar, Straus & Young, Inc., 1950. (Paperback–Noonday N211)
13. Gross, Alfred A., *Strangers in Our Midst: Problems of the Homosexual in American Society.* Public Affairs Press, 1962.
14. Hoffman, Martin, *The Gay World: Male Homosexuality and the Social Creation of Evil.* Basic Books, Inc., 1968. (Paperback–Bantam Q4492)
15. Magee, Bryan, *One in Twenty: A Study of Homosexuality in Men and Women.* Stein & Day, Publishers, 1966.
16. Masters, R. E. L., *The Homosexual Revolution: A Challenging Exposé of the Social and Political Directions of a Minority Group.* The Julian Press, Inc., 1962. (Paperback–Belmont 95-102)
17. Plummer, Douglas, *Queer People: The Truth About Homosexuals.* London: W. H. Allen & Co., Ltd., 1963; New York: Citadel Press, 1965. (Paperback–Compact C8)
18. Ruitenbeek Hendrik Marinus (ed.), *Homosexuality and Creative Genius.* Astor-Honor, Inc., 1967.
19. Stearn, Jess, *The Grapevine.* Doubleday & Company, Inc., 1964. (Paperback–Macfadden MB 95–107)

20. ——— *The Sixth Man.* Doubleday & Company, Inc., 1961. (Paperback–Macfadden MB 60–106)
21. Symonds, John A., *Studies in Sexual Inversion Embodying: "A Study of Greek Ethics" and "A Study in Modern Ethics."* Medical Press, 1964.
22. West, Donald James, *Homosexuality.* Aldine Publishing Company, 1968.
23. Westwood, Gordon, *Society and the Homosexual.* E. P. Dutton & Company, Inc., 1953.
24. Wildeblood, Peter, *Against the Law.* London: George Weidenfeld & Nicholson, 1955. (Paperback–Penguin 1188)
25. Wyden, Peter and Barbara, *Growing Up Straight: What Every Thoughtful Parent Should Know About Homosexuality.* Stein & Day, Publishers, 1968.

Pamphlets

26. Albany Trust, *Some Questions and Answers About Homosexuality,* 2d ed. London: Albany Trust, 1965.
27. Council on Religion and the Homosexual, *A Brief of Injustices: An Indictment of Our Society in Its Treatment of the Homosexual.* San Francisco: C. R. H., 1965.
28. ——— and others, *Homosexuals and Employment.* San Francisco: C. R. H. and others, 1970.
29. Group for the Advancement of Psychiatry, *Report on Homosexuality with Particular Emphasis on this Problem in Governmental Agencies.* Topeka: G. A. P., 1955. Report No. 30.
30. Gunnison, Foster, *An Introduction to the Homophile Movement.* Hartford, Conn.: Institute of Social Ethics, 1967.
31. Mattachine Society of Washington, *Federal Employment of Homosexual American Citizens.* Washington, D.C.: Mattachine Society, 1965.

32. Rubin, Isadore, *Homosexuality [A Study Guide]*. New York: Sex Information and Education Council of the United States, 1965.
33. Society for Individual Rights, *The Armed Services and Homosexuality*. San Francisco: S. I. R., 1968.
34. ——— *The Military Discharge and Employment Experiences of 47 Homosexuals*. San Francisco: S. I. R., 1969.
35. United States Congress: Senate. Committee on Expenditures in the Executive Departments—Subcommittee on Investigations. Interim Report: *Employment of Homosexuals and Other Sex Perverts in Government*. Senate Document No. 241, Dec., 1950.
36. United States Department of Health, Education, and Welfare. National Institute of Mental Health, *Final Report of the Task Force on Homosexuality* (the Hooker Committee). (Mimeographed paper, 1969)

Articles

37. Achilles, Nancy, "Development of the Homosexual Bar as an Institution," in John H. Gagnon and William Simon (eds.), *Sexual Deviance*, pp. 247–282. Harper & Row, Publishers, Inc., 1967.
38. Alverson, Charles A., "A Minority's Plea—U.S. Homosexuals Gain in Trying to Persuade Society to Accept Them," *Wall Street Journal*, July 17, 1968, pp. 1, 15.
39. Burke, Tom, "The New Homosexuality," *Esquire*, 73:178, 304–318 (Dec., 1969).
40. Collins, Carol, "Sex Deviates Menace Los Angeles," *Hollywood Citizen-News*, Feb. 4–8, 1964. (5 articles)
41. Doty, Robert C., "Growth of Overt Homosexuality in City Provokes Wide Concern," *New York Times*, Dec. 17, 1963, pp. 1, 33.

42. "Equality for Homosexuals?" *Christian Century,* 84:1587–1588 (Dec. 13, 1967).
43. Flacelière, Robert, "Homosexuality," in *Love in Ancient Greece,* tr. from the French by James Cleugh, pp. 62–100. Crown Publishers, 1962. (Paperback—Macfadden MB60–170)
44. Fonzi, Gaeton J., "The Furtive Fraternity," *Greater Philadelphia Magazine,* Dec., 1962.
45. Gagnon, John H., "Sexual Behavior: Sexual Deviation: Social Aspects," in *International Encyclopedia of the Social Sciences* (The Macmillan Company, 1968), 14:215–222.
46. Havemann, Ernest, "Homosexuality in America: Scientists Search for Answers to a Touchy and Puzzling Question—Why?" *Life,* 56:76–80 (June 26, 1964).
47. Helmer, William J., "New York's 'Middle-Class' Homosexuals," *Harper's,* 226:85–92 (March, 1963).
48. "The Homosexual in America," *Time,* 87:40–41 (Jan. 21, 1966).
49. "The Homosexual: Newly Visible, Newly Understood," *Time,* 94:56–67 (Oct. 31, 1969).
50. "Homosexuality: Coming to Terms," *Time,* 94:82 (Oct. 24, 1969).
51. Hooker, Evelyn, "Sexual Behavior: Homosexuality," in *International Encyclopedia of the Social Sciences* (The Macmillan Company, 1968), 14:222–233.
52. Kameny, Franklin E., "The Federal Government versus the Homosexual," *Humanist,* 29:20–23 (May–June, 1969).
53. Katz, Sidney, "The Harsh Facts of Life in the 'Gay' World," *Maclean's Magazine,* 77:18, 34–38 (March 7, 1964).
54. ——— "The Homosexual Next Door," *Maclean's Magazine,* 77:10–11, 28–30 (Feb. 22, 1964).
55. Kauffmann, Stanley, "Homosexual Drama and Its

Disguises," *New York Times,* Jan. 23, 1966, sec. 2, p. 1.
56. Kirkendall, Lester A., "Adolescent Homosexual Fears," in Isadore Rubin and Lester A. Kirkendall (eds.), *Sex in the Adolescent Years,* pp. 181–185. Association Press, 1968.
57. Parlour, R. R., and others, "Homophile Movement: Its Impact and Implications," *Journal of Religion and Health,* 6:217–234 (July, 1967).
58. Sagarin, Edward, "Homosexuals: The Many Masks of Mattachine," in *Odd Man In: Societies of Deviants in America,* pp. 78–110. Quadrangle Books, 1969.
59. Schott, Webster, "Civil Rights and the Homosexual," *New York Times,* Nov. 12, 1967, magazine section, pp. 44–72.
60. Schur, Edwin Michael, "Homosexuality," in *Crimes Without Victims,* pp. 67–119. Prentice-Hall, Inc., 1965. (Paperback–Spectrum S111)
61. Simon, William, and Gagnon, John H., "The Lesbians: A Preliminary Overview," in John H. Gagnon and William Simon (eds.), *Sexual Deviance,* pp. 247–282. Harper & Row, Publishers, Inc., 1967.
62. Smith, Julie, "The Lesbians' Story," *San Francisco Chronicle,* June 30 to July 2, 1969. (3 articles)
63. Star, Jack, "A Changing View of Homosexuality," *Look,* 33:68 (Dec. 2, 1969).
64. —— "The Sad 'Gay' Life," *Look,* 31:31–33 (Jan. 10, 1967).
65. Taubman, Howard, "The Subtle Persuasion in the American Theater," *Cosmopolitan,* 155:88–91 (Nov., 1963).
66. Welch, Paul, "Homosexuality in America: The 'Gay' World Takes to the City Streets," *Life,* 56:68–74 (June 26, 1964).
67. White, Jean, "Those Others: A Report on Homo-

sexuality," *Washington Post,* Jan. 31 to Feb. 4, 1965. (5 articles)
68. Wille, Lois, "Chicago's Twilight World–the Homosexuals," *Chicago Daily News,* June 20–23, 1966. (4 articles)
69. Wolf, Ruth, "The Homosexual in Seattle," *Seattle Magazine,* Nov., 1967, pp. 38 ff.

MATERIALS OF A RELIGIOUS AND ETHICAL NATURE

Books

70. Bailey, Derrick Sherwin, *Homosexuality and the Western Christian Tradition.* London: Longmans, Green & Co., Ltd., 1955.
71. Buckley, Michael J., *Morality and the Homosexual: A Catholic Approach to a Moral Problem.* The Newman Press, 1959.
72. Jones, H. Kimball, *Toward a Christian Understanding of the Homosexual.* Association Press, 1966. (Paperback–SCM Press)
73. Tobin, William J., *Homosexuality and Marriage.* Rome: Catholic Book Agency, 1964.
74. Weltge, Ralph W. (ed.), *The Same Sex: An Appraisal of Homosexuality.* The Pilgrim Press, 1969. (Paperback)
75. Wood, Robert Watson, *Christ and the Homosexual.* Vantage Press, Inc., 1960.

Pamphlets

76. Council on Religion and the Homosexual, *Churchmen Speak Out on Homosexual Law Reform.* San Francisco: C. R. H., 1967.

77. ——— *Consultation on Theology and the Homosexual.* San Francisco: C. R. H., 1967. (5 mimeographed papers)
78. ——— *CRH:1964–68, The Council on Religion and the Homosexual.* San Francisco: C. R. H., 1968.
79. Devlin, Patrick, *The Enforcement of Morals.* London: Oxford University Press, 1959. (Reprinted in *Proceedings of the British Academy,* 45:129–151, 1959).
80. Grey, Antony, *Christian Society and the Homosexual.* Oxford: Manchester College, 1966.
81. Heron, Alastair (ed.), *Towards a Quaker View of Sex.* London: Friends Home Service Committee, 1963; rev. ed. 1964.
82. Joint Committee on Homosexuality, *Report of the Diocesan Committee on Homosexuality.* San Francisco: Episcopal Diocese of California, 1966.
83. Kuhn, Donald, *The Church and the Homosexual: A Report on a Consultation.* San Francisco: C. R. H., 1965.
84. Lucas, Donald S. (ed.), *The Homosexual and the Church.* San Francisco: Mattachine Society, 1966.
85. Pittenger, Norman, *Time for Consent? A Christian's Approach to Homosexuality.* London: SCM Press, Ltd., 1967.
86. Roman Catholic Church in England, *Report on the Roman Catholic Advisory Committee on Prostitution and Homosexual Offences and the Existing Law.* London, 1956. (Reprinted in *Dublin Review,* 230: 57–65, Summer, 1956.)
87. Shackleton, Edward R., *Religion and the Law.* Ridbeugh, Kilbirnie, Ayreshire: E. R. Shackleton, 1966.
88. Treese, Robert L., *Homosexuality: A Contemporary View of the Biblical Perspective.* San Francisco: C. R. H., 1966.
89. United Church of Christ, Council for Social Action,

Civil Liberties and Homosexuality: An Issue in Christian Responsibility. December, 1967, issue of *Social Action.*

90. The United Presbyterian Church U.S.A., Office of Church and Society of the Board of Christian Education. *What About Homosexuality?* November–December, 1967, issue of *Social Progress.*
91. Wilkerson, David, *New Hope for Homosexuals.* New York: Teen Challenge, 1964.

Articles

92. Bailey, Sherwin, "The Problem of Sexual Inversion," *Theology,* 55:47–52 (1952).
93. Barth, Karl, "Freedom in Fellowship," in *Church Dogmatics,* Vol. III, Part 4, p. 166. Edinburgh: T. & T. Clark, 1961.
94. Bryce, Dean T., "The Unspeakables," *St. Joseph Magazine,* Jan. to May, 1965. (5 articles)
95. Casey, R. P., "The Christian Approach to Homosexuality," *Theology,* 58:459–463 (1955).
96. Cavanagh, John R., "Sexual Anomalies and the Law," *Catholic Lawyer,* 9:4–10 (1963).
97. Chikes, Thibor, "Christian Attitudes Toward Homosexuality," *Concern,* 15:8-11 (June 15, 1963).
98. "Clergy Shatter Another Taboo: Council on Religion and the Homosexual," *Christian Century,* 81:1581 (Dec. 23, 1964).
99. Coburn, Vincent, "Homosexuality and the Invalidation of Marriage," *Jurist,* 20:441–459 (1960).
100. Cole, William Graham, "Homosexuality in the Bible," in *Sex and Love in the Bible,* pp. 342–372. Association Press, 1959.
101. Connery, J. R., "A Theologian Looks at the Wolfenden Report," *America,* 98:485–486 (Jan. 25, 1958).

102. Cromey, Robert W., "Ministry to the Homosexual," *Living Church,* Jan. 8, 1967.
103. Cutler, S. Oley, "Sexual Offenses–Legal and Moral Considerations," *Catholic Lawyer,* 9:94–105 (1963).
104. Dart, John. "Church for Homosexuals," *Los Angeles Times,* Dec. 8, 1969, part 2, pp. 1–3.
105. Dempsey, William, "Homosexuality," *Dublin Review,* 239:123–135 (Summer, 1965).
106. "Depravity and Unbelief: The Christian Tradition and Unnatural Vice," *Tablet,* 202:570–571 (Dec. 12, 1953).
107. Driver, Thomas F., "On Taking Sex Seriously," *Christianity and Crisis,* 23:175–179 (Oct. 14, 1963).
108. Fiske, Edward B., "Episcopal Clergymen Here Call Homosexuality Morally Neutral," *New York Times,* Nov. 29, 1967, pp. 1, 39.
109. Gleason, R. W., "Homosexuality: Moral Aspects of the Problem," *Homiletic and Pastoral Review,* 58:272–278 (Dec., 1957).
110. Hagmaier, George, and Gleason, Robert W., "Homosexuality" and "Moral Aspects of Homosexuality," in *Counselling the Catholic,* (Sheed & Ward, Inc., 1959), pp. 94–112 and 228–235.
111. Harvey, J. F. "Current Moral Theology," *American Ecclesiastical Review,* 158:122–129 (Feb., 1968).
112. ——— "Homosexuality," *New Catholic Encyclopedia,* Vol. III, pp. 116–119. McGraw-Hill Book Company, Inc., 1967.
113. ——— "Homosexuality and Marriage," *Homiletic and Pastoral Review,* 62:227–234 (1961).
114. ——— "Homosexuality as a Pastoral Problem," *Theological Studies,* 16:86–108 (1955).
115. ——— "Morality and Pastoral Treatment of Homosexuality," *Continuum,* 5:279–297 (Summer, 1967).
116. "Homosexuality: Society's Attitude," *America,* 114:316 (March 5, 1966).

117. Hooker, Evelyn, "Homosexuality—Summary of Studies," in Evelyn M. and Sylvanus M. Duvall (eds.), *Sex Ways in Fact and Faith: Bases for Christian Family Policy,* pp. 166–183. Association Press, 1961.
118. ——— "Problems of Sex Ethics: Homosexuality," in Elizabeth S. and William H. Genné (eds.), *Foundations for Christian Family Policy,* pp. 167–189. National Council of Churches, 1961.
119. "How Should Homosexuality Be Viewed?" *Awake,* Jan. 8, 1964, pp. 14–16.
120. Kane, John J., "Understanding Homosexuality," *U.S. Catholic,* 31:14–18 (Jan., 1966).
121. Kelsey, M. T., "The Church and the Homosexual," *Journal of Religion and Health,* 7:61:78 (Jan., 1968).
122. Lowery, Daniel, "The Problem of Homosexuality," *Liguorian,* 54:18–24 (Sept., 1966).
123. Milhaven, J., "Homosexuality and the Christian," *Homiletic and Pastoral Review,* 68:663–669 (May, 1968).
124. Moody, Howard, "Homosexuality and Muckraking," *Christianity and Crisis,* 27:270–271 (Nov. 27, 1967).
125. Nouwen, Henri J. M., "Homosexuality: Prejudice or Mental Illness?" *Intimacy: Pastoral Psychological Essays,* pp. 38–52. Fides Publishers, Inc., 1969.
126. Perlmutter, Emanuel, "Catholics and Episcopalians Differ on Law for Sex Deviates," *New York Times,* Nov. 26, 1964, pp. 1, 34.
127. Phillips, G., "Hope for Homosexuals," *Homiletic and Pastoral Review,* 66:995–1001 (Sept., 1966).
128. "Religious Group Urges Recognition of Homosexuals' Rights," *Christian Century,* 85:744–745 (June 5, 1968).
129. Rhymes, Douglas, "The Church's Responsibility Towards the Homosexual," *Dublin Review,* 241:83–114 (Summer, 1967).

130. Ritty, Charles G., "Invalidity of Marriage by Reason of Sexual Anomalies," *Jurist,* 23:394–422 (1963), and *Catholic Lawyer,* 10:90–108 (1964).
131. Rosenbaum, J., "Religious and the Fear of Homosexuality," *Review for Religious,* 27:880–882 (Sept., 1968).
132. Sheedy, Charles, "Law and Morals," *Chicago Bar Record,* 43:373–378 (1962).
133. Shinn, Roger L., "Persecution of the Homosexual," *Christianity and Crisis,* 26:84:87 (May 2, 1966).
134. Smith, B. L., "Homosexuality in the Bible and the Law," *Christianity Today,* 13:7–10 (July 18, 1969).
135. Thielicke, Helmut, "The Problem of Homosexuality," in *The Ethics of Sex,* tr. from the German by John W. Doberstein, pp. 269–292. Harper & Row, Publishers, Inc., 1964.
136. "A Time for Moral Indignation," *Christianity Today,* 9:624–626 (March 12, 1965).
137. VanderVeldt, James H., and Odenwald, Robert P., "Homosexuality," in *Psychiatry and Catholicism,* 2d ed., pp. 422–438. McGraw-Hill Book Company, Inc., 1957.
138. "Was Jesus an Outsider?" *Newsweek,* 70:83 (Aug. 7, 1967).
139. "The Wicked and the Weak," *America,* 116:802–803 (June 3, 1967).
140. Williamson, H., "Sodom and Homosexuality," *Clergy Review,* 48:507–514 (Aug., 1963).

MATERIALS OF A LEGAL NATURE

Books

141. Mitchell, Roger S., *The Homosexual and the Law.* Arco Publishing Company, Inc., 1969.

142. Vedder, Clyde B., and King, Patricia G., *Problems of Homosexuality in Corrections.* Charles C. Thomas, Publishers, 1967.
143. *The Wolfenden Report: Report of the Committee on Homosexual Offenses and Prostitution.* London: Her Majesty's Stationery Office, 1957; New York: Stein and Day, Inc., 1963. (Paperback–Lancer 74–849)

PAMPHLETS

144. Council on Religion and the Homosexual and Others, *The Challenge and Progress of Homosexual Law Reform.* San Francisco: C. R. H. and others, 1968.
145. Draft Help, *Homosexuality: The Draft and the Armed Forces.* San Francisco: Draft Help, 1969.
146. Elliott, Richard H., *Enforcement of Laws Directed at Homosexuals: A Typical Metropolitan Approach.* Research paper, University of Pennsylvania Law School Library, 1961. (Reprinted in part in *Drum,* No. 26, pp. 10–13 and 26–28, Sept., 1967.)
147. Florida Legislative Investigation Committee, *Homosexuality and Citizenship in Florida.* Tallahassee: Florida Legislature, 1964.
148. Utley, Thomas E., *What Laws May Cure: A New Examination of Morals and the Law.* London: Conservative Political Center, 1968.

ARTICLES

149. American Law Institute, "Commentary," in *Model Penal Code–Tentative Draft Number 4,* pp. 276–281. Philadelphia: A. L. I., 1955.
150. Bickel, Alexander M., "Homosexuality as Crime in

North Carolina," *New Republic,* 151:5–6 (Dec. 12, 1964).

151. Bowman, Karl M., and Engle, Bernice, "A Psychiatric Evaluation of the Laws of Homosexuality," *Temple Law Quarterly Review,* 29:273–326 (1956).
152. Cantor, Donald J., "Deviation and the Criminal Law," *Journal of Criminal Law, Criminology, and Police Science,* 55:441–453 (1964).
153. Caprio, Frank Samuel, and Brenner, Donald R., "The Homosexual Problem" and "Psycho-legal Management," in *Sexual Behavior: Psycho-legal Aspects,* pp. 99–172 and 307–358. Citadel Press, 1961. (Paperback–Paperback Library 55–900)
154. Davidson, Janice R., "Regulation of Sexual Conduct by Withholding Government Benefits and Privileges," *University of San Francisco Law Reviews,* 3:372–388 at 372–375 and 377–381 (1969).
155. Donnelly, Richard C.; Goldstein, Joseph; and Schwartz, Richard D., "Consensual Homosexual Acts Between Adults in Private–A Crime: A Problem for the Legislature?" in *Criminal Law: Problems for Decision in the Promulgation, Invocation, and Administration of a Law of Crimes,* pp. 123–202. The Free Press of Glencoe, Inc., 1962.
156. Everhard, John A., "Problems Involving the Disposition of Homosexuals in the Service," *U.S. Air Force Judge Advocate General's Bulletin,* 2:20–23 (1960).
157. Ford, Stephen D., "Homosexuals and the Law: Why the Status Quo?" *California Western Law Review,* 5:232–251 (1969).
158. Gallo, Jon J., and others, "The Consenting Adult Homosexual and the Law: An Empirical Study of Enforcement and Administration in Los Angeles County," *University of California at Los Angeles Law Review,* 13:644–832 (1966).

159. Gebhard, Paul H., and others, "Homosexual Offenders Against Children, . . . Against Minors, . . . Against Adults, . . . [and] Homosexual Activity," in *Sex Offenders: An Analysis of Types,* pp. 272–357 and 623–653. Harper & Row, Publishers, Inc., 1965. (Paperback–Bantam D3279)
160. Glueck, Bernard C., Jr., "An Evaluation of the Homosexual Offender," *Minnesota Law Review,* 141:187–210 (1957).
161. "Government-created Employment Disabilities of the Homosexual," *Harvard Law Review,* 82:1738–1751 (1969).
162. Harris, Robert N., Jr., "Private Consensual Adult Behavior: The Requirement of Harm to Others in the Enforcement of Morality," *University of California at Los Angeles Law Review,* 14:581–603 (1967).
163. Hart, H. L. A., "The Use and Abuse of the Criminal Law," *Oxford Lawyer,* 4:7–12 (1961).
164. "Homosexual Law Reform," *America,* 114:278 (Feb. 26, 1966).
165. Jacobs, Harold, "Decoy Enforcement of Homosexual Laws," *University of Pennsylvania Law Review,* 112:259–284 (1963).
166. Kling, Samuel G., "Homosexual Behavior," in *Sexual Behavior and the Law,* pp. 97–128. Bernard Geis Associates, 1965. (Paperback–Pocket Books 77118)
167. Kyler, C. W., "Camera Surveillance of Sex Deviates," *Law and Order,* 11:16–18, 20 (1963).
168. Lamb, Paul L., "Criminal Law–Consensual Homosexual Behavior–the Need for Legislative Reform," *Kentucky Law Journal,* 57:591–598 (1968–1969).
169. "Law and Homosexuality," *America,* 113–71 (July 17, 1965).
170. "Laws Against Homosexuals," *Christianity Today,* 14:32 (Nov. 7, 1969).

171. McConnell, J. P., and Martin, J. D., "Judicial Attitudes and Public Morals," *American Bar Association Journal,* 55:1129–1133 (1969).
172. Pederby, G. R., "Homosexuality and the Law," *Medico-Legal Journal,* 33:29–34 (1965).
173. Ploscowe, Morris, "Homosexuality, Sodomy, and Crimes Against Nature," in *Sex and the Law,* rev. ed., pp. 182–201. Ace Books, 1962. (Paperback–Ace A2)
174. "Private Consensual Homosexual Behavior: The Crime and Its Enforcement," *Yale Law Journal,* 70:623–635 (1961).
175. Sadoff, Robert L., " 'Psychopathic Personality' and 'Sexual Deviation': Medical Terms or Legal Catch-alls–Analysis of the Status of the Homosexual Alien," *Temple Law Quarterly,* 40:305–315 (1967).
176. St. John-Stevas, Norman, "Homosexuality" and "Laws of the States of the U.S., . . . of the United Kingdom, . . . and of European Countries Concerning Homosexual Offences," in *Life, Death and the Law: Law and Christian Morals in England and the United States,* pp. 198–231 and 310–335. Indiana University Press, 1961. (Paperback–Meridian M179)
177. Smith, Charles E., "The Homosexual Federal Offender, A Study of 100 Cases," *Journal of Criminal Law, Criminology, and Police Science,* 44:582–591 (1954).
178. West, Louis J., and Glass, Albert J., "Sexual Behavior and the Military Law," in Ralph Slovenko (ed.), *Sexual Behavior and the Law,* pp. 250–272. Charles C. Thomas, Publishers, 1965.
179. Woetzel, Robert K., "Do Our Homosexuality Laws Make Sense?" *Saturday Review of Literature,* 48:23–25 (Oct. 9, 1965).

MATERIALS OF A MEDICAL, PSYCHOLOGICAL, SOCIOLOGICAL, ETC., NATURE

Books

180. Bergler, Edmund, *Homosexuality: Disease or Way of Life?* Hill and Wang, Inc., 1956. (Paperback–Collier AS199X)
181. —— *One Thousand Homosexuals: Conspiracy of Silence, or Curing and Deglamorizing Homosexuals?* Pageant Books, Inc., 1959.
182. Bieber, Irving, and Associates, *Homosexuality: A Psychoanalytic Study*. Basic Books, Inc., 1962. (Paperback–Vintage V291)
183. Cappon, Daniel, *Toward an Understanding of Homosexuality*. Prentice-Hall, Inc., 1965.
184. Cavanagh, John Richard, *Counseling the Invert*. Bruce Publishing Company, 1966.
185. Churchill, Wainwright, *Homosexual Behavior Among Males: A Cross-Cultural and Cross-Species Investigation*. Hawthorn Books, Inc., 1967.
186. Ellis, Albert, *Homosexuality: Its Causes and Cures*. Lyle Stuart, Publisher, 1965.
187. Ellis, Havelock, *Sexual Inversion* (Part IV of Vol. I of *Studies in the Psychology of Sex*). Random House, Inc., 1936.
188. Hauser, Richard, *The Homosexual Society*. The Bodley Head, 1962.
189. Henry, George William, *All the Sexes: A Study of Masculinity and Femininity*. Rinehart & Company, Inc., 1955. (Paperback–Collier 07684 and 09590)
190. —— *Sex Variants: A Study of Homosexual Patterns*. Paul B. Hoeber, Inc., 1948.
191. Humphreys, Laud, *Tearoom Trade: Impersonal Sex in Public Places*. Aldine Press, 1970.

192. Krich, Aron M. (ed.), *The Homosexuals: As Seen by Themselves and Thirty Authorities.* Citadel Press, 1954. (Paperback)
193. Marmor, Judd (ed.), *Sexual Inversion: The Multiple Roots of Homosexuality.* Basic Books, Inc., 1965.
194. Martin, Harold, *Men and Cupid: A Reassessment of Homosexuality and of Man's Sexual Life in General.* London: Fortune Press, Ltd., 1965.
195. Ollendorff, Robert H. V., *The Juvenile Homosexual Experience and Its Effect on Adult Sexuality.* The Julian Press, Inc., 1966.
196. Rees, Tudor, and Usill, Harley V. (eds.), *They Stand Apart: A Critical Survey of the Problems of Homosexuality.* The Macmillan Company, 1955.
197. Ruitenbeek, Hendrik Marinus (ed.), *The Problem of Homosexuality in Modern Society.* E. P. Dutton & Company, Inc., 1963. (Paperback–Dutton D127)
198. Schofield, Michael George, *Sociological Aspects of Homosexuality.* Little, Brown & Company, 1965.
199. Socarides, Charles W., *The Overt Homosexual.* Grune & Stratton, Inc., 1968.
200. Stekel, Wilhelm, *The Homosexual Neurosis,* tr. from the German by James S. Van Teslaar. Emerson Books, Inc., 1950.
201. Westwood, Gordon, *A Minority: A Report on the Life of the Male Homosexual in Great Britain.* Longmans, Green & Co., Ltd., 1960.
202. Willis, Stanley E., *Understanding and Counseling the Male Homosexual.* Little, Brown & Company, 1967.

Pamphlets

203. Amicus Curiae Brief, *Boutilier v. Immigration and Naturalization Service.* Philadelphia: Homosexual Law Reform Society, 1967.

204. Crompton, Louis, *Homosexuals and the Sickness Theory*. London: Albany Trust, 1969.

Articles

205. Bakwin, Harry, "Deviant Gender-Role Behavior in Children: Relation to Homosexuality," *Pediatrics,* 41:620–629, (1968).
206. Bluestone, Harvey; O'Malley, Edward; and Connell, Sydney, "Homosexuals in Prison," *Corrective Psychiatry and Journal of Social Therapy,* 12:13–24 (1966).
207. Bowman, Karl M., and Engle, Bernice, "Sexual Psychopath Laws," in Ralph Slovenko (ed.), *Sexual Behavior and the Law,* pp. 757–778 at 762–763 and 770–771. Charles C. Thomas, Publishers, 1965.
208. Braaten, Leif J., and Darling, C. Douglas, "Overt and Covert Homosexual Problems Among Male College Students," *Genetic Psychology Monographs,* 71:269–310 (1965)
209. Bromberg, Walter, and Franklin, Girard H., "The Treatment of Sexual Deviates with Group Psychodrama," *Group Psychotherapy,* 4:274–289 (1952).
210. Brown, Julia S., "A Comparative Study of Deviations of Sexual Mores," *American Sociological Review,* 17:135–146 (April, 1952).
211. Bychowski, Gustav, "The Ego and the Object of the Homosexual," *International Journal of Psychoanalysis,* 42:255–259 (1961).
212. Cavan, Sherri, "Interaction in Home Territories," *Berkeley Journal of Sociology,* 8:17–32 (1963).
213. Chang, Judy, and Block, Jack, "Study of Identification in Male Homosexuals," *Journal of Consulting Psychology,* 24:307–310 (1960).
214. Curran, Desmond, and Parr, Denis, "Homosexual-

ity: An Analysis of 100 Male Cases Seen in Private Practice," *British Medical Journal,* 1:797–801 (1957).

215. Dean, Robert B., and Richardson, Harold, "Analysis of MMPI Profiles of 40 College-educated Overt Male Homosexuals," *Journal of Consulting Psychology,* 28:483–486 (1964).
216. DeLuca, Joseph N., "The Structure of Homosexuality," *Journal of Projective Techniques and Personality Assessments,* 30:187–191 (1966).
217. Dickey, Brenda A., "Attitudes Toward Sex Roles and Feelings of Adequacy in Homosexual Males," *Journal of Consulting Psychology,* 25:116–122 (1961).
218. Doidge, William T., and Holtzman, Wayne H., "Implications of Homosexuality Among Air Force Trainees," *Journal of Consulting Psychology,* 24:9–13 (1960).
219. Druss, Richard G., "Cases of Suspected Homosexuality Seen at an Army Mental Hygiene Consultation Service," *Psychiatric Quarterly,* 4:62–70 (1967).
220. Feldman, M. P., and MacCulloch, M. J., "The Application of Anticipatory Avoidance Learning to the Treatment of Homosexuality: 1. Theory, Technique, and Preliminary Results," *Behaviour Research and Therapy,* 2:165–183 (1965).
221. Fitzgerald, Thomas K., "A Theoretical Typology of Homosexuality in the United States," *Corrective Psychiatry and Journal of Social Therapy,* 9:28–35 (1963).
222. Ford, Clellan S., and Beach, Frank A., "Homosexual Behavior," in *Patterns of Sexual Behavior,* pp. 125–143. Harper & Brothers, 1951. (Paperback—Ace Star K1285)
223. Freud, Anna, "Clinical Observations on the Treatment of Manifest Male Homosexuality," *Psychoanalytic Quarterly,* 20:337–338 (1951).

224. Freud, Sigmund, "Certain Neurotic Mechanisms in Jealousy, Paranoia, and Homosexuality," in Ernest Jones (ed.), *Collected Papers of Sigmund Freud,* tr. from the German by Joan Riviere, 2:232–243. London: Hogarth Press, 1933; New York: Basic Books, Inc., 1959.

225. Freund, Kurt, "Diagnosing Homo- or Heterosexuality and Erotic Age Preference by Means of a Psychophysiological Test," *Behaviour Research and Therapy,* 5:209–228 (1967).

226. Gershman, Harry, "Homosexuality and Some Aspects of Creativity," *American Journal of Psychoanalysis,* 24:29–38 (1964).

227. Ginsburg, Kenneth N., "The 'Meat Rack': A Study of Male Homosexual Prostitution," *American Journal of Psychotherapy,* 21:170–185 (1967).

228. Glueck, Bernard C., Jr., "Psychodynamic Patterns in the Homosexual Sex Offender," *American Journal of Psychiatry,* 112:584–590 (1956).

229. Grams, Armin, and Rinder, Lawrence, "Signs of Homosexuality in Human-Figure Drawings," *Journal of Consulting Psychology,* 22:394 (1958).

230. Greenspan, Herbert, and Campbell, John D., "The Homosexual as a Personality Type," *American Journal of Psychiatry,* 101:682–689 (1945).

231. Group for the Advancement of Psychiatry, Committee on the College Student, "Homosexual Behavior," in Harrison P. Eddy (ed.), *Sex and the College Student,* pp. 66–75 and 126–127. Atheneum Publishers, 1966. Report No. 60. (Paperback–Fawcett Crest t968)

232. Grygier, T. G., "Psychometric Aspects of Homosexuality," *Journal of Mental Science,* 103:514–526 (1957).

233. Hadden, Samuel B., "Treatment of Male Homosexuals in Groups," *International Journal of Group Psychotherapy,* 16:13–22 (Jan., 1966).

234. Hemphill, R. E.; Leitch, A.; and Stuart, J. R., "A Factual Study of Male Homosexuality," *British Medical Journal,* 1:1317–1323 (1958).

235. Hirschfeld, Magnus, "Introduction to the Theory of Homosexuality," "Forms of Homosexuality," "Diagnosis of Homosexuality," "Causes of Homosexuality," and "Feminine Homosexuality," in Norman Haire (ed.), *Sexual Anomalies and Perversions,* pp. 225–295. London: Encyclopaedic Press, Ltd., 1952.

236. Holemon, R. Eugene, and Winokur, George, "Effeminate Homosexuality: A Disease of Childhood," *American Journal of Orthopsychiatry,* 35:48–56 (1965).

237. Hooker, Evelyn, "An Empirical Study of Some Relations Between Sexual Patterns and Gender Identity in Male Homosexuals," in John Money (ed.), *Sex Research: New Developments,* pp. 24–52. Holt, Rinehart & Winston, Inc., 1965.

238. ——— "The Homosexual Community," in John H. Gagnon and William Simon (eds.), *Sexual Deviance,* pp. 167–184. Harper & Row, Publishers, Inc., 1967.

239. ——— "Male Homosexual Life Styles and Venereal Diseases," in *Proceedings of the World Forum on Syphilis and Other Treponematoses,* pp. 431–437. Washington, D.C.: Public Health Service, 1964. Public Health Publication No. 997.

240. ——— "Male Homosexuality in the Rorschach," *Journal of Projective Techniques,* 22:33–54 (1958).

241. ——— "Parental Relations and Male Homosexuality in Patient and Non-Patient Samples," *Journal of Consulting and Clinical Psychology,* 33:140–142 (1969).

242. ——— "A Preliminary Analysis of Group Behavior of Homosexuals," *Journal of Psychology,* 42:217–225 (1956).

243. Kallmann, Franz J., "Comparative Twin Study on the Genetic Aspects of Male Homosexuality," *Journal of Nervous and Mental Disease,* 115:283–298 (1952).
244. Kendrick, D. C., and Clarke, R. V., "Attitudinal Differences Between Heterosexually and Homosexually Oriented Males," *British Journal of Psychiatry,* 113:95–99 (1967).
245. Ketterer, Warren A., "Venereal Disease and Homosexuality," *Journal of the American Medical Association,* 188:11–12 (1964).
246. Kinsey, Alfred C., *et al.,* "Homosexual Outlet," in *Sexual Behavior in the Human Male,* pp. 168–172, 285–289, 315, 357–362, 383–384, 455–459, 482–483, and 610–666. W. B. Saunders Company, 1948.
247. ——— "Homosexual Response and Contacts," in *Sexual Behavior in the Human Female,* pp. 19–21, 106, 113–114, 140, and 446–501. W. B. Saunders Company, 1953. (Paperback–Pocket Book 99700)
248. Kitsuse, John I., "Societal Reaction to Deviant Behavior: Problems of Theory and Method," *Social Problems,* 9:247–256 (1962).
249. Krippner, Stanley, "The Identification of Male Homosexuality with the MMPI," *Journal of Clinical Psychology,* 20:159–161 (1964).
250. Liddicoat, Renée, "Homosexuality: Results of a Survey as Related to Various Theories," *British Medical Journal,* 2:1110–1111 (1957).
251. Loeser, Lewis H., "The Sexual Psychopath in the Military Service: A Study of 270 Cases," *American Journal of Psychiatry,* 102:92–101 (1945).
252. Martin, Agnes J., "The Treatment of 12 Male Homosexuals with L.S.D.," *Acta Psychotherapeutica,* 10:394–402 (1962).
253. Monroe, Russell R., and Enelow Morton L., "The Therapeutic Motivation in Male Homosexuals,"

American Journal of Psychotherapy, 14:474–490 (1960).

254. Perloff, William H., "The Role of Hormones in Homosexuality," *Journal of the Einstein Medical Center,* 11:165–178 (1963).
255. Roper, Peter, "The Effects of Hypnotherapy on Homosexuality," *Canadian Medical Association Journal,* 96:319–327 (1967).
256. Saghir, M. T., and Robins, E., "Homosexuality: I. Sexual Behavior of the Female Homosexual," *Archives of General Psychiatry,* 20:192–201 (1969).
257. ——— and Walbran, B., "Homosexuality: II. Sexual Behavior of the Male Homosexual," *Archives of General Psychiatry,* 21:219–229 (1969).
258. Serban, George, "The Existential Therapeutic Approach to Homosexuality," *American Journal of Psychotherapy,* 22:491–501 (1968).
259. Sonnenschein, David, "Homosexuality as a Subject of Anthropological Inquiry," *Anthropological Quarterly,* 39:73–82 (1966).
260. West, Donald J., "Parental Figures in the Genesis of Male Homosexuality," *International Journal of Social Psychiatry,* 5:85–97 (1959).

LITERARY WORKS ON A HOMOSEXUAL THEME

261. Baldwin, James, *Another Country.* The Dial Press, Inc., 1962. (Paperback–Dell 0200)
262. ——— *Giovanni's Room.* The Dial Press, Inc., 1956. (Paperback–Signet 51559)
263. Barr, James, *Derricks.* Greenberg, Publisher, 1951.
264. ——— *Quatrefoil.* Greenberg, Publisher, 1950. (Paperback–Paperback Library 54-871)

265. Blechman, Burt, *Stations*. Random House, Inc., 1964. (Paperback—Mayflower 114709)
266. Burgess, Anthony, *The Wanting Seed*. W. W. Norton & Company, Inc., 1963. (Paperback—Ballantine U5030)
267. Cameron, Bruce, *The Case Against Colonel Sutton*. Coward-McCann, Inc., 1961. (Paperback—Paperback Library 54–266)
268. Crowley, Mart, *The Boys in the Band*. London: Martin Secker & Warburg, Ltd., 1969. (Paperback —Dell 0773)
269. Duggan, Alfred Leo, *Family Favourites*. Pantheon Books, 1960.
270. Dyer, Charles, *Staircase*. Grove Press, Inc., 1966.
271. Friedman, Sanford, *Totempole*. E. P. Dutton & Company, Inc., 1965. (Paperback—Signet Q3023)
272. Genêt, Jean, *The Miracle of the Rose,* tr. from the French by Bernard Frechtman. London: Anthony Blond, Ltd., 1966.
273. —— *Our Lady of the Flowers,* tr. from the French by Bernard Frechtman. Grove Press, Inc., 1963. (Paperback—Bantam Q2945)
274. —— *Querelle of Brest,* tr. from the French by Gregory Streatham. London: Anthony Blond, Ltd., 1966. (Paperback—Panther O27467)
275. —— *The Thief's Journal,* tr. from the French by Bernard Frechtman. Grove Press, Inc., 1964. (Paperback—Bantam N3046)
276. Hellman, Lillian, *The Children's Hour*. Alfred A. Knopf, Inc., 1936.
277. Herbert, John, *Fortune and Men's Eyes*. Grove Press, Inc., 1967.
278. Isherwood, Christopher, *A Single Man*. Simon and Schuster, Inc., 1964. (Paperback—Lancer 72–969 and 74–913)
279. Marcus, Frank, *The Killing of Sister George*. London: Samuel French, Ltd., 1965.

280. Monsarrat, Nicholas, *Smith and Jones.* William Sloane Associates, Inc., 1963. (Paperback–Pocket Book 75221)
281. Osborne, John, *A Patriot for Me.* London: Faber & Faber, Ltd., 1965.
282. Petronius, *The Satyricon,* tr. from the Latin by William Arrowsmith. University of Michigan Press, 1959. (Paperback–Mentor MD283)
283. Peyrefitte, Roger, *The Exile of Capri.* tr. from the French by Edward Hyams. Fleet Publishing Corporation, 1965.
284. Plato, "The Symposium," in Irwin Edman (ed.), *The Works of Plato,* tr. from the Greek by Benjamin Jowett, pp. 333–393. Modern Library, 1928.
285. Proust, Marcel, *Cities of the Plain,* tr. from the French by C. K. Scott Moncrieff. Modern Library, Inc., 1927.
286. Purdy, James, *Eustace Chisholm and the Works.* Farrar, Straus & Giroux, Inc., 1967. (Paperback–Bantam N3797)
287. Rechy, John, *City of Night.* Grove Press, Inc., 1963. (Paperback–Black Cat BC1296)
288. ——— *Numbers.* Grove Press, Inc., 1967. (Paperback–Black Cat BC171)
289. Renault, Mary, *The Charioteer.* London: Longmans, Green & Co., Ltd., 1953. (Paperback–Four Square 798 and Cardinal 75181)
290. ——— *The Mask of Apollo.* Pantheon Books, Inc., 1966. (Paperback–Pocket Book 95049)
291. Selby, Hubert, Jr., *Last Exit to Brooklyn.* Grove Press, Inc., 1957. (Paperback–Black Cat BC153)
292. Spicer, Bart, *Act of Anger.* Atheneum Publishers, 1962. (Paperback–Bantam S2607 and N 4016)
293. Storey, David, *Radcliffe.* London: Longmans, Green & Co., Ltd., 1963.
294. Thorp, Roderick, *The Detective.* The Dial Press, Inc., 1966. (Paperback–Avon N156 and W159)

295. Vidal, Gore, *The City and the Pillar Revised.* E. P. Dutton & Company, Inc., 1965. (Paperback–Signet T3603)
296. —— *A Thirsty Evil. Seven Short Stories.* Zero Press, 1956. (Paperback–Signet S1535)
297. Williams, Tennessee, *Hard Candy. A Book of Stories.* New Directions, 1954.
298. —— *One Arm, and Other Stories.* New Directions, 1948.
299. Windham, Donald, *Two People.* Coward-McCann, Inc., 1965.
300. Yourcenar, Marguerite, *Memoirs of Hadrian,* tr. from the French by Grace Frick. Farrar, Straus & Cudahay, Inc., 1954. (Paperback–Noonday N258)